OUT OF LINE

History, Psychoanalysis, & Montage
in H.D.'s Long Poems

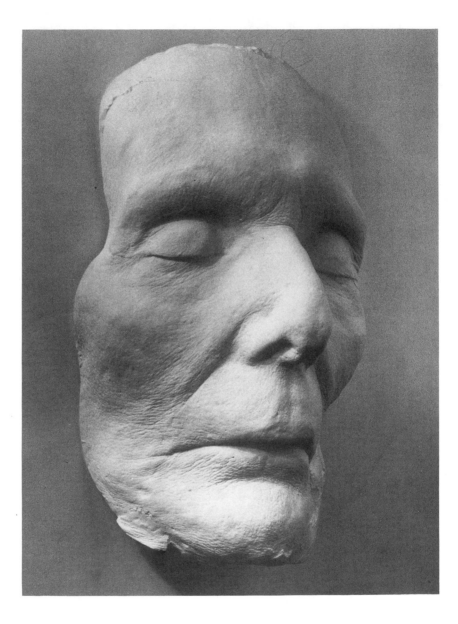

Out of Line

HISTORY,

PSYCHOANALYSIS,

& MONTAGE IN

H.D.'s LONG POEMS

Susan Edmunds

STANFORD UNIVERSITY PRESS
STANFORD, CALIFORNIA
1994

Stanford University Press
Stanford, California

© 1994 by the Board of Trustees of the
Leland Stanford Junior University

Printed in the United States of America

CIP data appear at the end of the book

Quotations from unpublished material by Bryher
Copyright © The Estate of Winifred Bryher.

Stanford University Press publications are distributed
exclusively by Stanford University Press within the United
States, Canada, and Mexico; they are distributed exclusively by
Cambridge University Press throughout the rest of the world.

Frontispiece: H.D.'s death mask, 1961.
Yale Collection of American Literature,
Beinecke Rare Book and Manuscript Library,
Yale University, New Haven, Conn.

to Beth and to Michelle

Acknowledgments

My first thanks go to the teachers and critics who helped me to shape this material into a book. Candace Waid, David Marshall, and Bryan Wolf all offered useful criticism along the way. Anonymous reviewers at *Contemporary Literature* and *Feminist Studies* brought flawless scholarship and a careful reading eye to bear on excerpted portions of my manuscript. The equally detailed and insightful comments of Margaret Homans, Wayne Koestenbaum, Rachel Blau DuPlessis, Eileen Gregory, and Adalaide Morris guided the manuscript into its final form. Special thanks go to Thomas Whitaker, whose high standards and good advice have seen me through many drafts; to John Hollander, whose hunches about H.D.'s literary influences have repeatedly paid off in the library; and to Harriet Chessman, whose own critical example and encouragement helped to sustain my faith in the value of the work at hand. I am lucky to be able to say that my teachers and colleagues include members of my family; their help with this project began years ago, when my mother overruled my decision to forgo learning how to read and write for the more immediate joys of make-believe. She and my father, as well as her mother and father before her, have set a lasting example of painstaking scholarship and joy in their work for me and my siblings. My thinking about H.D. owes an incalculable debt to Kathryn Riely, who has long been an eager and able consultant in the mysteries of make-believe and literary scholarship alike.

This book has profited enormously from weeks amid the papers of H.D. and her circle in the Yale Collection of American Literature at Yale's Beinecke Rare Book and Manuscript Library. Warm thanks go to Perdita

Schaffner and her son Timothy Schaffner for allowing me to cite unpublished manuscripts and correspondence from the estates of Hilda Doolittle and Winifred Bryher. Patricia Willis and Robert Babcock shared with me their expert knowledge and enthusiasm about Beinecke's collections, Marianne Moore, classical literature and H.D.; Kate Sharp, Lori Misura, Steve Jones, and Rick Hart provided ready help and cheerful encouragement from the front desk. Roz Carroll and Harriet Tarlo bridged the distance between the archives and the dinner table, enlivening a series of shared meals with their own knowledge and love of H.D. Through the generosity of the Mrs. Giles Whiting Foundation, I was given a crucial year of funding for research and writing; more recently, Syracuse University has provided funds to meet the costs of completing the project. And Helen Tartar, Ellen F. Smith, and Ann Klefstad have all helped to make the transition from writing to publishing a smooth and happy one.

The friends I made in graduate school have sustained me as no one else could. The example of their intellectual integrity and daring, the stimulation of their free-ranging conversation, and the pleasure of their love have made Adrienne Donald, Mary Renda, Lisa Cohen, Gigi Kunzel, Siobhan Somerville, and Bruce Hainley integral to the very fabric of my thinking. Finally, I would like to thank the two women to whom this book is dedicated: Michelle Bonnice, who continually revives my love of long books and longer (long-distance) conversation, and Beth Povinelli, who joins me in a life of thought and composition—part real, part pretend.

S.L.E.

Contents

Abbreviations

Works not listed here are cited in short form by author's surname, with title if appropriate, and are listed in the Works Cited, pp. 219–30.

DPA   Melanie Klein, Paula Heimann, Susan Isaacs, and Joan Riviere. *Developments in Psycho-Analysis.* Ed. Joan Riviere. London: The Hogarth Press, 1937.

HD   H.D. *Hermetic Definition.* New York: New Directions, 1972.

HE   H.D. *Helen in Egypt.* (1961) New York: New Directions, 1974.

LHR   Melanie Klein and Joan Riviere. *Love, Hate and Reparation.* London: The Hogarth Press, 1937.

SMK   Melanie Klein. *The Selected Melanie Klein.* Ed. Juliet Mitchell. New York: The Free Press, 1986.

T   H.D. *Trilogy.* Foreword by Norman Holmes Pearson. New York: New Directions, 1973.

OUT OF LINE

*History, Psychoanalysis, & Montage
in H.D.'s Long Poems*

So the first—it is written,
will be the twisted or the tortured individuals,

out of line, out of step with world so-called progress.

—H.D., "The Flowering of the Rod"

"*This unsatisfied duality*"

— Reading H.D. for (with) Ambivalence

> what is this mother-father
> to tear at our entrails?
>
> what is this unsatisfied duality
> which you can not satisfy?
>
> —H.D., "Tribute to the Angels"

They used to say the king had two bodies: one that lives a lifetime, and one that reigns forever. H.D. also has two bodies. One occupies the space of epiphany: it is hale, whole, holy. The other occupies the space of narrative or history, a body containing pain and contained by plot. We know them both. The first is a dancer, "perfect," "a rose flower / parted wide." She is "a dark lady" by the river, in "a clear-colored robe, yellow or faint-orange," "as abstract as a lady could be." She is Greta Garbo, an image of "purity and glamour," or she is Little Eva in a provincial play, a white child in a nightgown whose angel wings are painted on the curtain behind her. He is Amen, "upright, slender, / impressive as the Memnon mono-lith." Or he is a little boy with reddish curls, "the 'fiery moment' incar-nate." This body—hale, whole, holy—belongs equally to the convales-cent newly afoot and to the suicide: Hermione, whose feet trace a "wa-vering hieroglyph" of black prints on the white snow; and Natalia, who falls through the lake ice, her "body . . . still whirling down-ward" or "caught in a counter-current" having "reached the end." Male or female, this body may also be sexless or twinned in its sex. It belongs to the poet, who appears to herself in a dream as "a Virgin in the magic-mirrors" with "small buttocks" on both the front and back of her body. And it belongs to the unborn, the newly born, and the reborn: Rafton and Helen, prenatal "twins, lovers . . . held, sheltered beneath some throbbing heart"; the baby rabbits with their "eight pink bodies, eight unexpectedly furless and rigid bodies" awaiting Midget in the rabbit-hutch; or the smooth, blank "sun-disk" of "the re-born Sun" that emerges from the belly of the Ram.[1]

I

As for that other body, the body of pain and plot, its forms are more myriad still. This body is a Mamalie, capless, with mind adrift, a body that thirsts. It is wounded or scarred: Papa, with a bloody forehead and limp, "rag doll" arms; little Hilda with an ugly scar on her mouth, the side of her face "stung to death" by a snake in a dream; Hedylus, whose scarred forehead "brand[s] him primitive, disobedient"; or Achilles, dragging a heel of "bruised and swollen flesh" across the sand. "Twisted," "tortured," and "reviled," this is the body of "an unbalanced, neurotic woman," "un-maidenly" and "hardly decent." It "cries out in anger, // I am hungry," or it gives itself over to grief: a Mary who "weep[s] bitterly, / bitterly . . . bitterly"; or a Helen, blackening her face in the Greek gesture of sorrow. It is, most decidedly, an autobiographical body, H.D.'s own: first, the small child, "wispy and mousy," in a body that "did not fit it very well"; then the adolescent, "importunate, overgrown, unincarnated"; later, "a middle-aged woman, shattered by fears of tension and terror"; and finally, an old woman in her "decline," animated and emboldened with "unseemly, impossible, / even slightly scandalous" lust. But it is also, importantly, a body shared by other poets: D. H. Lawrence, "visibly an invalid," "an Orpheus head, severed from its body"; Ezra Pound, "The Poet in the Iron Cage"; and Sappho, who "twist[s] her two eyes unevenly" and "screws her face out of proportion," "this woman whom love paralysed."[2]

Given the persistence and the power of these two bodies in H.D.'s own writing, it is not surprising that they have figured so largely in the terms of her critical reception. In the prefeminist response to her work, the perfect, clear-colored, and pure body of epiphany surfaces in praise for her writing's luster, "realness," and flawless self-containment, while the ill-fitting, twisted, and reviled body of narrative and history peers forth in condemnations of her writing's deficiency, excess, weakness, or self-indulgence.[3] If this split reception betrays deep and widespread funds of critical ambivalence toward H.D.'s work, a hair-triggered logic of reversal has governed the relations between the positive and negative poles of such response. Thus, as Susan Stanford Friedman has argued, early reviewers "criticized precisely what so attracted them," and found in H.D.'s reputation for perfection "something to both adore and reject."[4]

Cassandra Laity has joined Friedman in demonstrating how this unstable pattern of response participated in the discourses of misogyny and homophobia underwriting the wider literary and critical effort to distinguish the "virile" and "exact" body of modernist writing from the "morbid" and "feminine" body of Romantic and Decadent writing.[5] The first feminist readings of H.D.'s work, precisely because they named as such the gendered oppositions informing the construction of literary value,

showed a new self-reflexiveness that permitted access to H.D.'s own ex-
tremely self-reflexive meditations on sexuality, gender, and writing.[6] But
feminist criticism has also, unexpectedly, continued to replicate both the
split and the logic of reversal governing earlier attempts either to shore up
H.D.'s writing as a space of achieved wholeness, authenticity, and virtue
or to expose it as a space of schism, alienation, and excess or lack.

Taking part in the wider U.S. feminist commitment to identity pol-
itics in the 1970's, critics such as Friedman, Rachel Blau DuPlessis, and
Alicia Ostriker argued compellingly for H.D.'s importance as a literary
precursor engaged in a specifically female "quest for wholeness," "au-
thentic female voice," self-recovery, and "inner integration."[7] The post-
structuralist response to these early feminist readings (a response in which
all three critics have to varying degrees participated) builds on their suc-
cess in generating a feminist readership for H.D. while challenging their
optimism. Thus, more recent critics, heavily influenced by Lacan and
Kristeva, value H.D.'s work precisely for the symptomatic or self-
diagnostic status of its crises, slippages, and failures. Elizabeth Hirsh ar-
gues that if H.D.'s "Helen sets out in quest of an authentic self-image, . . .
she finds . . . that no such thing exists except as a figment of the Imagi-
nation" (p. 8). Deborah Kelly Kloepfer finds in H.D.'s work an incestuous
and maternally connoted "language jarred free from the symbolic" (p.
169), while Dianne Chisholm argues on similar lines that H.D. confronts
"woman's exclusion from the universal, symbolic order," her "symbolic
deprivation." And Claire Buck values H.D. for her "representation[s] of
a split subjectivity," and her portrayal of "an oscillation which makes bi-
sexuality the mark of the difficulty or uncertainty of sexual identity, rather
than the foundation of an alternative identity."[8]

These latter critics have produced a series of theoretically rigorous
readings of H.D.'s work that pose important points: individual identity is
an (illusory) function of the social group rather than a refuge from it; the
unconscious enforces a split subjectivity that must be read rather than re-
paired; language itself "speaks the subject," whose authority depends on
and reinforces the patriarchal authority of the father while conspiring to
relegate the mother to a space outside history and on the outskirts of
speech. But in the transition from liberal-feminist to post-structuralist—
feminist readings of H.D., identity and fragmentation, authenticity and
self-alienation, adequacy and lack have remained the governing critical di-
chotomies, while the relative value of their component terms has simply
been reversed. Moreover, for all the declared opposition between these
readings, they are uniformly committed to recuperating H.D. according
to the preferred terms of each critic's chosen approach. Even when fem-
inists have located areas in H.D.'s work that could not be assimilated to

the positive poles of their respective evaluative frameworks, they have tended to position those areas as temporary nadirs in larger narratives of ascent.[9] This project of recuperation is at its most problematic in critics' intermittent or ongoing assumption that H.D. had the power to anticipate, without the benefit of our own experience, theoretical concepts and political stances that we critics are even now learning how to articulate.

A handful of critics have resisted such a project of recuperation, laying out the initial terms for a feminist reading of H.D. that responds to her own ambivalences ambivalently. DuPlessis has argued that "to all agendas given by others, H.D. is characteristically both complicit and resistant," and has aligned her bid to find "the deeper laws" behind modern life with "the larger Anglo-American modernist hopes" for "change without political struggle."[10] Similarly, Paul Smith has argued that "many of the demerits that I take the male modernists to exhibit are not unequivocally revised in H.D.'s work; they are also to a certain degree sustained, or replicated" (p. 78). And Sarah Schuyler admits that she "cannot say whether H.D. is best described as a critic of gender or as gendered," while noting astutely that "it is possible to view the dynamics in the older texts [such as H.D.'s] as versions of current feminist concerns, but only through a bilogical lens that reflects back at the woman critic her own desire and duplicity" (pp. 87, 90).

In the book that follows, ambivalence is the bi-logical lens I use to see H.D. through the glare of my particular desire and duplicity. In some sense, my project has been to render my ambivalence critical. As I look back at it now, it seems that this project began with the question of how to relate those two bodies—the twisted body of history and narrative and the radiant body of epiphany—while working outside the strict logic of opposition suggested by H.D.'s own dichotomy of "in-time" and "out-of-time" and the current critical dichotomies of fragmentation and identity, wholeness and lack. I have focused my study on three of H.D.'s late long poems: *Trilogy, Helen in Egypt,* and *Hermetic Definition.*[11] In these poems, H.D. makes bodies the locus through which narrative and history pass into epiphany and epiphany becomes available to the commemorative processes of narrative and history. Thus, H.D.'s representations of her own body and the bodies of earthly, mythic, and divine characters play an important structural role in these poems, providing the sites through which narrative and epiphany constitute one another. This structural role is in turn grounded in the montage structure of the poems themselves. H.D. closely links her poems' various montage strategies—repetition and reversal, reordering, and conflictual juxtaposition—to the body on the one hand and to the unsettling of the logic of rationalism on the other. Refusing the rational logic of linear narration, she makes access to ex-

tralinear—extratemporal—moments of transcendence and divine reve-
lation rhetorically possible. In these moments, poet and reader gain access
to a divine order of maternal plenitude that at once lies outside the order
of history and bestows on that order visionary solutions to specific social
conflicts.

Thus, in each of my readings, I try to account both for the social con-
flicts addressed in a given poem and for the poem's declared resolutions to
those conflicts. To put this another way, I try to decipher what specific
social conflicts certain bodies in the poems are embodying and how the
poem's epiphanic (maternal) bodies in turn embody their solutions. But I
work against the logic of the poems—a logic many feminist and psycho-
analytic analyses replicate as much as they diagnose—by refusing to grant
this epiphanic space of maternal plenitude a place outside the workings of
history. Instead, I argue that H.D.'s visionary solutions reveal fully his-
torical patterns of political bias, ambivalence, and incoherence.

To substantiate these claims, I place the poems in three new historical
contexts in addition to the already well-established context of H.D.'s en-
gagement with Freudian psychoanalysis. These contexts are: the contro-
versy over Melanie Klein's right to practice waged in the British Psycho-
analytic Society in the 1930's and 1940's; the film theory and practice of
Sergei Eisenstein, with their legacy of an art of revolution; and the African
independence movements of the 1950's and 1960's. Drawing on archival
materials, biography, war journalism, and theoretical and literary source
texts, I contend that the visionary politics of H.D.'s long poems cannot
be reconciled with the liberal-feminist and post-structuralist–feminist
agendas currently attributed to them. Deeply ambivalent, her late long
poems are out of line with radical and reactionary agendas alike precisely
because they are indebted to both. Thus, in using H.D.'s phrase "out of
line" to characterize her work, I mean to emphasize not only the nonlinear
method of her poems' montage narratives but also the irregular and con-
flictual nature of their politics. Ironizing a feminist tendency to endow all
acts of transgression, incoherence, and rupture with a univocal power to
contest the grounds of patriarchy, I argue that H.D. problematizes, even
as she solicits, our readiness to honor her poetry's self-proclaimed powers
of prophecy and social redemption.

In Chapter 1, I examine H.D.'s extended analysis with Walter Schmi-
deberg in the linked contexts of the mounting controversy in Britain over
Kleinian psychoanalysis and the wider literary and propagandist tradition
linking war with a dangerous femininity. I argue that the Schmideberg
analysis provides a key set of terms for H.D.'s meditation on war and fe-
male aggression in *Trilogy*. In the multiple narratives of this poem, H.D.
uses Kleinian concepts to challenge Freud's theoretical links between rep-

etition, reversal, female aggression, lesbian eroticism, and the death drive. In "The Walls Do Not Fall," she employs rhetorical strategies of reversal to generate a transcendental alternative to an earthly world of violence, division, and death. But the Kleinian figures of oral sadism that epitomize the terrors of this earthly world eventually contaminate H.D.'s representations of eternity as well. In "Tribute to the Angels," H.D. tries to forge new paths to eternity by reclaiming female aggression as a source of creativity and pleasure. Her alchemical transformation of the bitter maternal jewel doubles as a Kleinian act of reparation to the mother, and makes way for a coded scene of lesbian love-making, which rewrites Freud's associations between lesbian paranoia, repetition, and death. H.D.'s retelling of the story of Mary Magdalene in "The Flowering of the Rod" backtracks from a scene of divine reunion with the mother to confront the reality of loss and to reattempt the project to represent a doubly sexed god initiated in the poem's previous sections.

In Chapter 2, I argue that a Kleinian concern with fantasies of maternal violence continues to preoccupy H.D. in *Helen in Egypt*. Following Freud's lead in his revisionary Moses essays, H.D. recasts Helen of Troy as an Egyptian visionary entrusted with the task of reconstructing the destructive oedipal family on the ancient Egyptian model of the reunited family of Isis. Like Freud's hysteric and Eisenstein's montage filmmaker, who both rearrange the "proper order" of past events, Helen accomplishes the reconstruction of the family through the complex reorderings of her mythic memories. But the terms of such a reconstruction—which involves the transformation of the detested oedipal mother into a grieving Isis—are not particularly feminist. Moreover, in recovering the "memory forgotten" of the ancient family of Isis, H.D indirectly enforces the suppression of the contemporary "memory" of modern Egypt's struggle for independence from imperial Britain.

In Chapter 3, I turn to *Hermetic Definition* to analyze H.D.'s record of her relationships with Lionel Durand and St.-John Perse. I read H.D.'s fantasies about these two men against Perse's celebrated career as a poet of imperialism and Durand's own career as a political journalist. Durand's career ended abruptly when he died while covering the Algerian War for *Newsweek* before H.D. completed her poem. H.D. situates her sexual fantasies about Durand within a complex historical framework in which the modernist "journey to the interior," primitivist fertility myths, Africa's independence movements, and U.S. taboos against miscegenation compete to shape the terms of her desire. Yet she also struggles with the possibility that the modernist project to redeem society through primitivist myth-making may be implicated in the very violence of colonialism and decolonization that she would use such myth-making to resolve or mask.

H.D.'s fantasies of Durand thus become the occasion for an extraordinary interrogation of modernism from within, one that confounds current critical attempts to divide modernism itself into rival conservative and radical traditions. But the terms of this interrogation are largely occluded in the poem's final version, where H.D. cuts all explicit references to war in Africa and calls on the mother's mythical powers of resurrection to restore Durand to a life outside history.

I offer these synopses to provide a sense of the arguments that follow. It is more difficult to convey my sense of their critical significance; that story has become inseparable from the story of the poems' own personal significance to me, a significance shaped over several years' time as the experience of reading them gradually and erratically came clear. When I first read *Trilogy*, I thought it was a funny poem, full of jokes. On the last page, I laughed out loud. It took me a while to realize that it was also an angry poem, an angry poem by a woman, and a poem that consistently linked female anger and aggression with eating: gluttony, starvation, biting, bitterness. Later I realized the poem also linked joy with eating, joy and the memory of joy or the longing for it, for "the feasting, the laughter" (*T* 159). For me it became, unquestionably, a lesbian poem. Harriet Chessman's idea of using D. W. Winnicott's theories on children's play to read Gertrude Stein took hold in me (pp. 73–76), and when I traced his work back to the work of his teacher, Melanie Klein, I found this same world of eating, of anger moving to joy.

Often an awkward writer, Klein nevertheless compelled me to send her pages to friends, or to read them aloud over the telephone, at the kitchen table, in bed. But in what sense was her writing descriptively valid, authoritative, true? Lacanians have been quick to point out serious theoretical flaws in her work, points I often find convincing. Apparently indifferent to the "category of the signifier," she "lacks any adequate account of the relation between language and the unconscious."[12] She "assumes that the subject exists from the beginning." She assumes that the infant enters life with a capacity to relate to objects, not with the "primary narcissism" often attributed to the newborn in Freud's accounts. She assumes that desire can be satisfied. She interprets Freud's theory of the death drive to posit a separate "primordial instinct of aggression" whereas Lacanians have taken him to mean that "all instincts are characterised by their aggression, their tenacity or insistence (exactly their *drive*)." She assumes that "sexual identity is first given biologically and then developed and confirmed (or not) as the subject grows." She does not consider that the castration complex has "any fundamental bearing on sexual difference," nor does she link the production of sexual difference to the child's entry into language.[13] And she forgets to pay her respects to the Name of the Father. But Klein has influenced Lacan, as well as Julia Kristeva, greatly, and these theorists often forget to pay their respects to her.

Jacqueline Rose notes that "Lacan turns to Klein for confirmation of the aggressive component of the original imaginary operation." But his Imaginary owes Klein more than that.[14] Indeed, Fredric Jameson remarks that "it is from Melanie Klein's pioneering psychoanalysis of children that the basic features of the Lacanian Imaginary are drawn."[15] Klein argues that the infant must organize its internalized phantasies of the mother's "part-objects" into a "whole object" and that this construction of the mother as a whole being coincides with the infant's ability to see itself and its mother as separate.[16] Lacan reassembles these ideas in his scenario of the mirror stage: where the infant uses the mirror to create the illusion of a whole self out of its uncoordinated motor activities and fragmented drives; where this illusion of selfhood also divides the self; and where the mother's lap stands as the frame against which this activity is set or seen. Moreover, as several critics note,[17] Lacan's account of the transition from the Imaginary to the Symbolic owes a further debt to Klein. For it is Klein, not Lacan, who first makes Freud's isolated links between symbol-formation and the child's loss of the mother central to a theory of the child's entry into language, and who makes the child's first symbol-making activities a central function or product of the "depressive position" that coincides with the onset of the oedipal complex.

At times, Kristeva can acknowledge Klein more freely. She calls on "Kleinian theory" to "serve as a guide" when she posits that "the mother's body . . . becomes the ordering principle of the semiotic *chora*, which is on the path of destruction, aggressivity and death."[18] The "desirable and terrifying, nourishing and murderous, fascinating and abject inside of the maternal body" evoked in Kristeva's theories of abjection is also straight out of Klein, though here Kristeva does not say so. And the "ab-ject" it-self, "that non-introjected mother who is incorporated as devouring, and intolerable"? Here again, Klein surfaces as an unnamed influence.[19] Janice Doane and Devon Hodges point to Kristeva's increasingly conservative use of Klein in her later work. They relate several features in Kristeva's theories of depression to Klein's own work on the topic and trace her "sentimental evocation of Christian (specifically, Catholic Orthodox) forgiveness" back to Klein's theory of reparation (pp. 66, 73). More generally, they propose that "Julia Kristeva (following André Green) conflates" the work of Klein and her colleague D. W. Winnicott; this conflation, they argue, serves to collapse Klein's careful distinction between the infant's violent phantasies of its mother's actions and her actual behavior, and thus to hold the mother solely accountable for the pain of psychic life (p. 79).

The relative critical neglect of Klein's influence on the theories of Lacan and Kristeva, combined with the substantial influence of Kleinian concepts on H.D.'s late poetry, have several implications for H.D. criticism. In her recent study of Virginia Woolf's "engagement with the developmental narratives of both Klein and Freud," Elizabeth Abel speaks to the need "to dislodge the binary construction of the encounter not only between Woolf and psychoanalysis but also between literature and psychoanalysis as criticism habitually couples them" (p. xviii). H.D.'s familiarity with the heated debates over Kleinian theory in London indicates a parallel need for a more careful historicizing of her deployment of psychoanalytic concepts, one that acknowledges both her use of accounts now considered theoretically flawed and her selective (and not necessarily logically coherent) application of a number of competing theories simultaneously. The recovery of Klein's influence on H.D. breaks open the almost allegorical power of the pairing of Freud and H.D., disrupting the impulse to read the H.D.-Freud debates as a discrete, uncanny foretelling of the subsequent encounter between academic feminism and psychoanalysis, and complicating greatly our sense of the theoretical environment in which H.D. continued to receive or remember Freud after her analysis with him. Klein's considerable influence on Lacan diminishes the power of his rhetorical bid to go back and recover the radical Freud, and hence increases the difficulty in assuming that Lacanian concepts are somehow available to H.D. because Freudian ones were. At the same time, Klein provides a partial way of understanding why Lacanian and Kristevan approaches have been so profitable in H.D. criticism: all three writers share a common, as yet inadequately articulated, precursor in Klein as well as in Freud.

But restoring Klein to the picture also provides new ways to contest the authority that specific Lacanian and Kristevan concepts have acquired both in H.D. criticism and in feminist criticism more generally. Lacan's major complaint concerning Klein appears to be her "persistent failure to acknowledge that the Oedipal fantasies which she locates in the maternal body originate from the reality presupposed by the Name of the Father."[20] Behind this complaint lie Klein's and Lacan's competing ideas about the child's entry into language. Klein argues that the child turns to symbol-making in an attempt to reconstitute and recover the mother it feels it has shattered and destroyed in its own aggressive phantasies. Lacan objects that this grants no place to the intervening Law of the Father and hence to the threat of castration that severs the child from its mother and sets it, newly gendered, into the relay of the Symbolic. But pairing the theories also highlights problems in Lacan's own account.

Take, for instance, Lacan's reactionary and anti-Kleinian assumption that symbolic violence—the ability to threaten others with bodily harm—

is the exclusive mandate of the phallus-bearing father. Lacan assigns aggressivity to the infant, but only in the mirror stage and only aggressivity against one's—mistaken—self. Indeed, a careful comparison of Lacan and Klein suggests that the narcissistic aggression associated with Lacan's mirror stage replaces the reciprocal play of aggression that the Kleinian mother and child pursue in phantasy across the body's own "mirror"— the alimentary canal whose anatomy knows no sexual or generational difference. In substituting the blank artifice of an actual mirror for the organic reflexivity of the alimentary canal that attains such high visibility in Kleinian theory, Lacan eclipses the dense and long-standing cultural associations with female and maternal aggression that the alimentary canal carries, and thus obscures the cultural role the alimentary canal plays in gendering violence as well as desire.[21]

It is, I would suggest, because the alimentary canal has been occluded as a site of phantasy production that Lacan is able to conflate symbolic violence with the violence of the father's law, a law taking the threat to and from the phallus as its founding dynamic. This conflation, in turn, makes theoretically impossible any notion of symbolic resistance to the law and implies, among other things, that no one can threaten the father with harm. Furthermore, it gets the mother and the child off the hook, assigning their domain (be it domestic or Imaginary) an impossible purity when it comes to interpersonal violence. This tends to reinforce Victorian assumptions about maternal grace and childhood innocence, and gives unwelcome support to a feminist idea, occasionally voiced in H.D. criticism, that violence is a function of patriarchy.[22] Finally, a historical reading of Lacan's theories against Klein's allows us to question the inevitability of his idea, also given considerable play in H.D. criticism, that to enter language is to lose the mother; this is, in fact, a direct reversal of Klein's idea that to acquire the power to symbolize is to recover the mother (to make relations with the mother possible again) and might be suspect for the very neatness of that reversal.

An almost opposite set of problems emerges when we read Kristeva against Klein. All the capacity for aggression (symbolic or otherwise) that Lacan denies the mother Kristeva returns to her when she posits (in Jacqueline Rose's words) "a femininity whose over powerful and physical reality effectively places cultures at risk." But Kristeva also seems to place the mother at the far edge of human society, whose total resources of violence and death she then comes to represent. Defenders would object that Kristeva is diagnosing such a placement rather than endorsing it, but as Rose points out, there are troubling moments in her arguments when "the whole of her work seems to turn on itself, implicating her own concepts in the fantasies, ambivalences and projections which she describes."[23] The very instability of such moments, when cultural diagnosis reverts to cultural participation, can itself be read as part of Kristeva's debt to Klein, whose own work performs similar oscillations on similar issues, offering to analyze as such Western culture's most volatile fantasies of maternal good and maternal evil, but then grounding the production of such fantasies in a biological, and hence inevitable, theory of psychic development.[24] The ease with which both Kristeva's and Klein's theories can be interpreted to support the idea that the mother's powers of aggression put her uniquely in league with the forces of death, devilry, and horror (that maternal aggression is always destructive, never creative) should caution us about embracing either woman's theories wholeheartedly. This caution applies with particular force when we use Kristeva or Klein to elucidate H.D.'s writing, because their analyses tend to replicate, rather than problematize, H.D.'s own persistent and equivocal associations between motherhood and death.

If the investigation of Klein's influence on H.D. opens up her late poetry to new areas of psychoanalytic inquiry and hypothesis, the historicizing impulse behind such an investigation also permits us to read psychoanalytic theories themselves for their patterns of social complicity, duplicity, and resistance. Feminist psychoanalytic criticism has tended to confine this kind of reading to questions of sexual and gender identity and/or positioning, and—in direct opposition to recent trends in feminism as a whole—has paid less attention to the tendentious encoding of racial, national, and cultural identities or positions in psychoanalytic theories and practices. These latter encodings form an important part of H.D.'s poetic reception of psychoanalysis. For example, H.D. appears to have engaged the following ideas directly in her poetry: Walter Schmideberg's association of the Kleinian "bad mother" with the female image of Britannia on World War II posters; Freud's recurring associations of the unconscious with people of "coloured descent" and with "primitive" and ancient Eastern societies; and the convergence of imperialist and psychoanalytic discourses on the task of defining "normal" relations within the family.

While the first example informs my reading of *Trilogy*, the latter two become central to my reading of *Helen in Egypt*. For Freud's essays on hysteria and on Moses share with Eisenstein's accounts of montage filmmaking and spectatorship an investment in racialized as well as gendered notions of memory, vision, and creative thought; this common investment underwrites H.D.'s own unorthodox portrayal of Helen of Troy as a black woman. Trading on the many homologies between Freud's and Eisenstein's accounts, H.D. seizes upon a method for refiguring the pathologized hysteric as a politicized spectator empowered by visions of radical social change. With this attempt to synthesize and jointly transform insights of Freudian psychoanalysis and Marxist aesthetic theory, she anticipates the post-structuralist concerns of critics such as Althusser, Fredric Jameson, Stephen Heath, and Jacqueline Rose. But in substituting connotations of "social change" for those of "neurotic illness," H.D. also sends up a smoke screen that hides the more conservative logic of nostalgia at work in her poem's visionary reforms of the family.

Making an intriguing argument in her book *Gender Trouble*, Judith Butler calls on Freud's theories of melancholia to explain how heterosexuals come to identify with their same-sex parents. She portrays such identification as a grieving process gone awry, where the mourner attempts to recover a lost same-sex love by embodying it in his or her own person.[25] Against the backdrop of this argument, we might read the hysteric as a person grieving not the loss of one parent or another, but the loss or the risked loss of the family itself. Threatened by the family's secret past and threatening that secrecy with leakage, with grievance, with representation, the hysteric tries, as Freud says, "to play all the parts single-handed" (*Interpretation of Dreams* 149)—to identify with and embody all the familial loves she or he may lose, is losing, has lost. She is, he is, literally homesick, and embodies nostalgia, grief for the loss (the history) of the family. When I first read *Helen in Egypt*, I understood nothing but cried anyway in a burst of tears. When I began to know my way around the poem, my own nostalgia for the patriarchal family alarmed me. The patriarchal family (for it's that family H.D. seems to grieve in *Helen in Egypt*) is something most feminists are urgently trying to change, to render unrecognizable. How can we miss it? But if we bury it, if we lose it, how can we fail to grieve for it? And if we grieve for it, how can we be sure it is gone, or even that we want it gone? Theseus says: "where do they go, our old loves, / when love ceases?" (*HE* 148). And Paris says: "why remember Achilles?" (*HE* 142).

Isis in her grief does not bury her old loves. She revives them, in the form of Osiris—brother, husband, father, king. This is where I located my resistance to *Helen in Egypt*, a resistance I then strengthened along critical lines. H.D.'s bid to ground the nostalgic project of the patriarchal family's reconstruction in the recovery of the ancient Egyptian (hieroglyphic) story of Isis was highly overdetermined in the postwar era of decolonization. When Gayatri Spivak discusses Kristeva's exactly analogous bid to recover the mother in ancient "Chinese writing [which] maintained the memory of matrilinear pre-history (collective and individual) in its architectonic of image, gesture, and sound," she comments: "Reflecting a broader Western cultural practice, the 'classical' East is studied with primitivistic reverence, even as the 'contemporary' East is treated with realpolitikal contempt. . . . My final question about this macrological nostalgia for the pre-history of the East is plaintive and predictable: what about us?" (pp. 138, 140).

We can trace this link between H.D. and Kristeva back to a shared psychoanalytical tradition (though such a tradition is not the only thing they have in common). With less reverence, Freud also links ancient cultures (Mycenae, Egypt), ancient writing forms (hieroglyphs), and "archaic" powers of visual and sensory thought with the mother.[26] But then a nostalgic longing for the supposedly undiminished visceral and emotional thought patterns of "so-called 'Primitives' " and of women informs Eisenstein's program for a revolutionary cinematography as well. Again, it is important to point out that this nostalgia depends on the conviction that the power associated with these populations has been lost, a conviction that contemporary history has made, and continues to make, multiply suspect. For in associating white women and people of color with an irrational "prehistory" that the rational postures of civilized white men simultaneously displace and depend on, Freud and Eisenstein recast as a diachronic developmental struggle, waged across millennia with a victor named in advance, the synchronic political struggles against patriarchal imperialism waged in their own era with far less certain outcome by militant feminists on the one hand and anticolonial insurgents on the other.

Once again, Melanie Klein is strikingly alone among the theorists I place in conversation with H.D.'s poetry in her resolute refusal of nostalgia. When she wants to pose analogies between global politics and the child's relation to the mother's destroyed and reconstituted body, she turns to the "ruthless cruelty" of the West's history of exploration and conquest, its campaigns to exterminate whole peoples and to repopulate their lands with the explorers' own kind (*LHR* 104–5). And when she talks about the mother herself, she breaks open the nostalgic space of individual "prehistory" to place in the garden the warring images of maternal nourishment and maternal persecution.[27] Yet when H.D. calls upon Kleinian concepts in *Helen in Egypt*, she does so not to dismantle the nostalgic logic of her own argument but to provide its final, phobic justification. The good and bad mother become a good and bad Egypt, with modern Egypt, currently undergoing a revolution of its own, appearing to underwrite the demonized half of that splitting. As Jacqueline Rose suggests in another context, colonial discourses of the previous century had helped to prepare H.D. for this turn of events as well: in "late nineteenth century imperialist texts, . . . the Christian conquest of other worlds takes the form of an encounter with a deadly female principle."[28]

Together, Spivak and Rose propose that Westerners have historically projected our nostalgia for the mother onto the ancient East, our fear of

the mother onto "the 'contemporary' East." But in my own argument,
have I not projected my nostalgia—my very Western nostalgia for revo-
lution—onto modern Egypt? Is my resistance to the apparent suppression
of modern Egyptian history in *Helen in Egypt* a postcolonial political
stance or a displaced resistance to my impossible longing for the old family
to return, newly intact, with all its conflicts magically resolved? Has my
nostalgia for revolution (something outside my experience, something
which, when I hear other people fetishize it, enrages me, something which
reading has taught me to regard with suspicion) replaced—preserved—
my nostalgia for the family? All true, I suspect. But with that suspicion
has come a strong suspicion of the political aims of my own unconscious
desires, my fantasies, and of the frequently represented power of female
desire, fantasy, or writing, to constitute a "space elsewhere," a space of
subversion or liberation, rupture and renewal. Yes and no. One of the best
ways to hold onto the powers that be is to call those powers "revolution-
ary." The Reagan Revolution. For that matter, right-wing fundamental-
ists in the Moslem Brotherhood were leading participants in the Egyptian
Revolution.[29] And what about the unconscious? Freud said that it too is
profoundly conservative, its very purpose is to conserve, that it is a space
of buried protest because it protests change. At what risk, with what eva-
siveness, have we as feminists defined the unconscious as an unequivocally
radical, subversive space, a space of the unnamed, the unborn, or a space
elsewhere, outside the Law?

My first reading of *Hermetic Definition* embarrassed me. It seemed to
have a power to embarrass everyone who got near it.[30] When I started dig-
ging up the poem's dense connections to the Algerian War, I was fascinated
by what I found, but also a bit relieved. Now I would not need to talk
about lust, and the shame of loving someone who doesn't love you back.
But shame about lust, about loving the wrong person, reemerged as race
shame, my shame as a white woman about the racist and imperialist as-
sumptions I found in H.D.'s writing and, with more reluctance, in my
own ambivalent reactions to her. Rachel Blau DuPlessis, commenting on
an earlier draft of my argument, noted my tendency to pass judgment on
H.D.'s ambivalent responses to African decolonization, to assert from the
security of my own historical moment and political conviction that H.D.
"should not be resistant to the logic of history." An editor responding to
the same draft commented on my own resistance to the exploitive and ap-
propriative nature of H.D.'s erotic representations of Durand's black
masculinity.

I agreed with DuPlessis. I could not discuss H.D.'s ambivalence with-
out enacting an ambivalence of my own, an ambivalence caught up in
hers: an urge to say that such desire, desire that "resists the logic of his-

tory," is shameful, in need of discipline or reprimand, and an opposing urge to grant such desire a hearing, a history of its own. This meant that I balked somewhat at the words of the editor, who was nevertheless perceptive in reading the emotional undertones of my argument. Whose body exactly, I wondered, was H.D. exploiting, appropriating? Was this body, this body of words, Durand's or H.D.'s? Do I condemn the appropriation of bodies by desire, by representation? No, not entirely. The body's inability not to be appropriated by someone else's desire, by someone else's powers of representation, is the plight and the bliss of the body, what makes it vulnerable, sociable, lovable, what gives it a place in history. In *Helen in Egypt*, H.D. uses the image of a girl caught in a hunter's net to characterize the love that Helen finds with Theseus, her "godfather" and childhood abductor (*HE* 154). Years later, as H.D. mourned Durand's death, she also mourned her own desire's equivocal powers of appropriation; as she puts it:

> I didn't know you had fallen into a trap,
> the reddest rose;
>
> . . .
>
> . . . anyway,
> it was too late to cast you out.   (*HD* 52)

The (god-)father's incestuous desire for the girl-child, the white woman's ambivalently racist desire for the black man: these desires are exploitive, explosive, and cause harm. But all desires are exploitive, appropriative to some degree, making it impossible to carve out a space of desire that can escape all moral, or historical, suspicion. And it seems important that H.D. staged her desire for Durand in the realm of fantasy and representation, the realm of reflection. Some of the terms of that desire resist the logic of history (he did not accept them; we do not accept them), but they also enact or stage the logic of history; they "reflect the conditions of her time."[31] At the same time, in their loosely associative form, H.D.'s fantasies of Durand appear to stage the logic of the unconscious, to reflect—perhaps—her attempt to make that logic available to conscious reflection. If this is the case, should we hold H.D. responsible for the reactionary political commitments underwriting her fantasies of Durand or should we champion the pages of her notebook as an intentionally decensored space in which the transgressive positions of unconscious desire could be explored without necessarily being endorsed?

But to phrase the question this way is to assume that we are dealing with strictly demarcated alternatives. In fact, in H.D.'s erotic fantasies of Durand as a Lawrentian dark god, no such clarity exists. These fantasies draw on the racist modernist tradition of primitivist myth-making. But

Durand's persona as a dark god also functions in H.D.'s poem as a figure
of redemption, and answers to needs for healing and regeneration arising
in part from the very violence of colonialism and decolonization that this
same persona seems called upon to eclipse. In other words, Durand's per-
sona as a dark god functions in the poem as the visionary solution to the
historical crisis of decolonization, even as it serves as a symptom of and a
screen for this same crisis. Thus, this figure stands at the intersection of
an important doubling of purpose in H.D.'s late poetry: her use of writing
both to project visions of social redemption and to expose and explore her
own unconscious fantasies. Because she identifies the workings of the un-
conscious with the workings of eternity, H.D.'s visionary solutions to
current political crises draw authority from the very ambivalences and
contradictions of unconscious desire. Jacqueline Rose reminds us that
"there can be no direct politicisation of the unconscious since this is to
confuse political and psychic resistance or, more simply, struggle and
symptomatic distress."[32] Yet when we say that the represented terms of
H.D.'s desire for Durand both conform to and "resist the logic of his-
tory," where are we but inside that confusion, mixing up—sorting out—
the difference between political struggle and "symptomatic distress"?

If one set of questions adheres to the writing of *Hermetic Definition*, a
slightly different set adheres to its publication, which Norman Holmes
Pearson undertook after H.D.'s death. One reason we have previously
known so little about the historical context of this poem is that Pearson
did not want any extratextual meaning to accrue to Durand in the critical
introduction that accompanies the poem's published version. Rejecting re-
peated editorial requests for more information on Durand, he wrote to
James Laughlin at New Directions, "I may be wrong in keeping Durand's
profile down but I am sure, in fact, he does not regard himself, even after
death, as an hermetic figure."[33] We might read this as a cover-up, extend-
ing and complicating H.D.'s own decision to edit out of her poem all di-
rect allusions to the contemporary fighting in Africa. But whom was Pear-
son trying to protect? Was it H.D.? Or was he trying to protect Durand,
to represent him, to act in his interest? Was he afraid of what Durand had
become, what he might become, once he got mixed up with what H.D.
had written about him? Did he hope to keep the preposterous, animal,
mystical, possessed, epiphanic Durand of H.D.'s poem separate from Lio-
nel Durand's own history, the circle of what was proper to him, his
wishes, his life's work? Here again, we are faced with two bodies—this
time they "belong" to Durand—but the problem of constructing the re-
lation between them is no longer purely textual. For if I set out to histori-
cize and criticize H.D.'s visionary politics in *Hermetic Definition*, I ended

up collaborating with her—against the declared protest of Pearson, the projected protest of Durand—in a joint project to bring together two bodies that Durand himself may well have wished to keep apart. Thus, my argument inaugurates the public history of the very commemorative process it sets out to critique, and my own desire revives with shifting, even self-contradictory, loyalties the conflictual process of mutual regard and self-regard that, as Pearson so astutely notes, continues "even after death."

Durand appears in H.D.'s poem, in Pearson's letters to New Directions, and in my own argument as a man whose desires and intentions are largely unknown and yet of urgent concern and intense speculation for those who remember him. In this regard, he twins H.D., who was herself so reluctant to call a halt to the willfulness of the body at the threshold of death and who returns in this book as a woman of unruly passions, a wide and detailed knowledge of texts, and elaborate, even devious, intentions. If I have collaborated uneasily with H.D. in the business of remembering Durand, I have collaborated with her with far more presumption and for a far greater length of time in the business of remembering her own words, her own writing. In this sense, my readings of three of H.D.'s late long poems resemble the psychoanalytic encounter that provided her with a model for them. More precisely, I might say that these readings reproduce the presumptuous and uncertain terrain of the encounter between the analyst and the hysteric. At the center of that encounter lies the ambiguity over whose role will name the encounter, whose methodology will define it. In his first accounts, Freud opposes the hysteric's fraudulent, incomplete, and self-contradictory powers of memory to the circumspect, rational, and truth-loving investigations of the analyst. But as Jacqueline Rose points out, Freud's retraction of the seduction theory and his positing of a universal unconscious fantasy life initiate a crisis of indeterminacy, serving to confuse the difference between the hysteric's methods of remembering and those of the analyst.[34]

Somewhat surprisingly, even before he launches and retracts the seduction theory, Freud makes passing reference to the potential fraudulence of the life history the analyst reconstructs on the hysteric's behalf. In *Studies on Hysteria*, he notes that hysterics sometimes deny the validity of memories that the analyst retrieves for them and he asks: "Are we to disregard this withholding of recognition" or "are we to suppose that we are really dealing with thoughts which never came about, which merely had a *possibility* of existing, so that the treatment would lie in the accomplishment of a psychical act which did not take place at the time?" Along the same lines, he wonders "whether . . . we are not dating back to the period

of the illness an arrangement of the psychical material which in fact was
made after recovery." But then he asserts rather abruptly: "these are ques-
tions which I should prefer not to discuss as yet" (pp. 300, 287).

No longer here to "withhold recognition" from the array of textual
borrowings, revisions, and rebuttals I "recover" in reading her poetry,
H.D. is also no longer here to confirm the myriad intentions for which
she serves as host in my reconstruction of her poetic arguments. Not the
analyst exactly, but a hysterical participant in a process of reconstruction
that continues past H.D.'s death, I open myself to charges of accomplish-
ing psychical acts and arranging psychical material long after the fact. In-
deed, my very bid to claim the authority of the analyst in the beginning
stages of this project has necessitated these late self-disclosures of my own
hysteria. Meeting strong resistance to the arguments I was positing both
in my first circle of readers and in myself, I redoubled my efforts to doc-
ument my assertions, providing proof that H.D. read the texts or knew
of the events I myself had unearthed. To a degree, this legwork has paid
off, providing a fair amount of evidence for claims that at first seemed
unlikely. But such marshaling of evidence, while it may increase the con-
fidence of the analyst, only defers the larger, more urgent question of
whether H.D. read every one of these texts, whether she responded to the
knowledge of each of these events, in the particular, often intricate ways
I have proposed.

Chances are, of course, that she did not. But while I have had to throw
off an earlier wide-eyed and visionary ambition to see "the whole scope
and plan" of H.D.'s late poetry "all in minute detail" (*T* 154–55), I con-
tinue to keep faith—as Freud puts it—with the *possibility* that any one
reading I propose is sufficiently credible as to be illuminating. In most
cases, that is the best a critic can hope for. Furthermore, I think there is an
important distinction to be made between the claim that H.D. did engage
her source texts along the exact lines I propose and the claim that she was
capable of such an engagement. Doubts about H.D.'s intelligence, learn-
ing, and achievement have characterized her critical reception from the
start. This persistent doubt about H.D.'s intellectual and artistic capabil-
ities stands in stark contrast to the infinite credulity with which we con-
tinue to honor claims about the hermeneutic depth and encyclopedic range
of *Ulysses*, *The Waste Land*, and *The Cantos*. If for no other reason, the
readings of H.D. I offer here deserve a hearing for their very insistence on
the extremely high degree of conscious subtlety, specificity, and sophis-
tication we must be prepared to recognize in her work.

But perhaps it is only fair to point out in a book of this kind that on
the one occasion I had to gain indisputable evidence for my case, I lost my
nerve. The morning after I completed the book's first draft, I had a dream.

I was at a literary gathering in a college lecture room, where the usual large crowd had surrounded, and obscured, the person of an important living author. Alone and to the side, H.D. stood watching. She was tall—gigantic really—a full head above the others. I went up to her, exclaiming, "H.D.! I'm so glad to see you. I'm writing a book about you, about your long poems." She smiled distantly, but her eyes remained fixed on the crowd. "It's about your visionary moments in fact—when the gods turn up in your dreams." She looked over, her glance polite and unsearching. All of a sudden, I realized our encounter was coming to an end and I had yet to settle a small matter between us. "H.D.," I began, "did Melanie Klein really influence you as I said she did?" But then I thought of the dismay and embarrassment, the long years of new research, should her answer be no. I woke up, leaving the question unasked in my dream.[35]

"Stealing from 'muddies body'"

— War and Women's Aggression in *Trilogy*

A Yield of Pleasure from Words

I liked O. liking them and I think he really did.

    —H.D. to Norman Holmes Pearson (November 8, 1943)

Trilogy opens with a string of analogies between the stripped and broken London of the Blitz years, the recently excavated tombs at Luxor and Karnak, the child Samuel shivering before his lord's voice, a museum exhibit, the catastrophically preserved Pompeii, and a body, imagined without gender or history, whose catalogued components each meet a separate death: the brain bursts, the flesh melts, the heart burns out, the muscles shatter, and "the outer husk" is "dismembered" (*T* 4). Perhaps the most surprising term in the sequence is that of the museum exhibit. Asserting that "poor utensils" of a "sliced" London home "show / like rare objects in a museum" (*T* 4), H.D. toys with the fantasy of placing the city's, and the body's, devastation on display, making a show of it. Her sense of the appeal as well as the horror of this spectacle is evident not only in the descriptive attention she gives it but also in the joyless-ness of the questions that break off the fantasy and conclude the first section:

> yet the frame held:
> we passed the flame: we wonder
> what saved us? what for?   (*T* 4)

These lines introduce a figure H.D. will use again late in her wartime memoir of childhood, *The Gift*, where her tone of despair is even more explicit. She writes of the Blitz bombing raids:

> I had passed the flame, I had had my initiation, I was tired of all that. . . . [S]ometimes when the mind reaches its high peak of endurance, there is almost the hope—God forgive us—that the bomb that must fall on someone, would fall on me—but it could not—it must not. Because if the bomb fell on me, it would fall on Bryher, and Bryher must go on. That is the way we are trapped, that is the way I was trapped.[1]

If in the opening section of *Trilogy* the frame that holds testifies, however ambiguously, to a saving power, here in *The Gift* it offers only a double bind in which H.D. cannot wish for her own death without wishing death on her lesbian lover as well. Moreover, while the bombing of London provides the occasion for this double bind, H.D.'s own despair and ambivalence in the face of death enforce its power over her. What, then, are we to make of the fact that H.D. compels her reader to repeat her wartime experience of (self-)entrapment in the multiple narratives of "The Walls Do Not Fall"? Writing to Norman Holmes Pearson after completing the first sequence of poems in *Trilogy*, she notes, "Osbert [Sitwell] seemed to like the way they were written, he wrote Bryher to the effect that H.D. had neatly set traps, that snapped shut with the inevitable and unexpected idea or *mot* at the end. (These are not his exact words.) But I liked O. liking them and I think he really did" (*T* vii–viii).

Of course, it is not quite fair to say that H.D.'s neatly set traps repeat for her reader the double bind of living under fire. For if the yield of her Blitz trap was helpless "terror" that cut off even the hope of her own release, the yield of these traps is helpless pleasure—and the pleasures attendant on releasing another's pleasure. In fact they sound very much like Freud's description of jokes, whose "original intention" is "to obtain a yield of pleasure . . . from words" (*Jokes* 169). Freud suggests a further point of correspondence between H.D.'s word-traps and joking when he proposes that jokes leash violence to the ends of laughter, using a "disguised aggressiveness" to overwhelm their listeners' powers of conscious resistance so as "to release pleasure even from sources that have undergone repression" (*Jokes* 108, 134). The joke's interlocking structure of entrapment and release provides H.D. with a way to restage her traumatic Blitz experiences within the controlled play of language, even as it allows her to exchange the unexpected inevitability of death for the more fortuitous surprise endings wit can supply. Indeed, the snappy punch lines that conclude H.D.'s word-traps repeatedly act out the most surprising of all imaginable endings, that sacred reversal of rational expectation in which "we rise again from death and live" (*T* 87).

In current readings of *Trilogy*, these redemptive dramas of rebirth testify to H.D.'s feminism and pacifism, her gendered aversion to the violence of war. Susan Stanford Friedman proposes that "*Trilogy* argues fundamentally that a world at war has lost touch with the female forms of divinity and that the search for life amid death is inextricably linked with the recovery of the Goddess." More recently, Susan Schweik contends that Kaspar's visionary resurrection of the lost Atlantis near the end of *Trilogy* reveals "a register not defined by, provoked by, or responsive to men's wars." Both Friedman and Schweik are careful to qualify their arguments; Friedman notes that "*Trilogy* does not explicitly link war with patriarchy," while Schweik reminds us that H.D. "could not and would not entirely relinquish her own part in fashioning a war she saw not only as abhorrent but also as imperative."[2] But they each stop short of the possibility that World War II forced H.D. to confront the conflict between her pacifism and her own destructive and self-destructive tendencies. It is this possibility I propose to consider; indeed, I will argue that far from offering immunity against the criminal violence of "men's wars," H.D.'s gender provides the troubled occasion for her extended poetic investigation into the frightening implications of female aggression.

While any act of aggression can be frightening in a time of war, Sandra M. Gilbert suggests that during World War I the women who were largely barred from the front were more, not less, vulnerable to charges of a death-dealing malevolence than the men who were recruited to do the actual killing. Reviewing war propaganda, official documents, personal memoirs, and literary works by men and women in Britain and the United States, Gilbert traces the contours of a widespread cultural fantasy that made World War I "in some peculiar sense [women's] fault, a ritual sacrifice to their victorious femininity" (p. 199). Claire M. Tylee differs sharply with Gilbert's assessment of the extent both of British women's political and economic gains and of their militarism during World War I, but agrees that "part of the British government's Great War propaganda campaign was designed to make both men *and women* believe that women in general supported the government's war-aims and 'sacrificed' men gladly. Censorship was used to prevent women from denying this publicly, especially in print" (p. 209).[3] In her discussion of World War II propaganda, Susan Gubar suggests that images of women's heterosexual vulnerability, allure, and/or pollution replaced World War I images of threatening maternity,[4] but Susan Schweik's analysis of both popular and canonized writing of World War II points to the persistent literary pairing of mothers and war. Schweik proposes that while one group of "biblical war poems" from the 1940's typically "represents a maternity and a birth scenario before, beyond, and outside war," a second group "reveals moth-

erhood as the source and prop, as well as the subject, of [war's] atrocity"
(pp. 262–63).

In contrast to those critics who would place *Trilogy* securely within
Schweik's former category, I want to suggest that the poem grapples am-
bivalently and repeatedly with the assumptions of the second category.[5]
The matriarchal dramas of rebirth that *Trilogy* so insistently performs
speak not to H.D.'s belief that women inherit a culture—or constitu-
tion—free of all violent intent, but rather to her attempt to reconcile both
the fact and the fear of female aggression with a necessary faith in women's
powers of life. Two psychoanalytic accounts of female aggression provide
H.D. with a crucial set of terms for such a project. The first account is
Freud's; while he usually avoids the topic altogether, preferring to align
femininity with passivity and masochism, a scattered network of associ-
ations in his writing posit disturbing links between repetition, aggressive
female (and particularly lesbian) sexuality, and death. Introducing a new
intellectual influence on H.D.'s thinking, I argue that Melanie Klein's the-
ories of the early mother-child dyad provide H.D. with a provocative al-
ternative to Freud's account. In the years leading up to World War II, H.D.
underwent an analysis ambivalently indebted to Klein's example, in which
her analyst, Walter Schmideberg, aligned her paralyzing "war phobia"
with wider cultural fantasies of the good and bad mother, such as those
since analyzed by Gilbert, Culleton, and Schweik.[6] At the same time,
Klein's bitter professional struggle with her daughter and Walter's wife,
Dr. Melitta Schmideberg, formed an important contemporary backdrop
to H.D.'s own inquiry into the vicissitudes of the mother-daughter
relationship.[7]

While Klein's accounts of the early mother-child dyad play into, as
much as they resist, wartime fantasies of female malevolence, they also
provide a model for reconceiving female aggression as productive and cre-
ative. I am proposing that this model informs H.D.'s own poetic pro-
gression past the persecutory world on view in "The Walls Do Not Fall,"
through the stabler world of pleasure and vision in "Tribute to the An-
gels," and into the renewable world of "The Flowering of the Rod,"
where the reality of loss and grief tempers but no longer overpowers the
poet's faith in life's resurgence. Throughout the poem's three montage se-
quences, H.D. uses Kleinian concepts to engage and transform the neg-
ative connotations of repetition, reversal, and return underlying Freud's
association of women's aggressive sexuality with the death drive.[8]

Thus, the playful word-traps of "The Walls Do Not Fall," whose
jokelike peripeteias double as dramas of rebirth, constitute only the first
in a series of H.D.'s attempts to reclaim her aggression as a cause for re-
joicing. Like any good performer, H.D. manages to save her best joke for

last. With its seemingly innocuous equation of the Christ Child and a "bundle of myrrh" (*T* 172), the poem's final epiphany sets a trap yielding pleasure from sources so deeply repressed that their brief emergence in the reader's consciousness carries with it all the unexpected and inevitable force of a divine manifestation. If, in the involuntary instant of getting the joke, the reader is unable to distinguish between the pleasures of witnessing the repressed return and those of witnessing the Child return, that, I will argue, is the joke's point. That H.D.'s strategy of confusing the reader's sense of where this moment's pleasure is coming from holds particular interest for feminist readers of *Trilogy* is largely due to the content H.D. assigns to the returning repressed: female aggression, desire, and periodicity—or returning—itself.

A Bit on the Warpath: The Schmideberg Analysis

In a way I adore her sheer and perfect aggressiveness but it is also troublesome and I dont pretend to be able to handle her.

　　—Bryher to Walter Schmideberg (February 29, 1940)

Between October of 1935 and May of 1937, H.D. pursued analysis with Walter Schmideberg "five times a week" for "9" and then for "7 straight months."[9] In the only discussion of this analysis to date, Susan Friedman downplays its importance. Extrapolating from Bryher's and H.D.'s own testimonies of affection for Schmideberg, Friedman characterizes him as a "comfortable, homey friend" who helped H.D. to "fill in the gaps" in the "framework" provided by her analysis with Freud.[10] But H.D.'s records of her almost daily sessions with Schmideberg over a two-and-a-half-year period trouble the smooth face she occasionally put on this analysis and contradict the supposition that Schmideberg kept within lines of interpretation previously laid out by Freud. Instead, these records suggest that H.D. used the years leading up to World War II to focus on the unorthodox topic of female aggression in an analysis that ambivalently engaged the work of Melanie Klein, Schmideberg's mother-in-law.[11]

During the same years, Klein's pioneering speculations on aggression, paranoia, and reparation in the mother-child dyad became the object of increasing controversy in the British Psychoanalytic Society. As Pearl King has summarized, this controversy came to a head in the Extraordinary Meetings held in early 1942 when several Members of the Society prepared resolutions voicing their

anxiety concerning the discrepancy between Melanie Klein's approach to psychoanalysis and what they referred to as "Freudian psychoanalysis," and the

consequent anxiety that students and the public should be exposed to her the-
ories which they felt were in many ways alien to their understanding of psy-
choanalysis. . . . These resolutions made it clear to Melanie Klein and her col-
leagues that some Members of the Society would like to remove her from it,
or at least to prevent her work from being taught to candidates.[12]

In this controversy, Dr. Melitta Schmideberg emerged as her mother's
"arch opponent."[13] While Melitta's first professional essays reveal an initial
sympathy with Kleinian theory, Klein's biographer, Phyllis Grosskurth,
reports that she and Edward Glover began to campaign against Klein as
early as 1933, when Melitta became an elected member of the Institute (p.
212).[14] Although Melitta grounded her attacks on her mother in carefully
reasoned theoretical disagreements and professional reservations about
Kleinian practice, her public airing of their differences was, by all ac-
counts, extremely personal, violent, and bitter.

While Melitta had already turned against her mother in 1935 when
H.D. began analysis with Walter, H.D.'s letters to Bryher suggest that
Walter (whom she called Uhlan and Bear) continued to make use of Klein-
ian concepts during this period. From the start, Walter gravitated to "the
war period" of "good old '18" and H.D.'s "deep fund of repressed aggres-
sion."[15] With H.D. as with his other clients, he took up Klein's focus on
the violent psychic life of early infancy; a year into her analysis, H.D. re-
ports to Bryher Silvia Dobson's comment that Walter "is a good analyst,
he brings it back to the nursery, every time."[16] In one of his first inter-
pretations in H.D.'s own analysis, Walter employed Klein's idea that in its
early position of paranoia the infant carries out phantasy raids on its moth-
er's body, robbing it of precious babies and other riches that it feels the
"bad mother" has unjustly withheld. In early November 1935, H.D. in-
forms Bryher that Walter "thinks I have a deep, very early guilt suppres-
sion about wanting to steal a baby, a brother or cousin, and that I had a
lot of that when I 'stole' you and went to Greece. I think this is a new and
very sound idea and it means a certain amount of exploring. S. and I talk
chiefly [about] this guilt and the suppressed rage."[17]

H.D.'s analytic focus on her wish to steal a child culminated in the
following spring with her "out-burst" of protest when Bryher conveyed
her mother's request to spend the day with H.D.'s daughter, Perdita, on
Perdita's seventeenth birthday in March of 1936. Walter attributes H.D.'s
rage to her unconscious fear that Bryher's mother was stealing Perdita just
as H.D. had long ago stolen Bryher herself: "Sch. seems to think it is a
valuable snag in the UNK [unconscious], baby stolen by bad-mother,
mixed up with good-mother protecting same."[18] On March 10, 1936,
H.D. reiterates to Bryher: "The UNK great problem is the pup [Perdita]

and stealing of same, in which you double for PUP." And on March 12, 1936, she reports that she and Walter have traced this fantasy back to H.D.'s early childhood attachment to a "huge doll" named Dolly: "You and Pup apparently double in the UNK for myself, or the Dolly . . . South A. at first, was to UNK a sort of Ali Baba cave with treasures . . . fear of getting shut in, stealing from 'muddies body' and so on . . . very clever Uhlan" (H.D.'s ellipses).[19] A year into the analysis, in October of 1936, H.D. is still discussing her aggression in the Kleinian terms of the child's jealousy over the mother's hidden funds of "treasure" and power. She informs Bryher, "I am in such an aggressive bear-layer, it is as well, to shift it out. He says an important point was reached and passed—I told you—with externalization of the 'hidden phallus.' But it seems to me endless."[20]

This sustained focus on aggression allowed H.D. to supplement Freud's account of her unconscious terror of male sadism toward women with fresh evidence of her own aggressive impulses, toward men and women alike.[21] On November 14, 1936, she tells Bryher, "Bear is most kind, I am getting terribly up-stage and 'aggress' at him." A month earlier, on October 8, 1936, she notes to Bryher that Silvia Dobson "was getting released like mad, I suspect the B[ear] will suspect you of incendiary bombs in her UNK, as evidently she threw communism versus faschism at him, her whole hour. . . . Both of us seem to be a bit on the war-path but I am taking it out in a more subterranean manner." At one point Bryher gleefully reports to H.D. that "Pup [Perdita] is shaking with terror at prospect of a grim, devouring Bear." However, H.D.'s letters indicate that Bear, far from showing his own teeth, kept himself busy unpacking "a sort of lesb[ian]-clutch between pup and me" in which aggressive, if loving, feelings abounded. In March of 1936, H.D. writes to Bryher of Perdita: "I am torn, as Sch. said between wanting to eat her up, and being afraid lest I get too attached—so please forgive all the ambi-stiff [ambivalence-stuff]"; and in April of the following year she reports on Walter's efforts to redirect the teenage girl's "amorous onslaughts" on her mother and to "help her 'aggression'" by encouraging her passion for driving.[22]

In addition, Walter may have used his wife, Melitta, as a lightning rod to expose H.D.'s aggression toward her own mother. On June 15, 1937, H.D. complains to Bryher, "Bear very nice but a little snappy. I get so tired of Oedipus, it now appears I must hate Melitta." Walter's move to interpret H.D.'s hostility toward Melitta along the standard Freudian lines of the little girl's sudden hatred for the mother at the advent of the oedipal complex surprises the reader too quickly convinced that he took a thoroughly Kleinian approach in H.D.'s analysis. In fact, Walter's reception of

Klein was intensely ambivalent, as was Bryher's. Both explicitly balked at aligning themselves with the London school of psychoanalysis, increasingly associated with Klein, over the Viennese school, still loyally backing Freud. In a 1936 letter in which she asserts her own distance from "Albion" in these matters, Bryher questions Walter as to why he and Melitta "include yourselves with the English group? The Professor [Freud] himself assured me you were brought up most carefully according to the strictest Viennese principles."[23]

Bryher's question reinforces the evidence in H.D.'s letters suggesting that Walter Schmideberg equivocated in his alliances in 1936. Phyllis Grosskurth recounts, however, that by the Extraordinary Meetings of 1942 he was discussing Klein's theories in hostile terms. Such a stance would suggest that he did in fact align himself with the Viennese. Yet this alignment is itself ambiguous since it was his contention in 1942 not that Klein's theories were heretical but that they plagiarized established concepts of continental Freudians.[24] H.D.'s own take on the matter appears to have been less divisive and partisan than either Bryher's or Walter's. She writes to Bryher in 1936, "I needed to get together IN London on psa-[psychoanalysis], and the Bear is perfect as he combines Wien and London."[25]

H.D.'s letters to Bryher support this diagnosis of her analysis, and suggest that Walter was practicing an uneasy hybrid of Freudian and Kleinian thought, which emphasized precisely those areas in Freud's theories that Klein would greatly expand upon, and mixed in specifically Kleinian terms and postulations with those that were originally Freud's. Even Bryher seems to have been more knowledgeable and accepting of Klein's theories than she was wont to let on. In 1936 she declares to Walter that she knows "all the books of Susan Isaacs," one of Klein's main disciples, "and agrees with them partly"; in 1937 she jokes with him along Kleinian lines: "it is so depressing to think one has spent years in acute agony just because one wanted to be a cannibal." And in 1940 she writes asking him to clarify the meanings of the Kleinian terms "depressive" and "manic defence."[26] Moreover, when H.D.'s letters to Bryher begin to fill up with Kleinian terms—"hidden phallus," "good" and "bad mother," "muddies body"—Bryher responds in kind with passing references to "infantile fantasies" and "sado-masochistic infantile tendencies."[27]

While it is thus possible to establish both Bryher's and H.D.'s familiarity with major concepts of Kleinian psychoanalysis, their friendship with the Schmidebergs provided another, more intimate and voyeuristic, vantage point on Klein's career during this period. From the start, Bryher was eager to soak up the gossip surrounding Klein and her estranged daughter and to fan the flames of controversy. In fact, Bryher may have

dubbed their new friends "Polar Bears" because their reception of her re-
quests for "dirt" were so chilly. Punning on their patronym, Bryher re-
ports to H.D. on the eve of the 1936 International Congress that "the Polar
Bears are an iceberg of dignity. . . . No dirt *whatever*."[28]

The Schmidebergs' reticence here seems understandable, since Bryher
had been beside herself with mirth since March over a sadistic plan to bait
the Bears in public by "reading a paper on paranoia in polar bears at the
Congress." In an unmistakable allusion to the current controversy be-
tween British and continental camps over Klein's theories of infantile
paranoia and oral sadism, she outlines her plan for H.D.: "I refuse to allow
them to take this all so seriously. . . . I think with the connivance of Anna
[Freud], we'll probably give the sad story of the English analyst who was
devoured by his polar bear, and the poor bear that died under the attack
of Wien. As puppets perhaps, silhouettes or a film." Adding that "I should
think that the Congress will all end in one superb fight," she concludes by
noting that she "gave Anna some dollars to get all Wien there, to resist the
English heresies."[29] By the Congress of 1938, Bryher managed to get the
fight she was looking for—by starting it herself with London's own Er-
nest Jones. Bryher's report to H.D. on this fight, as well as another with
Anna Freud, ends with her triumphant boast that she now has the upper
hand as far as "dirt" goes: "I got an impassioned note from Mrs Bear [Me-
litta] imploring me to bring her the dirt. . . . Have to unload the dirt on
someone and have all the same to be a bit discreet with the Bears."[30]

In H.D.'s relationship with Bryher, it was generally understood that
Bryher, whom Freud described as excessively "warlike," was the more
openly aggressive of the two.[31] With this caution in mind, we might still
read Bryher's heady enthusiasm here as an indication of the pleasure H.D.
and her circle could take in exploring their "carnival aggression" in the
relative safety of the analytic dyad and the increasingly topsy-turvy court
of "Queen Victoria Melanie."[32] But these explorations could also be ter-
rifying. H.D. repeatedly testifies to the power of the Schmideberg analy-
sis to call up "perfectly damnable and perfidious dreams" and to leave her
"completely abandoned to my own fiery guilt and terror."[33]

A complex network of associations between female aggression and
war gleaned from H.D.'s records of her analysis provides an important
context for this "fiery guilt and terror" as well as for the themes of hunger,
oral violence, and persecution that abound in the first part of her wartime
Trilogy. Because the hungry Kleinian infant begins life experiencing the
absence of the breast as an active maternal assault, H.D. was vulnerable
to suggestions that she had played the role of the persecutory mother in
Perdita's early fantasies. Letters to Bryher in the early months of 1937 re-
port that H.D. and Walter discussed her "guilt that I did not feed Puss

[Perdita] after death of father," and her unconscious need to be assured that her first, stillborn daughter (delivered in the spring of 1915) "was 'wanted.' "[34] In late February, she had a dramatic and frightening nose-bleed in the bathtub, an incident that she linked to her current negotiations with Ian Parsons of Chatto and Windus for the publication of her translation of Euripides' *Ion*. It was this incident—"some sort of birth and guilt, I suppose"—which became the immediate catalyst for H.D.'s feelings of "fiery guilt and terror" and an important focal point in her discussions with Walter about "the first pup, who arrived also in the spring."[35]

The plot of *Ion* not only provides a necessary context for understanding these feelings and memories but also suggests why the play would emerge as a powerful site of symptom-formation and interpretation in an analysis indebted to Kleinian thinking: the play's protagonist Kreousa—who is raped and abandoned by Apollo, abandons her child Ion in turn, and later comes close to poisoning him—provides a literary embodiment of the Kleinian infant's phantasies of maternal negligence and persecution. Several months later, the theme of maternal abandonment emerges again in H.D.'s analysis when she records Walter's connection between the adolescent Perdita's recent outburst—"you are tearing me from my mother's arms"—and the time H.D. spent apart from her daughter in infancy. Noting that she has finally begun "to see the joke of it," she nevertheless passes on to Bryher Walter's speculation that " 'perhaps Perdita really DID feel the early separation' etc."[36]

While Walter Schmideberg was eager to uncover—or induce—guilt in H.D. for her refusal to comply with conventional expectations in mothering Perdita, he also encouraged H.D. to explore her infantile grievances against her mother, Helen Wolle Doolittle. Apparently, Walter believed that H.D.'s war-terror had been grafted onto her own early fantasies of the bad mother. It is not clear whether H.D. herself supplied any fantasies of this sort, but she does record that Walter was able to muster evidence for his case from the representations of threatening maternity on British war posters, which Sandra M. Gilbert has since analyzed along similar lines (pp. 209–13). In a chilling letter to Bryher, dated March 28, 1936, H.D. discusses her reactions to the current political "situation" of impending war:

> [I] am not going to allow myself to be bullied by any "situation," whatever. Blast them all. It couldn't be worse than the last and I survived that . . . and who wants to survive i[f] it IS worse. I don't believe in it anyhow . . . will simply hold my own against the "bad mother" as Sch. calls that incarnation of Brittania on the war-posters. There is also the good mother . . . and the joke king, as the world knows. (H.D.'s ellipses)

Three later letters to Bryher flow in and out of an elliptical style that makes it difficult to pin down all of H.D.'s references precisely. Nevertheless, these letters strongly suggest that Walter associated war with "weaning" along lines spelled out in Klein's recently articulated theory of the "depressive position." This theory redefined weaning as the time of transition from the infant's early position of paranoia to its subsequent, depressive position; in the former position, the infant perceives its own hunger as a kind of "air-war" attack by the persecutory mother's biting breasts and her burning and explosive excrement, while in the latter, it perceives its hunger as a destructive force directed against the mother. Phantasies attached with both positions can result in eating difficulties, according to Klein, either because the infant fears that the mother's food (or lack of it) is a harmful weapon or a poison sickening it from within, or because it fears that its desire to bite and chew up the mother will kill her. These ideas seem to underwrite H.D.'s comment of May 2, 1936, to Bryher on the subject of her analysis: "its all war-starvation material . . . . perhaps air-war does not mean starvation . . . I don't know" (H.D.'s ellipses). On May 6, 1936, she continues:

> The bear . . . gets up a lot about food and cleaning the house, having to do with the war having not made it worth while to eat or in any way, make an effort. Weaning of course, but applied direct to Cuth [Aldington] and the general slump in tinned beans etc. Anyhow, I am no longer sick of a morning, but all the same find food hard to chew, ~~but~~ that will come back now, I think.

And on October 5, 1936, she writes that she is "doing all the time, one way and another, food, starvation, and so on."[37]

It should be clear that H.D. devoted her analysis with Walter Schmideberg to a sustained investigation of the links between her war phobia and fantasies of aggression in the early mother-child dyad. But the substance of that analysis was completed by May of 1937 and H.D. would not begin "The Walls Do Not Fall" until 1942. What evidence is there that Kleinian concerns continued to occupy H.D.'s thoughts as she entered a second period of world war? Here, we might turn to an ongoing series of letters about her dog Claudi that Bryher sent to H.D. and Walter Schmideberg in the opening months of World War II.[38] In a letter to Walter dated February 29, 1940, Bryher (herself nicknamed "Dog") comments on Claudi, "In a way, I adore her sheer and perfect aggressiveness but it is also troublesome and I dont pretend to be able to handle her." In the spring, Bryher reports to both H.D. and Walter on her fears that a hostile neighbor has left out poisoned meat for Claudi, as well as on a comic but frightening episode in which Claudi chased two enemy Germans up a tree.[39] When Claudi becomes pregnant, Bryher reports to H.D. (who has already commented "Poor Claudie. . . . I too, had pups in war-time") that Claudi is "a thoroughly unwilling mother."[40] Bryher's summer letters fill up with news on Claudi's violent happiness "over not feeding her family anymore" and on the puppies' own inordinate sadism.[41] In August, after Claudi bites yet another workman, Bryher writes to Walter, "I am afraid we must send her away for training because this is too unsafe, if she bites anybody else, they can order her to be killed." In early September, Bryher finally did send away Claudi to the local military barracks, telling H.D., "It was time as she terrified everyone but ourselves."[42]

H.D.'s unflagging empathy for "poor Claudie" and her troubles challenges Susan Friedman's sense that the poet continued to associate her World War I pregnancies exclusively with female victimization at the hands of male sadists during this period. By the outset of World War II, H.D. was instead identifying, however playfully, with a mother whose life was endangered most immediately by the threat of reprisals for her own aggression.[43] And indeed, the thoroughly Kleinian landscape of poisoned food, maternal violence, infantile sadism, and fears of persecution evoked in Bryher's Claudi tales turns up again two years later in the animal narratives of "The Walls Do Not Fall." In the meantime, however, this landscape had also swallowed up the ordinary proceedings of the British Psychoanalytic Society.

By 1941, the battle between Klein and her daughter had erupted into a more general crisis, giving rise to the five Extraordinary Meetings of 1942, designed to address the larger affairs of the Society, and the subsequent Controversial Discussions, begun in January of 1943 and lasting until March of 1944.[44] While the Extraordinary Meetings devolved into spite campaigns and personal attacks, the Controversial Discussions were more formal, and more fruitful, meetings in which Klein and several of her female disciples offered summary papers of her theories in an attempt to clarify her debts to, and departures from, Freudian thought. There was general agreement, however, that both series of meetings, in which feelings often ran high, served as displaced sites for expressing deeper anxieties about World War II. In April of 1942, Sylvia Payne told the Society, "The conflict is extraordinarily like that which is taking place in many countries and I feel sure that it is in some way a tiny reverberation of the massive conflict which pervades the world."[45]

For H.D., in regular contact with the Schmidebergs throughout this period, both the terms of Klein's and her daughter's antagonism (reproduced in the wider debates, dominated by women, to which it gave rise)[46] and that antagonism's microcosmic mirroring of global conflict could well serve to confirm a capacity for aggression and injury among women as great as that being tapped by the male architects and antagonists of

World War II. Furthermore, the destructive nature of Klein's battles with Melitta formed a readily available counterpoint both to Bryher's and H.D.'s own destructive and self-destructive impulses before and during the war period, and to the pain these impulses brought them both.[47]

At the center of the professional crisis surrounding Klein stood the problem of whether a woman could claim to be using aggression productively or creatively at all. At a historical moment when all of Europe witnessed a return to war for the second time in half a century, the question of whether people in general could use aggression productively was an acute one. But as Walter Schmideberg himself suggested to H.D. and as recent feminist critics have substantiated, in the fantasy lives of the British public (stimulated by the misogynist offerings of the War Office) the question of human aggression was rarely settled with reference to people in general. Instead, two decades of war propaganda and literature routinely collaborated with Klein's theories on the infant's phantasies of the good and bad mother by deploying images of maternal nurturers innocent of all aggression to guarantee the possibilities of peace while simultaneously deriving the injury of war from women's uncommon appetite for destruction. (Indeed, in a reversal of Walter Schmideberg's move to read war propaganda in the context of Kleinian theory, we must read Klein's theoretical developments in their historical context of world war before we understand fully what they are trying to explain.) H.D., with her triple vantage points on the war effort, the controversy over Kleinian theory, and her own relationships with Bryher and Perdita, had multiple opportunities to observe the particular difficulty women have in representing the difference between productive and destructive aggression to themselves and their communities; both the difficulty of this task of representation and the escalation of retaliatory violence against women who do not (or cannot) succeed in it made their experience an exceptionally pertinent one to explore in a time of war.[48]

Eating a Way Out of It: H.D.'s Hunger Stories

I am hungry, the children cry for food
and flaming stones fall on them

— H.D., "The Walls Do Not Fall"

In "The Walls Do Not Fall," H.D. draws widely on a number of heterogenous traditions, exerting syncretic pressure on the icons and explanatory myths of gnosticism, Christianity, Judaism, ancient Egyptian mythology, and astrology. Juxtaposing Biblical settings—desert, shore, highway, and temple—with scenes from wartime London, she also ventures into landscapes shaped and misshapen by dream, vision, and fantasy. The patchwork world she assembles shows strong debts to Freud's theories of paranoia and Klein's related account of the infant's early paranoid position, not only in its otherwise curious association of world war with oral sadism, but also in the unpredictable patterns of fragmentation, repetition, reversal, and return that govern its deployment of imagery. These structural patterns replace progressive, linear development as the sequence's logic of succession; combined with prominent discontinuities of narrative, setting, character, and address, such a logic clearly aligns "The Walls Do Not Fall" with the wider modernist cultivation of montage and collage strategies of composition. But if H.D.'s strategies of composition here are familiar, the effects she achieves can seem quite new. Take, for instance, her consistent use of the first-person narrator throughout the sequence: Are we to read the sequence as a series of testimonies of different "I"'s or as the chronicle of the shifting fortunes of a single, metamorphosizing "I" who speaks in turn as mollusk, lover, worm, poet, religious initiate, dreamer, witness, ram, lamb, beggar, lunatic, and prophet? T. S. Eliot intervenes directly to resolve a similar ambiguity in *The Waste Land*, explaining in a footnote that "Tiresias, although a mere spectator and not indeed a 'character,' is yet the most important personage in the poem, uniting all the rest."[49] In "The Walls Do Not Fall," we receive no such assurances of unity.

The very indeterminacy of the status of the narrating "I" serves H.D. well in her repeated attempts to stage the drama of resurrection in this sequence, for each new section enforces the possibility of its speaker's rebirth. But this indeterminacy equally arouses anxieties about the stability and integrity of bodily life and of selfhood; in this sense, the ambiguous fragmentation of the narrating "I" across disparate sections participates in the ongoing drama of *sparagmos*, or the self in pieces, which gains such high visibility in the Kleinian infant's early phantasy life. H.D. explores this drama in recurring scenes of somatic and conceptual integrities violated not only by acts of outright destruction, but also by acts of metamorphosis and revelation. Playing out the drama of the self in pieces at the level of structure, she breaks open the integrity of individual sections by repeatedly lifting fragments from one section and lodging them in another. Detached from its original narrative context, a given word or image seems to float out of sight for shorter or longer distances, and then settle in another narrative that reincorporates it to startlingly new effect. This transnarrative action of reincorporating textual fragments in later sections is itself reproduced at the level of the sequence's literary subtexts; alluding to a specific passage in a source text in one section, H.D. stages the return of a neglected accompanying passage in a later section in ways that challenge and transform her initial appropriation.

H.D.'s highly manipulative attempts to define and redefine the reader's relationship to "The Walls" constitute perhaps the most obvious and dramatic instance of this strategy of dislodging and reincorporating fragments across the sequence's disjunctive narratives. The narrator of "The Walls" is an "I" who continually claims to merge into a "we," a plurality that itself functions not as a loose confederation of individual voices but as a fused community, almost a fused self, of "nameless initiates" who together take one "Name" (*T* 21). Generated in opposition to this "we," a hostile, uninitiated, and equally uniform "they" also occupies the sequence's narrative landscapes. Addressed by turns as part of the narrator's "us" and as a hostile "you" aligned with "them," the reader is positioned within the text as an unstable fragment bouncing between two antagonistic communities, and thus continually falls in and out of the narrator's circle of sympathy and trust. Once again, H.D. leaves indeterminate here whether different narrators address different readers at different points or whether her readers themselves are understood to be enacting rapid reversals of status and affiliation.

It is within this space divided by rival communities, whose common boundary we as readers constantly find ourselves transgressing, that H.D. "neatly set[s] traps" for us. The traps themselves typically employ rhetorical strategies of reversal, such as irony and peripeteia, to create a snapping action upon the delivery of "the inevitable and unexpected idea or *mot* at the end" of individual sections (*T* viii). These traps are at their most haunting and delightful when they invite us to transgress the boundary between life and death and then surprise us with epiphanic reversals of perspective that supply resurrection as the hidden gift of the grave. But such reversals of perspective also function as symptoms of insanity, as in the extended sequence that spans sections 30–32, where the speaker's "mind dispersed" is

> lost in sea-depth,
>
> sub-conscious ocean where Fish
> move two-ways, devour.   (*T* 40)

In this sequence, H.D. launches into a derogatory critique of poetic methods that sound increasingly like her own. Because this critique is assigned to no speaker other than the "I" who opens section 30 (*T* 40), readers might assume that the sections represent H.D.'s hostile feelings toward her own writing. In section 32, however, the speaker abruptly swerves from a poetic description of poetry dangerously aligned with "madness" to ask the reader: "you find all this?" (*T* 43, 44). This question catapults the foregoing critique into the reader's own mouth, and reassigns the entire series of remarks to the hostile judgments of an unsympathetic critic. Flipping our extratextual apprehension of her self-critique into her intratextual apprehension of our critique of her without warning, H.D. dodges the implications of her own argument by accusing us of making it. The trick is effective but dirty, and leaves both poet and reader with a startled and ambivalent sense of its success. As Susan Friedman notes, H.D. disowned these sections as the work of her poet-persona, "H.D.," writing to George Plank on June 15, 1945, "XXIX and XXX are not 'H.D.' but they wrote themselves and I did not like to tamper with the idea."[50] She writes as well to Norman Holmes Pearson:

> XXX, XXXI, XXXII may seem rather long—but oddly, XXXI, XXXII actually did tap-off all in one—rather startled me to write all that in one fell swoop and made no changes, save for ordinary tidying-up—it rather startled me, so I let the thing stand—it is a bit larger "trap," I suppose, for a larger, bulkier animal—but it does snap-shut neatly—with (XXXII) "you find all this?" (*T* viii)

While H.D. urges Pearson to regard this somewhat "larger 'trap,' " set across successive sections "for a larger, bulkier animal," as different in degree but similar in kind to the neat traps she sets elsewhere in "The Walls," I want to read these sections that "wrote themselves" "in one fell swoop" as a trap H.D. devises in a moment of genuine crisis, as her strategies of reversal spin out of control and threaten to backfire on herself in a realm governed not by the skillful turns of thought characteristic of irony or peripeteia but by the more disturbing operations of projection, which Freud and Klein both associate with paranoid defense. But to make this argument, I will need to define more precisely what H.D. is here defending against, and to answer that question, I want to turn back to some of the sequence's earlier traps in order to examine how their construction and progression begin to generate anxieties that their own epiphanic strategies of reversal and closure cannot fully contain.

The scene or setting for the anxieties expressed in "The Walls" is on view as early as section 2, where we learn that "Evil was active in the land, / Good was impoverished and sad," and that "they were angry when we were so hungry / for the nourishment, God" (*T* 5). This world of good and evil, anger and hunger, resonates sharply with the phantasy life of the Kleinian infant in the paranoid position; hence a brief overview of Klein's account will provide a useful interpretive framework for the close analyses of H.D.'s word-traps to follow. Klein's theory of infant paranoia offers two major departures from Freudian theory. First, Klein backdates the onset of the oedipal conflict from the genital to the oral stage and the time of weaning, which Klein sets midway through the infant's first year of life. This shift eclipses the role of Freud's castrating father and brings the breast-feeding mother newly into view.[51]

Klein then rejects Freud's representation of the pre-oedipal phase as a time of blissful fusion with the mother. Instead, she argues, the infant's relationship with its mother in its first three to four months of life revolves around highly sadistic phantasies in which bodily "part-objects," such as breasts, penises, fetuses, and excrement, act as both the agents and objects of constant attack (*DPA* 201). Unable to tolerate mixed feelings for the same object, the infant splits its part-objects into good and bad aspects and uses the mechanisms of introjection and projection to ingest good objects, such as the nourishing breast, and expel bad objects, such as its own burning and poisonous waste (*DPA* 40, 62). The need to stock up on good objects leads the infant to carry out phantasy raids on its mother's body, in which it robs the mother of her hidden wealth, claiming the breasts, penises, and children inside her for itself. In turn, the infant uses the mother's raided body as a dumping ground for the bad objects that it wants to rid itself of.

Two factors defeat the infant in this project, however. Because it perceives any lack as positive injury, the inevitable recurrence of its own hunger automatically transforms its good objects, such as the nourishing breast, into persecutors biting it from within (*DPA* 47). And because its attempts to raid and loot the mother's body invite phantasies of retaliation, it must fear reincorporating bad rather than good objects with every feeding.[52] This cycle of paranoia, set in motion by the infant's own aggression, is kept in motion by the splitting of objects into good and bad aspects and by the reversal of agency (whereby the infant becomes the object rather than the subject of aggressive attacks). Under the hold of this cycle, the infant's internal and external worlds both become terrifying and it enters a state of psychotic anxiety.

This double world gains intermittent visibility throughout "The Walls Do Not Fall," intruding on more hopeful declarations of communal survival to reassert the isolating power of hunger. Derived from the actual conditions of wartime London, with the long food-lines, short rations, and constant threat of attack, H.D.'s scenes of hunger equally evoke the Kleinian infant's fears of its mother's biting breasts and burning and explosive excrement; thus, lines such as the following easily encompass both experiences:

> but the old-self,
>
> still half at-home in the world,
> cries out in anger,
>
> I am hungry, the children cry for food
> and flaming stones fall on them.   (*T* 39)[53]

The world of "The Walls" is a world stalled at the oral stage, whose inhabitants are frequently small and always genderless, at once vulnerable, needy, and self-obsessed. In this world, disaster takes three forms—going hungry, getting poisoned, and being chewed to bits—while heaven is the chance to

> feed forever
> on the amber honey-comb
>
> of your remembered greeting.   (*T* 39)

Then again, in such a world, the gods may choose at any moment to devour rather than nourish their worshippers. And it is this world that makes a hero of the mollusk who proclaims,

> so I in my own way know
> that the whale
>
> can not digest me   (*T* 9)

—and of the worm who rejoices,

> I profit
> by every calamity;
>
> I eat my way out of it.   (*T* 12)[54]

But if abilities such as these constitute supreme virtues in the opening sections of "The Walls," that is only to say there are no virtues greater than these, a fact perhaps not surprising in a world itself constituted by the twin axes of oral desire and oral rage. While the mollusk and worm enjoy the triumphs of the fittest survivor, they also suggest the limits of this model of behavior as a sufficient description of earthly life; indeed, we might read their narratives as exemplary instances of H.D.'s strategies of entrapment, for gracefully ironic reversals at the ends of their sections sharply underline the limitations of earthly life itself and prepare the reader for triumphs of an entirely different order. The mollusk in particular would seem to comment ironically on Freud's discussion of human consciousness in *Beyond the Pleasure Principle*, a work whose postulation of the death drive and discussion of introjection and projection would make it a crucial point of reference for Klein and her followers.[55]

H.D.'s mollusk comes to voice with the lines:

> I sense my own limit,
> my shell-jaws snap shut
>
> at invasion of the limitless,
> ocean-weight.   (*T* 9)

In doing so, it appears to speak for Freud's primitive ego, or rather for the "little fragment of living substance" encased in a "protective shield," which stands as evolutionary ancestor, embryonic antecedent, and structural analogue to the ego:

> This little fragment of living substance is suspended in the middle of an external world charged with the most powerful energies; and it would be killed by the stimulation emanating from these if it were not provided with a protective shield against stimuli. . . . By its death, the outer layer has saved all the deeper ones from a similar fate—unless, that is to say, stimuli reach it which are so strong that they break through the protective shield. *Protection against* stimuli is an almost more important function for the living organism than *reception of* stimuli. (*Beyond the Pleasure Principle* 27)

Freud goes on to argue that, weighed against the living fragment's greater need for protection, "it is enough to take small specimens of the external world, to sample it in small quantities" (*Beyond the Pleasure Principle* 27). Employing similar strategies of selective sampling, H.D.'s mollusk

> unlocks the portals
> at stated intervals:
>
> prompted by hunger,
> it opens to the tide-flow:
>
> but infinity? no,
> of nothing-too-much.   (*T* 8)

In passing, Freud defines this defensive strategy of periodic sampling as the origin of conscious perception and time-perception, which he contrasts to the "timeless" nature of unconscious processes (*Beyond the Pleasure Principle* 28). Four years later, he returns to the matter to argue in more detail that "this discontinuous method of functioning . . . lies at the bottom of the origin of the concept of time" ("A Note upon the 'Mystic Writing-Pad'" 231).

As Freud's cautious organism passes into H.D.'s hands, the open/shut rhythm of its activity and (through this mediating image) of human consciousness continues to function as a time-producing meter, but a meter that in the name of self-defense has become a method of self-delusion. For the "limitless, / ocean-weight" that the mollusk's monitoring locks out recalls Freud's description of the "sensation of 'eternity,' a feeling as of something limitless, unbounded—as it were, 'oceanic'" in *Civilization and Its Discontents* (p. 64). There, Freud traces "oceanic feeling" to the "infant at the breast," whose sense of its own boundaries is "uncertain," even "incorrect" (*Civilization* 66–67). Yet any attempt to reject the experience of eternity as more illusory than the experience of time is undermined in advance by Freud's definition of temporal perception as an arbitrary side-effect of the primitive ego's attempts to limit its exposure to external stimuli through periodic sampling. Within H.D.'s narrative rehearsal of Freud's argument, the mollusk's ability to "sense [its] own limit" points less to an achieved maturity or realism than to sensation's own involuntary and self-limiting action. An ocean creature whose self-generated rhythms fend off any feeling of the ocean, the mollusk is not a rationalist, she implies, but a fool.

H.D.'s worm also recalls Freud's account of the little fragment of living substance, but with somewhat different effect. The "death" of his organism's outer layer, suffered to save its interior regions "from a similar fate," becomes a "shroud" spun from the "nourishment" of "vine-leaf and mulberry" which the voracious silkworm rakes in from its calamitous environment (*T* 12). Yet where the protective shell serves Freud's organism as a temporary shield against death only to embody and foreshadow that death's inevitability, the cocoon serves H.D.'s silkworm as vehicle and symbol of "how the worm turns" in death and from death to second life (*T* 13)—a possibility flatly denied to the Freudian ego. Thus, the worm invokes the butterfly as Graeco-Christian symbol of the resurrected Psyche or Christ, proclaiming at the end of its narrative:

> I am yet unrepentent,
>
> for I know how the Lord God
> is about to manifest, when I,
>
> the industrious worm,
> spin my own shroud.   (*T* 12)

Of course, the mollusk itself has performed a similar reversal or "turn" in the last line of its own section. Its self-preoccupied closed-mindedness turns out to be the necessary condition for begetting self-out-of-self,

selfless,
that pearl-of-great-price   (*T* 9)

—the kingdom of heaven which cost the merchant all he had.[56] Here, the ironic reversals in perspective at the ends of both sections 4 and 6 are redemptive. Luring us into narratives that initially present earthly survival as the only game in town, H.D. successfully springs her traps on readers for whom the good news of eternity is unexpected.

H.D. confides in Pearson: "I think [section] IX is very neat, on re-reading" (*T* viii); and, indeed, it seems to offer the same kind of redemptive irony that governs the ends of sections 4 and 6. Section 9 illustrates the claim of section 8 that only those who "understand what words say" can judge "what words conceal" (*T* 14). H.D. first invites the reader to share her despair over the war effort's reappropriation of "books, // folio, manuscript, old parchment" in order to make paper "cartridge cases." But by the end of the section, she leaves us rejoicing that the word for these lethal containers conceals not explosives but the French word "cartouche," taken up as the name for the bullet-shaped capsules enclosing the immortal names of ancient Egyptian royalty. Thus, H.D. writes:

> irony is bitter truth
> wrapped up in a little joke,
>
> and Hatshepsut's name is still circled
> with what they call the *cartouche*.   (*T* 16)

Revealing in modern containers of death ancient testimony to the sacred and immortalizing power of the written word, she repeats the worm's trick of pulling proof of second life from a shroud.

In the pivot on which section 9 turns, H.D. places irony itself within another container: "irony is bitter truth / wrapped up in a little joke." Once again, the trope is Freud's, who writes in *Jokes and Their Relation to the Unconscious*, "The [repressed] thought seeks to wrap itself in a joke because in that way it recommends itself to our attention and can seem more significant and more valuable, but above all because this wrapping bribes our powers of criticism and confuses them" (*Jokes* 132). On the opposing page of the *Standard Edition*, Freud itemizes at length the "aggressive purposes" served by this strategy of bribery and confusion. A joke can turn its indifferent listener "into a co-hater or co-despiser, and creates for the enemy a host of opponents where at first there was only one." "It overcomes the inhibitions of shame and respectability," and it "shatters respect for institutions and truths in which the hearer has believed" (*Jokes* 133). In section 9, H.D. neatly subverts Freud's argument, offering us, as the

repressed content that returns through *her* irony, the vanquishing of the
cartridge's "aggressive purposes" by the cartouche's display of the names
of the immortal Egyptian pharaohs.

But closer inspection reveals a more troubling cargo to her irony,
which works against its redemptive assertions and instead suggests that
hidden things are never what they seem. For the name H.D. sets within
her cartouche, Hatshepsut, is the name of a woman who "pretended to be
a man."[57] As an ancient Egyptian ruler destined to become a god in death,
Queen Hatshepsut opens up a space of doubleness and reversal between
mortal and immortal states. As a woman who passes as a man, she opens
up a similar space of doubleness and reversal between the genders.[58] The
parallel invites us to regard the Queen's twin projects to attain immortality
and to undo or exceed the fixity of her given gender as linked attempts to
escape the constraints of earthly life. With this reading, her various role
reversals would align her with the mollusk and the worm as a positive
model of redemption. At the same time, she implicitly serves as the
poem's first evocation of a doubly sexed god, the "androgynous Divine
One transcending all dualisms," whose nature Susan Friedman identifies
as "the fundamental premise of hermetic tradition."[59]

But H.D.'s comment to Bryher that Hatshepsut merely "pretended"
to be male suggests that the ancient queen is only able to pull off her re-
demptive reversals through pretense and deceit: her portraits may present
a bearded man, but H.D. knows she's a woman. Yet if Hatshepsut was
not really male, can we be sure she was really immortalized? H.D. does
not explore this doubt in section 9. In placing within the sacred enclosure
of the cartouche the name of a woman who "pretended to be a man,"
however, she lays the ground for the poem's later inquiries into the nature
and authenticity of divine being, inquiries that will themselves repeatedly
return to the problem of sexual and gender division.

Appearing first as the sexless pearl hidden in the mollusk's shell, the
ungendered silkworm hidden in the cocoon, and the royal pretender hid-
den in the cartouche, Amen, "the hidden-one,"[60] does eventually appear
as himself:

> the world-father,
> father of past aeons,
>
> present and future equally.   (*T* 25)

No questions here—"it appears obvious" and "very clear" that he is male
(*T* 27, 29). In fact, maleness appears to be Amen's only positive attribute
when he shows up in the dream recounted in section 16, for he is otherwise
defined almost entirely by negation. "Beardless, not at all like Jehovah,"
he is "not out of place" in the dream scene's eighteenth-century meeting-

house (*T* 25), itself notable only for its emptiness. A double for Christos, Amen appears without Christ's usual attributes of "pain-worship and death-symbol" (*T* 27). Even his eyes turn out to be not quite the same as the eyes of "Velasquez' crucified," which have themselves never been seen directly; "lowered" in Velázquez's painting, these other eyes, if open,

> would daze, bewilder
> and stun us with the old sense of guilt
>
> and fear, but the terror of those eyes
> veiled in their agony is over.   (*T* 28)

With this last assurance, rendered somewhat dubious by the accumulating pressure of so many negatives, the dreamer finally enjoins us in section 19 to look into the eyes that *are* there:

> I assure you that the eyes
> of Velasquez' crucified
>
> now look straight at you,
> and they are amber and they are fire.   (*T* 28)

But these are the eyes of the vengeful Son of Revelation, whose "eyes were as a flame of fire."[61] And, in fact, the narrator's claims that "the terror . . . is over" soon prove to have been premature. For an adjoining piece of John's Book of Revelation, neglected in section 19, returns in section 21 to destroy the certainty with which H.D. has proclaimed Amen's gentleness and his masculinity. John's full verse reads: "His head and his hairs were white like wool, as white as snow; and his eyes were as a flame of fire." When Amen-Christos shows up again in section 21, he is "the Ram," "bearer of the curled horns" of the Moses patriarch, who charges, butts, and bellows at a childlike seeker begging both to be taken home and to be eaten alive (*T* 30, 31). Where Freud consistently traces childhood animal phobias back to a fear of the castrating father, the seeker's fantasy of self-annihilation resembles the alternative paradigm associated with the cannibalistic Kleinian mother, who acquires phallic traits when she swallows the father's penis during intercourse. Thus, the "wail[ing]" seeker of section 22 pleads:

> hide me in your fleece,
> crop me up with the new-grass;
>
> let your teeth devour me,
> let me be warm in your belly,
>
> the sun-disk,
> the re-born Sun.   (*T* 31)

The speaker's plea conflates two ancient Egyptian myths of creation. In one, "the sky was . . . pictured as a goddess of colossal size stooping over the world, her head being in the west, and her thighs, between which [the Sun-God] Rā was reborn daily, in the east."[62] This sky-woman is "the great cow-goddess Nut,"[63] whose powers of oral conception and anal birth gain in fascination and terror on the Kleinian infant's phantasies of the mother's cannibalistic sexuality in that Nut nightly consumes not the father's penis but the child itself. In ancient Egyptian iconography, however, the "sun-disk" that H.D. here equates with "the re-born Sun" is the emblem not of Rā, but of Aten, the abstract, only faintly male solar god popularized by the pharaoh Akhenaten, and placed by Freud at the origin of Jewish monotheism in his controversial Moses essays. For H.D., the sun-disk god carried additional associations, drawn from her reading of James Strachey's essay, "Preliminary Notes Upon the Problem of Akhenaten," which immediately follows Freud's second Moses essay in the January 1939 issue of *The International Journal of Psycho-Analysis*.[64]

In this essay, Strachey uses the evidence of a statue portraying Akhenaten as a woman and the pharaoh's worship of the almost asexual sun-disk to build a case for his effeminacy, repressed homosexuality, and paranoia. His argument refers to Freud's theory that paranoiacs defend against repressed homosexual feelings by projecting them outward with reverse affect as persecution fantasies involving a same-sex parental figure. Thus, Strachey takes the faceless benevolence of the new god, Aten, as evidence of the positive trend in Akhenaten's paranoiac split between "the loving and destructive elements in his relationship to his father," but reads his "systematic erasing of the name of Amun from every accessible inscription throughout . . . the land" as evidence of the opposite trend (pp. 40–41). On two counts, sections 21 and 22 of "The Walls" offer direct inversions of Strachey's argument. Where Strachey interprets Akhenaten's acts of vandalism as the effeminate son's revenge on a castrating father, H.D. turns to Klein's theory of paranoia to model her Ram after the hungry infant's paranoid apprehension of the devouring mother. Similarly, where the solar father-god Aten "is carefully de-anthropomorphized," carrying only vestigial traces of a masculine gender, H.D.'s Ram takes on the double aspect of both mother and father and it is rather the seeker who longs to assume the somatic blankness of the sun-disk.

More to the point, however, are the links H.D. forges between Amen's newly emerging sexual ambiguity or doubleness and his sudden show of violence. Just as the Kleinian infant perceives its parents' sexual organs and sexual proceeds (breasts, penises, womb-stomach, and unborn children) as agents of persecution, the Ram portrays its phallic horns and womblike "belly" as weapons of assault used to "toss" and "smother" the seeker (*T* 31, 30). Here, the very fact of sexual and gender difference seems productive only of violence (though violence of a particularly seductive sort), while the seeker's desire to "hide" (*T* 31) and to be reborn as blank and sexless as a sun-disk seems to express neither homosexual nor heterosexual, neither sadistic nor masochistic, yearnings, but rather the yearning for release from the dichotomous logic of these very choices, and a corresponding refusal of the oedipal injunction to "commit" to one sex or the other.[65]

Yet there is still another register to the violence displayed when the Amen shows up a second time. As he

> bellows from the horizon:
>
>   . . .
>
> time, time for you to begin a new spiral,
> see—I toss you into the star-whirlpool   (*T* 30)

Amen transforms the planetlike mollusk's "limited" "orbit // of being" and "stated intervals" of hunger (*T* 9, 8) into the gigantic, whirling orbits of stars whose motions trace the contours of a sucking and bellowing mouth. Alerted by his tolling of the word "time," we can assign this mouth to Time the Devourer, linked by a conventional pun with the Greek father-god, Cronus, who tried to secure his power against the rise of the next generation by swallowing up all his children. Yet, as we have seen, under the syncretic pressure necessary to conflate *chronos*, Cronus, Nut, and Amen, the spiraling mouth of time assumes a double sex; resembling (or perhaps being) the curled horns of the Ram, it is phallic, while as a whirlpool it connects back with Charybdis, the virgin destroyer, and the *vagina dentata*.

In this fantasy, H.D. makes the very aspects of life she seems most eager to escape—sexual difference, temporal periodicity, and oral sadism—into agents of the death that would release her from them. Thus, the body's self-limiting "orbit // of being," the violent dichotomies of sex and gender, and time's "stated intervals" whose rhythms cut off access to eternity, are all combined and refigured in the Ram's star-studded and whirling jaws, which would "crop" the seeker "up with the new-grass." Yet while the seeker longs to pass between the teeth of a doubly sexed time in order to be reborn with the sun-disk's immortal and sexless perfection, the doubt implicit in this strategy has already been voiced at the opening of section 21. There, the seeker echoes the Kleinian infant's fear that the broken and angry fragments of its paranoid phantasy life will never cohere and that its undamaged "good objects" will never return. For once "the crystal of identity" is "splintered" and "the vessel of integrity" is "shat-

tered" by the devouring teeth of Mother-Father Time (*T* 30), what guar-
antee is there that the seeker will merge with the more perfect oneness of
divinity, and not remain in pieces?

Recounting an air-raid vigil in *The Gift*, H.D. writes, "It is true that
the psyche, the soul can endure anything. But one did not want the body
broken—we must not think about that" (138). This, though, is the very
thought associated with "the One, *Amen*, All-father" in section 25:

> *Amen,*
> only just now,
>
> my heart-shell
> breaks open.   (*T* 34, 35)

In the sequence spanning sections 25–29, where the speaker's heart lodges
the grain and tree of the kingdom, H.D. dramatizes Christ's own inter-
pretation of his parable of the sower: "The sower soweth the word . . .
in their hearts."[66] Imagining the grain of heaven splitting and scalding the
heart and consuming its core as "nourishment" (*T* 35), the speaker tes-
tifies to the painful ecstasy of yielding up the flesh of the body to god's
voracious word. But this same fantasy might suggest, more subversively,
that the hope of heaven simultaneously inflicts and feeds on the heart's
suffering, cheating it of redemption, in much the way a Kleinian infant
understands its own hunger as a hostile breast tearing and devouring it
from within. Literally brokenhearted, the speaker moves from a spiritual
stance of self-sacrificing devotion to one of frailty and "anger" in section
29 (*T* 39). As the scalding grain dropped from above in sections 25 and 28
becomes the "flaming stones" of the air-raids that fall on children crying
for food, the good news of heaven turns into the threat of persecution and
death, and the body's own hunger remains unsatisfied.

Thus, just as the Kleinian infant's attempts to split its mother's breast
into good and bad aspects set in motion the vicious cycle of reversal by
which good will always revert to bad, H.D.'s initial attempts to dissociate
all violence and suffering from Amen's gentle aspect in the dream recorded
in section 16 bring on their own subversion as he returns in section 21 as
the bellowing and devouring Ram. In turn, Amen's divine manifestation
as an oral sadist releases further fantasies of heavenly persecution when
the speaker again addresses him in section 25. Yet if by section 29 the
speaker can demand that god confront the speaker's own anger and hun-
ger, an even more frightening reversal stems from the fantasy of satiety
born of such intense need. This latter reversal leads directly into the se-
quence of sections 30–32 whose sources we set out to investigate. Praying
to Christ in section 29 to

say again, as you said,

the baked fish is ready,
here is the bread   (*T* 39),

the speaker painfully conveys the severity of both its physical and spiritual
hunger by equating the messiah's return with the chance for a hot meal.
Section 30, however, immediately transports the speaker into the "sub-
conscious ocean where Fish / move two-ways, devour" (*T* 40). With this
last narrative reversal of the speaker's attempt to transform the fear of
being eaten into the hope of being full, the sacred meal itself becomes the
eater, and the speaker's ability to direct the course of its own imagination
spins out of control.

In sections 30–32, the speaker returns to a carnivorous ocean world
like that described by the mollusk in section 4. But for the mollusk firmly
committed to "living within," the ocean and its occupants represent the
hostile elements of its external environment; "the shark-jaws" that
threaten to devour it are those of "outer circumstance" (*T* 9). In contrast,
the speaker "lost in sea-depth" in section 30 falls into the ocean of its inner
life: that is, into the "depth of the sub-conscious" whose "sea-floor" har-
bors "illusion, reversion of old values, / oneness lost, madness" (*T* 40, 44,
41). Moreover, when the sacred meal of baked fish and bread returns in
section 30 as the devouring Fish that "move two-ways" (*T* 5, 40), the or-
der of eternity merges catastrophically with the order of the unconscious.
With this merging, the terrifying fantasies of oral sadism generated in the
unconscious overwhelm H.D.'s attempts to imagine eternity, which, far
from offering mystical union with divine oneness, now itself becomes
aligned with

illusion of lost-gods, daemons;
. . .

reversion of old values,
oneness lost, madness.   (*T* 43)

In resituating the limitless ocean of eternity within the human uncon-
scious, H.D. sets the stage for yet another catastrophic return of a ne-
glected piece from one of her source-texts: in this case, Freud's discussion
of the primitive ego in *Beyond the Pleasure Principle* that she has successfully
ironized in the narratives of the mollusk and the worm. After Freud dis-
cusses the primitive ego's dependency on a shieldlike surface to protect it
from the world without, he goes on to say that the ego is powerless before
the world within, toward which "there can be no such shield." By neces-
sity, the organism deals with such unpleasurable "internal excitations" by

"treat[ing] them as though they were acting, not from the inside, but from the outside, so that it may be possible to bring the shield against stimuli into operation as a means of defence against them. This is the origin of *projection*, which is destined to play such a large part in the causation of pathological processes" (*Beyond the Pleasure Principle* 29). It is this defensive strategy of projection, given a central role in Freud's accounts of paranoia, that H.D. uses to escape the nightmarish results of her equation of unconscious and eternal orders. Thus, in section 32 she accuses the reader of authoring her own critique of a poetic style too closely aligned with madness in an attempt to locate both the charges and the possibility of madness outside herself.

The speaker of section 30 initially promises us that

> the elixir of life, the philosopher's stone
> is yours if you surrender
>
> sterile logic, trivial reason.   (*T* 40)

However, "the alchemist's key" that "unlocks secret doors" ends up admitting us not to the secrets of immortal life but rather to a world of violated boundaries and collapsed distinctions: life set loose from its hinges. In this world, the sky threatens to sink into the ocean as the shifting positions of the orbiting stars drag its zodiacal figures toward "the abyss" below the horizon (*T* 40). Similarly, the "invasion of the over-soul" threatens to crack open the body figured as "a cup / too brittle, a jar too circumscribed" (*T* 42). This drama of transcendental violation initially suggests nuptials in which the seeker, "bride of the kingdom" (*T* 43), yields to Christ the bridegroom; but returning figures of oral sadism trouble the fantasy. By section 32, the virginal jar bursting with

> the out-flowing
> of water-about-to-be-changed-to-wine
>
> at the wedding   (*T* 42)

becomes a spewing oceanic mouth:

> Depth of the sub-conscious spews forth
> too many incongruent monsters
>
> and fixed indigestible matter
> such as shell, pearl; imagery
>
> done to death; perilous ascent,
> ridiculous descent; rhyme, jingle,   .
>
> overworked assonance, nonsense,
> juxtaposition of words for words' sake,

without meaning, . . .
               . . .

over-sensitive, under-definitive,
clash of opposites, fight of emotion

and sterile invention—
you find all this?   (*T* 44)

H.D. here describes a poetic technique exactly like her own, whose word-play exploits unconscious processes of displacement, condensation, and overdetermination in an attempt to convey eternity in words—to achieve "finite definition // of the infinite" (*T* 42). Condemning this technique for its failures, she refigures the divinely inspired mouth of the epic singer or the pronouncing Pythian (*T* 4) as a mouth that indiscriminately vomits up the monstrous creations of the unconscious, the pearl of the kingdom, and the stuff of poetry. The horrific (self-)image of this ejecting mouth calls for yet a further ejection, and H.D. immediately holds her reader responsible for thoughts she will no longer claim as her own. Yet what ultimately becomes so terrifying in section 32 is not the content of H.D.'s fantasies, nor her violent projection of them onto us, but the bind of reversal itself. Where the "neat" ironies and peripeteias governing the ends of the mollusk's and worm's sections use reversal to reveal an afterlife their narratives of oral violence and oral conquest otherwise eclipse, H.D.'s subsequent acts of reversal create a rebound effect that repeatedly returns to view the acts of oral violence she initially uses reversal to escape. Thus, in section 32 the very action H.D. must defend against is also the action she must take in her defense, as she attempts to escape the sacred meal's reversion into a devouring Fish and then into a vomiting oceanic mouth by reversing the location of her own thoughts with the sudden address to her reader: "you find all this?"

Throughout these sections, H.D. explores her ambivalence toward the boundaries and divisions of earthly life in figures of the mouth whose action paradoxically ruptures the body's integrity in sustaining it: the mouth's hunger for nourishment threatens the body with invasion from without, its teeth grind up the food it admits, and its regurgitations level life's variety to a lifeless and shapeless pulp. In "The Walls Do Not Fall," boundedness and division are themselves sources of pain and loss, whether we speak here of the division of eternal oneness into the discrete "heart-beat[s]" of temporal life (*T* 38), or into the discrete bodies of men and women. The ironies of the early sections and the syncretic conflations of the Amen sections initially offer H.D. a way out of the trap of boundedness and division by opening up a space of doubleness and reversal like that of Queen Hatshepsut's cartouche. However, that space itself even-

tually turns out to be only another trap "for a larger, bulkier animal." For
it is intrinsic to the unconscious logic of reversal that one term will always
supply its split-off opposite; while this logic can afford H.D. free passage
over "the regrettable chasm" between male and female, past and future,
time and eternity (*T* 54), it also commits her to crossing those chasms
forever.

Furthermore, because the repressed thought split off from conscious-
ness returns *within* the nexus of thoughts maintaining the repression,[67] re-
peated acts of reversal between opposing terms eventually bring about the
breakdown of difference. Thus, H.D.'s strategy of opposing the conscious
and temporal realm of this life to the unconscious and eternal realm of the
next life, and then moving from one to the other by rhetorical acts of re-
versal, ends up communicating the contents of temporal existence to eter-
nity. When the "star-whirlpool" of section 21 returns as the spewing
"sub-conscious" ocean of eternity in section 32, eternity's own mouth,
unlike the mouth of the sky-goddess Nut, receives the dead but cannot
revive them. Instead, it succeeds only in regurgitating all the ill-sorted liv-
ing fragments "done to death" by the repetitive action of time's devouring
teeth (*T* 44).

Drawing back from the disintegrating effects of madness, the speaker
concludes section 32 in a fragile mood that admits to a new measure of
compromise and uncertainty. The last lines of the section offer up the im-
age of an "erratic burnt-out comet" that nevertheless maintains "its pe-
culiar orbit" (*T* 45). Conflating in this image the nameless body's "dead
ember" of a heart in section 1, the seeker's scalded heart in section 25, and
the flaming stones falling from the sky in section 29, the speaker effects
the fusion between the persecuted body and its persecutors necessary to
bring their dynamic of opposition to an end. With a new tolerance for
flawed states, orbiting takes on positive value; if orbiting condemns a
moving body to predictable rounds of repetition, at least it saves it from
the more terrifying possibility, so recently explored, of losing track al-
together. With the admission "hunger / may make hyenas of the best of
us" (*T* 47) in section 34, the speaker further acknowledges the raging
strength of hunger rather than fantasizing its quiet end, and abandons faith
in any simple purity of love for the mixed powers of "Isis, the great en-
chantress, / in her attribute of Serqet"—a goddess as willing to kill as she
is to cure (*T* 47).[68]

Granting important recognition to the mother's own powers of sa-
distic aggression (already on view in the Amen-Ram fantasy) while ex-
tending a welcome reminder to women readers that our sex need not en-
force our position as victims of male violence, the seeker invokes

> the original great-mother,
> who drove
>
> harnessed scorpions
> before her.   (*T* 47)

But to acknowledge life's inherent violence—regardless of one's sex—is also, at this point in *Trilogy*, to acknowledge a residue of division and strife that is not only unassimilable to the concept of eternal oneness, but has managed to contaminate even that possibility with its pervasive negative effects.

H.D. ends "The Walls Do Not Fall" with a concerted attempt to achieve a vision of eternal oneness through a play on words, a little joke. But the joke seems strained. The speaker of section 40 who pries open the name of Osiris to "find the meaning that words hide" discovers that the resurrected father-god bears both a male and a female aspect: "O-Sire-is" and "Sirius," the Dog Star of Isis (*T* 53,54). This naming game renders explicit the sexual ambiguity associated with Hatshepsut, whose own name is set within the immortalizing cartouche in section 9. By the end of the section, however, the speaker moves from the successful doubling of Osiris's sexual identity to

> recover the secret of Isis,
> which is: there was One
>
> in the beginning, Creator,
> Fosterer, Begetter, the Same-forever.   (*T* 54–55)

Here the speaker's visible struggle to free the names of divine oneness from any trace of sex or gender, closely following (and reversing) the attempt to render Osiris both male and female, reveals the persistent anxiety that a god who cannot transcend the divisions of sex and gender can be neither truly one nor truly eternal.

In section 41, the speaker recalls the floods and drought of its broken heart's internal landscape (*T* 38), addressing Osiris as the sacred "grain" of the kingdom sprouting anew:

> where heat breaks and cracks
> the sand-waste,
> you are a mist
> of snow: white, little flowers.   (*T* 56)

In a letter to Norman Holmes Pearson, H.D. glosses this last image as "the ever-lasting miracle of the breath of life" (*T* vii). But by section 43, the redemptive image of the dry earth breaking to reveal breath's mist is again reversed into a hellish image of the earth rising to fill our lungs with dirt, as the grave overleaps its bed to invade the collapsing houses of the living:

> *we are powerless,*
>
> *dust and powder fill our lungs*
> *our bodies blunder*
>
> *through doors twisted on hinges,*
> *and the lintels slant*
>
> *cross-wise.*   (*T* 58)

In between these positive and negative refigurings of Yahweh's creative act of mingling breath and earth, H.D. restages her claim to know "the meaning that words hide" through another play on words that finds in the name of Osiris evidence of redemptive union with a higher oneness. But in fact her strategy only manages to make the effects of division more evident; in an internal repetition of the montage method she uses to organize the sequence as a whole, section 42 once again breaks open the name of the male Osiris, "the *answerer*,"[69] to expose a question, a need to know, a doubt: "O, Sire, / is this union at last?" (*T* 57).

Reparation; Or, The Lady Who Came Instead

and the faint knocking
was the clock ticking.
   —H.D., "Tribute to the Angels"

In "The Walls Do Not Fall," H.D. attempts to oppose the liberating oneness of eternity to the deadly limitations of sequential time and dichotomous sex and gender. Yet this opposition itself falls prey to the radical instability of defensive splitting, and her opposed terms begin to take on each other's attributes. The anxiety that eternity and the unconscious share the power to grind up body and self, repeatedly contained within individual sections, manages to reappear in subsequent sections and to require new efforts at containment. Both the action and the content of this anxiety link it with Freud's theory of a death drive that manifests itself through the compulsion to repeat.

Rachel Blau DuPlessis notes that although "The Walls Do Not Fall" "is, in the main, about Amen, the father God," the mother-goddesses maintain "a muted presence."[70] The ongoing focus on "food, starvation, and so on" in the sequence supports her point, while suggesting that the very mutedness of the mother's role here may stem from the sequence's wider strategies of suppression and containment. Only intermittently visible as a named presence, the mother's influence instead persists at the level of the sequence's montage structure. For H.D., like Klein, casts the structural dynamic of opposition and reversal in "The Walls" in terms of the oral stage, and locates the recurring fact of hunger as the force underlying that dynamic's instability. As long as "nourishment" and satiety are not everlasting, as long as hunger returns, rage at the persecuting nourisher and fear of annihilation will return as well. What ultimately makes the force of hunger so formidable, however, is not its own implacability but H.D.'s initial reluctance to understand the anger and aggression it incurs as sources of strength, and even of release. Until the late entreaty to an Isis of scorpions, "The Walls" tries to maintain a further opposition between the "Word" and the "Sword," the writer's vocation and that of the warrior (*T* 17, 18). Attempting to foreclose any potential for violence in her own vocation as a writer, H.D. in fact generates a mirroring play of suspicion and antagonism between narrator and reader, and a pattern of returning disruption and persecution within the poem's ostensibly heterogeneous collection of sections.

It is quickly apparent that "Tribute to the Angels" proceeds from a different set of givens. In this sequence, the narrative heterogeneity of "The Walls" gives way to the sustained themes of alchemical transformation and poetic tribute to the seven angels who flank Christ in the Book of Revelation. The emphasis on oral aggression, so pervasive in "The Walls," is all but absent in "Tribute," which also makes very little use of rhetorical devices of reversal such as irony. And the narrator's relationship with the reader, while still somewhat crisp, becomes explicitly collaborative by the end of this second sequence. Moreover, in "Tribute," H.D. brings the mother out of hiding and forges positive links between women's sexuality, time, and repetition, terms which are no longer understood as antithetical to eternal oneness, but in fact provide the site of its successful manifestation within the poem. These changes stem from a new willingness to acknowledge and value both childhood and adult experiences of frustration, anger, and grief, and a new resolve to make all three emotions integral to the poet's work of creativity and healing.

Here again, H.D.'s poetry poses striking parallels to Kleinian theory, though the second sequence of *Trilogy* reverberates most strongly not with Klein's theories of infant paranoia but with her theory of the depressive position. According to Klein, at weaning the infant pulls out of an initial phase of paranoia and enters a phase of guilt and mourning, in which it fears "the loss of the loved object" (*SMK* 119) and desires to make reparation to the mother whose body it feels it has destroyed in its

early phantasies (*DPA* 203). Deterred by its own anxiety from approach-
ing the mother's body directly, the infant appropriates other objects as
symbolic substitutes for her.[71] Acting out both its sadistic and its reparative
phantasies with these symbols, the infant learns to tolerate its aggressive
feelings and to realize their limited capacity for harm. As the infant gains
faith in other people's integrity and ability to survive its assaults, its
sharply divided world of good and bad part-objects gives way to an in-
tegrated world of whole people who can be both good and bad, present
and absent, loved and hated.[72] Likewise, a world in which all good expe-
riences are canceled out by the inevitable return of hunger and pain gives
way to one in which the infant's memories of good experiences endure
and accumulate, providing the materials (good internal objects) by which
it can replenish and repair the mother's body in phantasy.[73]

Klein defines the depressive position as "the central position in the
child's development" (*SMK* 145), and defines the child's acts of symbol-
making as the position's major developmental achievement. In her ac-
count, anxiety, aggression, and grief, rather than standing as barriers to
the child's healthy development, become its necessary conditions. Klein
argues that "a sufficient quantity of anxiety is the necessary basis for an
abundance of symbol formation"; furthermore, because she believes that
"the epistemophilic impulse aris[es] and coexist[s] with sadism," a certain
amount of aggression is required to fuel the infant's inquisitive passage
from object to object (*SMK* 98). Similarly, grief over the lost mother
stands at the origin of the infant's creativity; Klein's follower Hanna Segal
explains that "symbol formation is the outcome of a loss, it is a creative
work involving the pain and the whole work of mourning,"[74] while Klein
herself proposes that "the desire to re-discover the mother of the early
days, whom one has lost actually or in one's feelings, is . . . of the greatest
importance in creative art" (*LHR* 105).

In "Tribute" H.D. takes over the Kleinian child's creative work of
reparation in her alchemical transformation of the "bitter jewel" into
"Star of the Sea, / Mother" (*T* 72, 71). In fact, the main image of this po-
etic fantasy, the bitter jewel, resonates suggestively with Klein's own ter-
minology. In *Love, Hate and Reparation*, under the page heading "Bitter-
ness of Feeling," Klein analyzes bitter feeling into its component emo-
tions of "frustrated greed," "resentment, grievances, and hatred." She
derives emotional bitterness from the child's grievances toward its par-
ents, which originate in its earliest phantasies of maternal aggression and
persecution. The work of reparation is to turn "bitterness of feeling" into
love and inner "contentment": "if we have become able, deep in our un-
conscious minds, to clear our feelings to some extent towards our parents
of grievances, and have forgiven them for the frustrations we had to bear,

then we can be at peace with ourselves and are able to love others in the true sense of the word" (*LHR* 116, 118, 119).[75]

For H.D., the effort to confront and transform a residual childhood bitterness toward the mother is both conditioned and complicated by her own status as a mother who "had pups in war-time" and by a wider culture of wartime propaganda and fantasy linking war with a threatening maternity. While these cultural fantasies find a clear counterpart in Klein's theories of infantile paranoia, they also find a counterpart in the controversy over Kleinian theory itself. Several members of the British Psychoanalytic Society, including Klein's daughter, perceived Klein's use of Freud as an attack on his memory, one that threatened the integrity and longevity of his achievement with illicit trespassing, corruption, or falsification. In "Tribute to the Angels," H.D. seems to have Klein in mind as she explores both what it means for a woman to propose changes or "additions" to a man's vision understood to be complete and final, and what it means for a woman to acknowledge and use her aggression in a culture where any female aggression can feel like too much. The ease with which both private and public fantasies of motherhood split into mutually exclusive images of nurturing self-sacrifice and murderous self-assertion during the two world wars speaks to a widespread cultural refusal of the distinction between creative or life-enhancing, and destructive or deadly, female aggression. In an attempt to restore a positive pole to the experience of female aggression, H.D. focuses on the nexus of psychoanalytic identifications linking temporal, unconscious, and female repetition with the compulsory activity of the death instinct. By breaking down the associations between repetition, returning, and death that she herself has begun to lay out in "The Walls," she is able to revalue as pleasurable what she has previously found terrifying about the mother's body.

H.D. foregrounds her use of Kleinian concepts in "Tribute to the Angels" from the start. She begins the sequence by invoking "Hermes Trismegistus / . . . patron of alchemists," whose "metal is quicksilver" (*T* 63). Noting further that "his clients" are "orators, thieves and poets," she commands us: "steal then, O orator, / plunder, O poet." These lines resonate with H.D.'s early childhood fantasies of "stealing from 'muddies body,'" analyzed by Walter Schmideberg along the lines Klein lays out in works such as *Love, Hate and Reparation*. There, she argues that the infant "has, in his aggressive phantasies, injured his mother by biting and tearing her up" (*LHR* 61). H.D. takes these infantile phantasies as an interpretive model for "the new-church" of Christianity which "spat upon // and broke and shattered" the icons of its predecessors. And where Klein goes on to state that the infant "may soon build up phantasies that he is putting the bits together again and repairing" his mother's body (*LHR* 61), H.D.

calls for her fellow thieves and poets to "collect the fragments of the splin-
tered glass" and to "melt down and integrate, // re-invoke, re-create" the
lost mother-goddesses (*T* 63).

In section 3, the poet invokes the curse John placed on any who would
"add" to his vision of the New Jerusalem, only to contrast this curse with
Christ's own declaration: "*I make all things new*" (*T* 65). H.D.'s compar-
ison of John and Christ here reverberates strongly against the current con-
troversies in the British Psychoanalytic Society. Riccardo Steiner has sug-
gested that the multiple losses suffered by continental analysts, who parted
with their homelands and their founder in short succession, increased their
need to claim an "exclusive and extremely idealized possession of Freud's
truth and work,"[76] to say, in effect:

> *I John saw. I testify;*
> *if any man shall add*
>
> *God shall add unto him the plagues.*   (*T* 65)

Kleinians, on the other hand, understood themselves to be attempting
not a rejection of Freud but his expansion and renewal; whether building
on his premises or diverging from them, they argued they were only sus-
taining the example of Freud himself, who "greatly expanded and revised
his metapsychology in successive contributions."[77] In siding with Christ
and against his church in section 3 of her poem, H.D. conflates his anti-
ecclesiastical project of continually renewed spirituality with the Kleinian
project of reparation: "He of the seventy-times-seven / bitter, unending
wars" (*T* 65), like the Kleinian child, must "make all things new" to es-
cape the repeating cycles of retaliation encoded in the Mosaic law of "an
eye for an eye, and a tooth for a tooth."[78] But if this is a fairly normative
interpretation of Christ's message, H.D. becomes more subversive when
she suggests that Christ, again like the Kleinian child, can only make
things new by restoring the old—by repairing a failed relationship with
the lost body of the mother.

In section 5, H.D. names the first "three of seven" angels who receive
the tributes structuring the rest of the sequence (*T* 67). Critics have con-
sistently identified two organizing themes in this segment of the poem:
the alchemical transformation of the bitter jewel into the newly venerated
mother, and the transgressive and empowering naming of the seven un-
named angels guarding the Lamb's throne in the Book of Revelation.[79] In
fact, these two themes are one. The sequence's seven angels serve as re-
gents of the seven "planets" that rule over the stages of the alchemical
work.[80] Thus, the candles the poet lights in tribute to the angels also feed
the flame under the crucible during each stage of the alchemical work. In

section 28, H.D. reveals that she initially planned to arrange this "sequence of candle and fire" according to the strict course laid down by "the law of the seven" (*T* 92) that leads to the production of the precious philosopher's stone. But a fantasy of the bitter jewel, a vision of the flowering may-tree, and a dream of the Lady disrupt these plans; while she eventually names all seven angels, only Uriel, Annael, and Zadkiel receive full tributes. Each of the sequence's three interpolated episodes orbit around a female presence, and it is according to a feminizing logic that H.D. constructs her revisions to the normative course of the alchemical work.

Traditionally, the alchemist must follow a rigid and exacting program, which begins with the stage of Mercury (or quicksilver) and moves to the three stages of the "lesser work," ruled by Saturn, Jupiter, and the moon. This phase of the work is feminine and yields *materia prima*, or pure matter without form. Then come the three stages of the "great work," ruled by Venus, Mars, and the sun. This phase is masculine and culminates in the production of the philosopher's stone. The philosopher's stone reimprints pure matter with the perfect and immortal forms of the universal spirit by purifying the corrupt and feminine action of universal nature—an "all-embracing rhythm" of creation and destruction that preserves the immortality of matter but repeatedly condemns its forms to death.[81]

Stripping down the seven stages of the work to three, H.D. reorders their sequence, reversing the alchemist's traditional valuation of masculinity above femininity. With her tributes to Uriel, Annael, and the lunar Lady, she focuses exclusively on the sixth, fifth, and fourth stages of the work (with a last fleeting nod toward the third stage in her tribute to Zadkiel). Running these stages in reverse order, she ignores the masculine solar phase of the great work and places greatest emphasis on the lunar stage that crowns the lesser work. H.D.'s promotion of the feminine lunar stage to the place of climax in her version of the work stands as the first redemptive use of the strategy of reversal itself, which caused such terror in "The Walls Do Not Fall." Furthermore, with her reorderings, the "dim, luminous disc" of the bedside clock in her lunar dream of the Lady usurps the place of perfection previously held by "the sun-disk" both within the alchemical tradition, with its climactic solar phase, and within the Amen sections of the poem's previous sequence (*T* 89, 31). As such, H.D.'s "little clock" becomes the new philosopher's stone (*T* 90). But where the traditional philosopher's stone is hermaphroditic, H.D.'s clock is triply coded as feminine: its tick, echoing the feminine rhythm of universal nature, explicitly links up with the "pulse" of the maternal jewel as well as the Lady's knock, while its "phosphorescent face" recalls Phosphorus, the dawn face of Venus, invoked in section 10 (*T* 76, 90). Standing in its littleness as the essence of the lesser work, the clock-as-philosopher's stone would thus reclaim for women all the magnificence formerly attributed to the great work and to men.

Feminist wit notwithstanding, such glorification of a bedside clock needs further explanation. We might begin by looking at the clock's precursors within the sequence. As Susan Friedman points out, the clock finds its immediate prototype in the "bitter jewel."[82] In turn, the jewel, placed "in the heart of the bowl," recalls the scalding grain of heaven "lodged in the heart-core" of the seeker in "The Walls" (*T* 72, 35). But where its acts of consuming the seeker's heart for nourishment align the grain with all the other transcendent devourers of that sequence, the jewel's bite is confined to its bitterness: the ferocity and oral violence of "The Walls" here fades into a distant memory-trace, a taste left in the mouths of those "who rebel" (*T* 72). With this transition from biting to bitterness, H.D. pulls out of the terrifying, persecutory world of "The Walls" to enter a more self-reflective space in which to examine the residue of her own anger, frustration, and grief.

In section 8, H.D. associates this residual bitterness with the mother through wordplay. Placing "a word most bitter, *marah*, / a word bitterer still, *mar*" in the alchemical bowl, she "melt[s]" these words into

> mer, mere, mère, mater, Maia, Mary,
>
> Star of the Sea,
> Mother.   (*T* 71)

In *The Unspeakable Mother*, Kloepfer makes two points that bear directly on a Kleinian reading of the bitter jewel sequence. First, she introduces the idea that the daughter's own negative feelings toward the mother gain representation in the bitter maternal jewel:

> *Trilogy* is significant as the space in which H.D. begins to work through the intense ambivalence of her early work, taking early conflicting aspects of the mother and attempting to fuse them, change them, alter them, passing through maternity and bitterness and illusion and divinity until the *word*—Mother—lies in the crucible. To extract her requires this transmogrification through *language*, a textualization, alchemy worked not upon the lost maternal form itself but on the words that both contain and release her. (p. 130)

Kloepfer emphasizes her second point about language as part of a Kristevan reading that recognizes in the rhythmic pulsings of the jewel "the space of the *chora*," with its links to the semiotic and the lost bond to the

mother's body (p. 133). The same point, however, also recalls Klein's the-
ories of reparation in which the child, too anxious to approach its mother's
gutted body directly even in phantasy, carries out its first acts of restitu-
tion on her symbolic substitutes.[83]

In her initial address to a mother bitter like the sea, and like the sea a
"breaker, seducer, / giver of life, giver of tears" (*T* 71), H.D. rehearses
the Kleinian infant's first impulse to hold the mother personally respon-
sible for all of life's ills as well as its pleasures (*DPA* 127, 159). H.D.'s links
between mother and sea recall the oceanic images of "The Walls," asso-
ciated there with the destructive and maddening powers of the uncon-
scious and eternity. Here, she brings to the surface the association between
oceanic and maternal violence ("breaker, seducer") lurking in her earlier
conflation of the sucking mouth of the "star-whirlpool" and the sky
mother who devours in order to create in sections 21 and 22 of "The
Walls." The links between the mother, heartbreak, bitterness, and the sea
also carry established lesbian connotations for H.D. In "The Wise Sap-
pho," Sappho "is the sea itself, breaking and tortured and torturing, but
never broken." Sappho finds Eros a "bitter, bitter creature, . . . who has
once more betrayed her"; in turn, her own "manners" and "gestures are
crude, the bitterest of all destructive gibes of one sensitive woman at the
favourite of another."[84] And in her translation of Euripides' *Ion* (which,
as we have already seen, played a role in her analysis with Walter Schmi-
deberg), H.D. ascribes to Kreousa an "inner fire and concentrated bitter-
ness."[85] As a mother who both longs for the safety of her abandoned child
and attempts to murder him, Kreousa adds Kleinian associations of the
good and bad mother to H.D.'s earlier association of bitterness with les-
bian betrayal, jealousy, and aggression. Finally, Walter Schmideberg's
interpretation of the female "incarnation of Brittania on the war-posters"
as a "bad mother" stands behind this fantasy of the jewel.[86] For H.D. uses
repetition to trace adult aggression—our capacity to harbor "passionate,
bitter wrongs" and to conduct "bitter, unending wars" (*T* 65)—back to
the "bitter jewel" and the child's unresolved "bitterness of feeling" to-
wards the persecutory mother.

In section 9, the poet begins to explore where the sources of her bit-
terness toward the mother lie, addressing a series of frustrated questions
to the "bitter jewel":

> what do you offer
>
> to us who rebel?
> what were we had you loved other?
>
> what is this mother-father
> to tear at our entrails?

what is this unsatisfied duality
which you can not satisfy?   (*T* 72)

Here, H.D. explicitly spells out the grievances we had to decipher for our-
selves in the "star-whirlpool" section of "The Walls." The "unsatisfied
duality" of "mother-father"—that is, sexual difference as the condition of
human reproduction—is itself a form of punishment, a source of violence
and frustration. With the figure of a "mother-father" that "tear[s] at our
entrails," the poet conjures up the image of the "combined parental fig-
ure" joined in coitus, which the Kleinian infant imagines has invaded its
own body, tearing and devouring it from within (*DPA* 164).[87] For Klein
the combined parental figure represents the infant's resentful sense that its
parents take pleasure in one another at the expense of the infant. In con-
trast, for H.D. it is not the parents' act of coitus but the "unsatisfied dual-
ity" of that act—the fact that mother cannot be father, nor father mother,
even in their act of coming together—which occasions the child's
frustration.

If in section 9 the poet mourns the mother's and father's involuntary
bequest of a single, limiting sex to each of their children, in section 10 she
makes peace with her lot through a surprising and ingenious revision of
her own earlier figures of orbiting. Translating the "unsatisfied duality"
of "mother-father" into the two contrasting names of the planet Venus,
"Phosphorus at sun-rise, / Hesperus at sun-set" (*T* 73), she plays on the
fact that these male attendants of the goddess of sexual love are actually
alternate aspects of her, and only appear to be separate entities because
they manifest in different parts of the sky at different times of day. Just as
the planet Venus is one planet whether it appears in the east or the west,
as male or as female, so, the implicit analogy runs, our bodies' earthly as-
pects both obscure and point to a oneness beyond temporal and sexual
division in another, higher dimension.

With this resolution in hand, the poet is newly able to reject hostile
accusations against a maligned Venus, associated with "poison" and
"witches" in section 11, and to call for the "return" of a newly "vener-
ate[d]" Venus in section 12 (*T* 74, 75). In the following section, the poet
exclaims over her jewel: "it lives, it breathes, / it gives off—fragrance?"
(*T* 76). Proof of a new blossoming of Eros in "Love's sacred groves" (*T*
81), the jewel's "green-white" color and fragrance reappear in H.D.'s vi-
sion of the flowering may-tree in section 17. Their whiteness and fra-
grance make both may-tree and jewel coded symbols for *materia prima* or
purified quicksilver—matter rinsed of mortal rhythm—which is the
product of the lesser work. The fifteenth-century alchemist Bernardus
Trevisanus reports, "I tell you, with God as my witness, that this Quick-

silver, when it was sublimated, was clothed in so pure a white, that it looked like snow on top of a very high mountain. It had a fine, crystalline lustre, from which, when the vessel was opened, there emanated a perfume so sweet that nothing resembling it could be found on earth."[88] For H.D. the unearthly fragrance of purified quicksilver carried another connotation as well. In her autobiography, St. Thérèse of Lisieux (who called herself the "Little White Flower of Jesus") repeatedly figures the presence of Jesus in her life as a precious perfume.[89] Where the Saint attributes to the divine son the power to make "sweet even that which is most bitter,"[90] H.D. attributes this power to his holy mothers—the Virgin Mary, whose month is May, and her ancient precursor, the amorous Venus.

But H.D.'s emphasis on the sweetness of love should not blind us to her insistence that the bitter flame of aggression plays an "inexorable" role in bringing about love's fragrant flowering. Just as Sappho called Eros the "bitter-sweet,"[91] H.D. lights a candle to war and one to peace on either side of the bitter jewel sequence, arguing that the

> one must inexorably
>
> take fire from the other
> as spring from winter.   (*T* 80)

Thus, while she associates the bitter maternal jewel with "the anger, frustration, / bitter fire of destruction" at the opening of "The Flowering of the Rod," H.D. also associates it with "the fire // of strength, endurance, anger / in [the] hearts" of the heroic Londoners who prefer "daring the blinding rage // of the lightning" to abandoning their city during the Blitz (*T* 114, 68–69, 79). Source of the self-respect, courage, and resistance among these Londoners of "unbroken will" and "unbowed head" (*T* 68), bitter anger and aggression receive the poet's praise in her tribute to Uriel. H.D.'s very decision to give thanks to the angel of war, left unhallowed until now, parallels Klein's sense that aggression plays a necessary and productive role in human development (*T* 70). Similarly, her vision of the flame passing from the candle of Uriel, angel of war, to the candle of "*Annael*, / peace of God" ("the Venus name"—"companion of the fire-to-endure" [*T* 79, ix]) parallels Klein's belief that young children's successful entrance into love, language, and the human community depends on their willingness to accept, in symbolic form, the give-and-take of both aggression and nurture in their relations with the mother.[92]

In "Tribute to the Angels," the bitter jewel might stand as a symbol of the nurturing or sustaining power of aggression itself in the mother-daughter relationship. With its "pulse uncooled that beats yet" (*T* 76), the jewel displays the repetitive action of Freud's death drive; but its beat also

lies at the erotic center of the sequence. Under its steady pressure, the
poet-alchemist reconstitutes the jewel as a point not of grievance but of
dreamy pleasure between mother and daughter. Thus, in section 14 the
poet watches the jewel's

> faint
>
> heart-beat, pulse-beat
> as it quivers   (*T* 77)

Before long, she too is privy to a "new sensation" that

> strikes paralysing,
> strikes dumb,
>
> strikes the senses numb,
> sets the nerves quivering.   (*T* 85)

For the rest of the sequence, the jewel's pulsing rhythm exerts a similarly
uncontrollable effect on those who watch it: like candle-fire, its beat is
catching. In fact, the jewel's repeating beat acts as the intradiagetic source
of H.D.'s pervasive use of repetition throughout "Tribute." Loading the
sequence with formal repetitions ranging from a single word to several
lines in length, H.D. also sets it drumming with a host of mental sounds,
associated not only with the pulsing jewel but also with a ticking clock, a
knocking Lady, ringing bells, and quivering flames. This, surely, is rep-
etition with a vengeance.

Freud's small essay, "A Case of Paranoia Running Counter to the
Psycho-Analytic Theory of the Disease" (1924), provides not only a pos-
sible source text for all this ticking and knocking, but also a clue to H.D.'s
insistence on the epiphanic and redemptive power of such repetitive ac-
tion. In his essay, Freud tests his theory that repressed homosexual feelings
lie behind the persecution fantasies of paranoiacs against a case that would
initially seem to contradict it. The young woman who consults Freud
wants to prosecute a male coworker for secretly photographing her during
an afternoon liaison in his apartment. As Freud reports, "in the midst of
this idyllic scene she was suddenly frightened by a noise, a kind of knock
or click. . . . She had at once asked her friend what this noise meant, and
was told, so she said, that it probably came from the small clock on the
writing-desk" ("A Case of Paranoia" 264). The woman herself insists that
this "knock or click" came from a camera snapping pictures. On a second
consultation, Freud decides that the woman's suspicions center not on the
young man, but on their "elderly superior" at work, a "motherly old
lady" who treats the woman as "her particular favourite," but who, she
now fears, has turned against her ("A Case of Paranoia" 266). Arguing

that these suspicions stem from the woman's repressed homosexual attachment to her mother, Freud revises the woman's own story even further to claim that there was neither a camera nor a clock to be heard in the apartment:

> I do not believe that the clock ever ticked or that there was any noise to be heard at all. The woman's situation justified a sensation of a knock or beat in her clitoris. And it was this that she subsequently projected as a perception of an external object. Just the same sort of thing can occur in dreams. A hysterical woman patient of mine once related to me a short arousal dream to which she could bring no spontaneous associations. She dreamt simply that someone knocked and then she awoke. Nobody had knocked at the door. . . . There had been a "knock" in her clitoris. In the case of our paranoic patient, I should substitute for the accidental noise a similar process of projection. ("A Case of Paranoia" 270)

"Just the same sort of thing can occur in dreams," but not in just the same way if the dreamer has any stake in revising Freud's theory of paranoia's repressed subtext of homosexuality. And when H.D. dreams of a Lady whose "faint knocking" turns out to be "the clock ticking" "at my bed-head" (*T* 90, 89), the revisions abound.[93] In identifying the Lady of her dream as "the Troubadour's or Poet's Lady" (*T* ix), H.D. directly engages Denis de Rougemont's argument in *Passion and Society*. In this book, de Rougemont condemns the long-standing cult of Eros in Europe on the grounds that its seekers' yearning for "fusion or ecstatic dissolving of the self in God" is actually nothing but a glorified "wish for death";[94] and he further denounces the unapproachable lady love of Provençal poetry as man's own "*spiritual* element, that which the soul imprisoned in his body desires with a nostalgic love that death alone can satisfy."[95] Freud's description of the office worker's knocking clitoris poses a similar link between the desire for a forbidden lady and the drive toward death. In *Beyond the Pleasure Principle*, he reassigns the unconscious "compulsion to repeat" to the "daemonic" workings of the death drive, which seeks "to restore an earlier state of things" (36).[96] While Freud never explicitly links the office worker's paranoid hallucination of the ticking clock with her death drive, the repressed content of her hallucination—the desire to make love to her mother—replays in sexual terms the death drive's aim to return to the origin, just as the camera or clock's displaced rhythm of clitoral orgasm keeps the beat associated with the death drive's repetitive action.

H.D.'s account of the lunar Lady breaks down both Freud's and de Rougemont's arguments point by point. Where Freud tells the story of a woman whose repressed lesbianism leads her into a malevolent world of clandestine surveillance and betrayal, H.D. tells the story of a lifted repression leading to joyous contact with the "cool beneficence" of the Lady (*T* 96). Where Freud distinguishes between paranoid hallucination and psychoanalytic theory—that is, between the clock (or camera) and the clitoris—H.D. fuses the two; just as its tick encodes the beat of the clitoris, the clock's "phosphorescent face" encodes the dawn aspect of Venus and sexual love (*T* 90).[97] Where Freud insists, in an analogous patient's case, that "nobody had knocked at the door," H.D.'s dream furnishes two other witnesses—"we three together"—who agree that someone has, and that "she is actually standing there" (*T* 90). And where Freud situates the office worker and her "elderly superior" within the divisive triangle of oedipal rivalry, H.D. assures us that her Lady is free of all other attachments. With the dreamer's claim—

> but the Lamb was not with her,
> either as Bridegroom or Child;
>
> her attention is undivided,
> we are her bridegroom and lamb   (*T* 104)

—the "unsatisfied duality" of "mother-father" resolves into the "undivided" attention of a woman who doubles as the daughter's mother and lover.

Under the moon, which governs the alchemical stage in which all conflict between matter's elements ceases,[98] H.D. merges the Lady's "faint knocking," the clock's ticking, and the "pulse-beat" of her own arousal to reinterpret paranoid "projection" in alchemical terms.[99] As she lies dreaming and waking on her bed in the clock's "luminous light" (*T* 90), she uses this triple rhythm to elevate her whole body to that "luminous essence" that signifies the "fusion or ecstatic dissolving of the self in God," sought alike by practitioners of the alchemical "royal art" and by the initiates of the cult of Eros whom de Rougemont condemns.[100] Like *materia prima*, said to mirror perfectly the universal spirit,[101] H.D.'s dimly lit body mirrors the bright Lady of her dream. In turn, the Lady emerges, like Venus, from the oceanic realm of the unconscious and of eternity to replace the male herald of Christ's holy conception. H.D. impishly demands from her readers an explanation for this surprising turn of events:

> I had been thinking of Gabriel,
>
>   . . .
>
> how could I imagine
> the Lady herself would come instead?   (*T* 92)

Susan Friedman has established important connections between H.D.'s dream of the Lady's coming and an earlier, lesbian and possibly masturbatory dream of Artemis, the "moon-mother," recorded during her therapy with Freud. We might add to Friedman's account further connections between this dream of the Lady and H.D.'s dream, also discussed during the Freud sessions, of kissing the breast of a Venus who appeared to her in the guise of her daughter Perdita. However, Friedman goes on to argue that "the lesbian/masturbatory/erotic layer has been distilled out of the relatively impersonal discourse" of the Lady sequence in *Trilogy*.[102] In a similar vein, Deborah Kloepfer reads the Lady as an "asexual" precursor to Mary Magdalene, who, she argues, allows H.D. to resolve "the two conflicting aspects of the mother—the erotic and the maternal"—and to explore the daughter's incestuous desire for the mother in "The Flowering of the Rod" (pp. 133, 135, 139). With the recovery of the dream texts underlying H.D.'s epiphanic encounter in "Tribute" we can now identify the Lady herself as "a woman of pleasure" (*HE* 12) who, like the later Helen of Troy, embodies the mother's and daughter's erotic fantasies of one another.[103]

Here, it is important to note that H.D.'s representations of lesbian orgasm within the mother-daughter dyad—like the cryptic alchemical texts she takes as her model—are highly encoded; you have to be up on your Freud (to say nothing of St. Thérèse) to catch her drift. Even in its hiddenness, however, this dream is redemptive. Refiguring the terrifying aspect of Amen, "the hidden-one," who butts and bellows at the asexual seeker before smothering and devouring it, the very codedness of H.D.'s dream resurrects and redeems the possibility first ascribed to Hatshepsut's cartouche: that hidden things bear not harm but eternal life. Dissolving the paranoid world of the cannibalistic Ram-as-mother, the dream of the Lady sets in its stead an epiphanic space of aggressive eroticism between mother and daughter that flowers in an immortalizing ecstasy.

But as if to counteract de Rougemont's argument that the pleasures of the Lady's love are not available to the living, that they can only be enjoyed among the dead, H.D. insists on locating this space of epiphany in the repetitive flow of earthly time. She marvels over the Lady's "miraculous" ability to "relate herself to time here" (*T* 91) and constitutes this ability as a transcendental mirroring of time's own latent ability to relate "our life, this temporary eclipse / to that other . . ." (*T* 88; H.D.'s ellipses). This intimate relation of clock and Lady, time and everlastingness, revises a long-standing network of associations between clocks, death, male violence, and female homoeroticism in H.D.'s earlier writings.[104] One novel stands out among them: *Nights*, which charts Natalia's twelve nights of sadomasochistic lovemaking with a young man and her eventual suicide.

After her lover fails to satisfy her and leaves for the night, Natalia masturbates to a climax in which a "high-powered deity" "crept up the left

side, [as] she held it, timed it, let it gather momentum, let it gather force"
until "at the nape, it broke, distilled radium into the head."[105] If Natalia
here "times" her orgasm, when she plunges to her death in a frozen lake
she leaves time on the shore in the form of a watch she's borrowed from
her lesbian sister-in-law, Renne. The novel's first narrator, stodgy John
Helforth, urges us to submit this gesture to a Freudian reading, proposing
that the borrowed watch signifies Natalia's desire to be Renne. But the
reader suspects John of falling somewhat short here. His description of
the suicide scene—"a small, mannish platinum or platinum-plated watch,
with a wide strap, was left on a strip of dark fur [Natalia's 'muff'], by the
side of a small lake on the edge of the road"[106]—clearly inscribes a sym-
bolic typography of the female genitals, with the lesbian Renne's "small,
mannish . . . watch" standing in as the clitoris, to which Freud himself
assigns a "virile character" ("Female Sexuality" 228).

Susan Friedman links Natalia's heterosexual masochism to her death
wish, and reads the suicide itself as a desperate attempt to return through
a "dark gash" in the ice to her mother's womb.[107] In this reading, which
makes explicit homophobic tendencies within Freud's own theories of les-
bian desire, the libidinous wish to return to the mother coincides with the
death wish to "restore an earlier state of things" as the daughter's end co-
incides with her beginning. The message implied by this tight circle of
return can only be that lesbian incest equals death. On second glance,
however, Natalia's return to the womb/tomb does not effect perfect clo-
sure, but instead leaves a remainder, "something forgotten," "lost or left
over": the watch (*HE* 282, 281). Perched on the lip of the vertiginous de-
scent back to the mother-in-death, Renne's abandoned watch mediates be-
tween the "infinite" depth of the lake and the road leading back to Na-
talia's unhappy marriage. As the epiphanic site in which time and eternity,
the pulsing female body and the "high-powered deity," meet for a gath-
ering of force, the watch-as-clitoris stands as a neglected space of fanta-
sized interaction between mother and daughter where the aggressive, even
sadomasochistic, avenues of lesbian eroticism need not end in death. It is
to this watch and its possibilities, then, that H.D. returns in her dream of
the Lady.

Just as the Lady's ability to "relate herself to time here" offers H.D. a
way out of the supposed death trap lurking in her nostalgic desire to return
to her mother, the Lady also provides a way out of the traps associated
with earthly life in the first sequence of *Trilogy*. While there the poet was
held back from union with divine oneness by a body caught up in the con-
stitutive divisions *within* the orders of gender, sex, and time, H.D. here
springs the trap of the body by fusing the divisions *between* these orders;
as the clitoris's gemlike ardor, the clock's glow, and the Lady's brightness
unite at

> the point in the spectrum
> where all lights become one,
>
> . . .
>
> where the flames mingle
>
> and the wings meet, when we gain
> the arc of perfection,
>
> we are satisfied, we are happy,
> we begin again.   (*T* 109)

Circling back on her accusatory cry to the bitter maternal jewel—"what is this unsatisfied duality / which you can not satisfy?" (*T* 72)—H.D. reports a happier beginning, in which mother deeds to daughter a specifically female form of aggressive sexuality whose repetitions bypass death for heavenly joy.

In reworking Freud's account of the death drive, H.D. also revises his account of early female development. Claiming that the daughter's first phase of amorous "attachment to the mother ends in hate" when she blames the mother for "the discovery that she is castrated" ("Femininity" 121, 126), Freud's account stands as the direct inverse of Klein's account of the same relationship; where Freud's little girl must give up her "aggressive impulses" that "leave nothing to be desired in the way of abundance and violence" ("Femininity" 118) when she rejects clitoral masturbation for mother-hatred,[108] the Kleinian infant's early phase of paranoid hatred for a persecuting mother gives way to a second phase in which the daughter can leash her aggressive feelings toward the mother to the positive ends of language acquisition, creativity, and pleasure. In performing the reversal of Freud's account along Kleinian lines in her movement from the bitter maternal jewel to the final recognition that the Lady "must have been pleased // with the straggling company of the brush and quill" (*T* 100), H.D. once again redeems the strategy of reversal that wreaked such havoc on her attempts to portray eternity in "The Walls."

H.D.'s recognition of the mother's pleasure in the poet-daughter's gift for words also revises St. Thérèse's homoerotic dream of the "Venerable Mother" in which she inquires whether Jesus is pleased with her and the Venerable Mother answers, "God asks nothing more of you; He is pleased, very much pleased."[109] In H.D.'s dream, the Lady prefers to answer for herself. Yet the mark of the Lady's pleasure—a closed book whose pages we can only "imagine" "are the blank pages / of the unwritten volume of the new,"—provides the ground but not the terms of H.D.'s repeating attempts to say what "I wanted to say" in the final sections of "Tribute" (*T* 103, 106). Like the Kleinian child who appropriates a world of existing objects for its own symbol-making activities, H.D.

casts her love for the Lady in a playful naming game. Calling up in words and then rejecting the heritage of portraits[110] that do not quite convey her "as I saw her," H.D. finally chooses two images that are nonrepresentational; their resemblance to the Lady rests entirely on a symbolic connection posed by the poet, but left for the reader to decipher:

> when the jewel
> melts in the crucible,
>
> we find not ashes, not ash-of-rose,
>
> . . .
>
> but a cluster of garden-pinks
> or a face like a Christmas-rose.   (*T* 109–10)

Where "knaves and fools" had earlier found in the aphrodisiac root of mandragora "poison, / food for the witches' den" (*T* 74), H.D. now finds in the Lady's "face like a Christmas-rose" a divine remedy for all mortal, and mental, ills. Like the philosopher's stone, which promises healing power and longlasting life and whose floral symbol is the rose,[111] garden pinks bear the Greek name *Dianthus*, which means "heavenly flower," and the Christmas-rose blossoms on a plant called *Helleborus niger*, whose medicinal root yields a powder "used by the ancient Greeks and Romans in treating mental and other disorders."[112]

Femininity and Its Returns

This will happen again.
—H.D., "The Flowering of the Rod"

I have argued that "The Walls Do Not Fall" poses a sharp distinction between the unifying order of eternity and the divisive order of time, gender, and sex, only to bring about the return of a repressed order of eternal death. In contrast, "Tribute to the Angels" fuses the clock's tick, the dream Lady's knock, and the clitoris's pulse in the poet's ecstatic epiphany. With this fusion, H.D. newly accepts time, the unconscious, and female sexual aggression as vehicles not of division, limitation, and death, but of transcendence and divine (re-)union. But her very success in refiguring aggression between women as a source of creative ecstasy can leave one a little uneasy. In Klein's model of reparation, the child's act of mourning for the lost body of the mother brings about her recovery only if the child is able to acknowledge actual loss and the limits reality places on the reparative process. The manic child, according to Klein, fails to make such acknowledgment; instead, it exaggerates its power to restore its lost objects to life, and attempts not so much to repair loss as to overturn or reverse it, to escape its effects altogether (*SMK* 132–34). Similarly, in "Tribute" the very power of the poet's alchemy to convert war into peace, bitter into sweet, anger into joy allows us to get from violence to healing without encountering loss, its rawness, its despair. Loss occasions the sequence; it is because the mother is lost that we must "re-invoke, re-create" her (*T* 63). But loss receives surprisingly little attention in the sequence. As occasion, it stands occluded.

In "The Flowering of the Rod," loss itself comes out of hiding and becomes "unalterably part of the picture" (*T* 146). Writing at Christmas after D-Day, H.D. can be more certain that she will not die, will not be lost. But as a survivor she must, once again, confront the loss of others. Left behind by death, she learns the links between gifts, guests, and grief. She measures loss in the body's own terms: falling, spilling, seeping, leaking, weeping, loosening, and leaving. She allows loss to take place, refusing to deprive it of a history through denial (no loss has occurred) or accusation (loss recast as injury, a crime or a fault, a question of good and evil, right and wrong). Repeating the Kleinian child's act of reparation which transforms grievance against the mother into grief on her behalf, H.D. also reverses that act, performing the mother's redemptive mourning for the lost child. That such an act of redemptive mourning takes place within the poet's realm of wordplay is no accident; following both Klein and Freud in their accounts of symbolic reparation and of joking respectively, H.D. casts language itself as a maternalized field of loss and return.

In its focus on maternal mourning, "The Flowering of the Rod" echoes H.D.'s memoir of childhood, *The Gift*, itself written between 1941 and 1943. Dianne Chisholm argues that in this memoir "H.D. undertakes a (w)rite of passage from melancholia to mourning, from a frozen, incarcerated crying to a liberation of tears and, beyond that, to a revelation of what was originally lost—the gift. . . . What 'frees' [the child protagonist] Hilda from her defensive enclosure, her melancholic frigidity, is the memory and resurgence of a maternal, masochistic *jouissance*."[113] Traveling by a different interpretive path, Chisholm also arrives at a theoretical alignment between maternal grieving and joking in *The Gift*.[114] But where Chisholm locates the mother's gift of healing laughter in the ego-shattering force of a primary masochism, I would argue that for a wartime poet so recently threatened with destruction and self-destruction, the masochist's pain-seeking passivity proves too dangerous an erotic position to take up. Instead, H.D. again follows Klein in overturning the conventional representation of grief as a form of passive suffering by reconstituting it as a creative and even procreative act, an ultimately comedic labor of sorrow.[115]

At the same time, however, H.D.'s very association of mourning with maternity replicates one of the most common conventions in contemporary war propaganda and literature. Susan Schweik demonstrates the vulnerability imposed on women by the gendered relationship between losers and lost in poetry of World War II; making male bodies into lost bodies and female bodies into the bodies of losers, weepers, such poetry places maternalized mourners on the edge of the scene of male loss only to hold them ultimately accountable for it. Schweik suggests that H.D. writes "The Flowering" to protest this conventional positioning of weeping woman as "intolerable":

> *Trilogy* finally banishes its wailing version of Mary, retaining only a Mary of Magdala who comments sternly, self-reflexively, perhaps even sardonically on her role as weeper, all the while with her "voice steady" and her eyes dry (*F* 17 [*T* 136]). . . . We can read these deletions [of the weeping woman], then, in part, as an attempt to find a way within the master plot of Western male sacrifice for a woman in a narrative of violence, for a narrative itself, to say no. (pp. 252, 259)

There is much that is compelling in this argument. But some of Schweik's assumptions go against what I understand to be the premises of *Trilogy* as a whole. First, insofar as H.D. uses her war sequence to explore women's own capacity for aggression, she must forgo faith in a body (male or female) free of all violence. And so she must forgo the hope that one can just say no to narratives of someone else's violence; when violence lies inside the narrator, the piety of such a no is as much a narrative of violence as any story it might refute or deter. By the same token, the narrator who says no to her role as weeper, griever, admirably rejects her complicity in a scene of suffering; but she also risks rejecting grief itself, and the reality of loss. Such a narrator occupies a double bind. Living in a world "where Fish / move two-ways, devour" (*T* 40), she must learn to say yes and no.

Drawing on Schweik's argument, I would modify it in the following ways. When women accept rhetorical positioning as weepers in cultural narratives of loss, we accept the work of acknowledging loss, representing it, and fending off its denial. But we also risk incurring the wrath of those who would prevent grief as a way of preventing loss itself. Accepting grief as women's work, we embody desolation, depletion, dissolution for an entire society, and so stand vulnerable to the charge that we unleash these forces onto the world. This might suggest that women need only refuse grief to refute our rhetorical positioning as agents of loss, discontinuity, and departure. But the risks of this refusal—personal, cultural—are just as high, even higher, than the risks of complicity, and the chances for success in such a venture are small, given the ease with which "woman" circulates in the absence—or denial—of women's own say in the matter. Better to accept the work of grief, H.D. seems to say in "The Flowering," and try to redistribute it across lines of sexual difference. Better to repeat grief than refuse it. Better to treat grief as an investment, on which one might expect a return. Better to put grief into the flow of circulation, to pass it around—like women, like gifts, like guests, like ecstasy—than to declare oneself the ground on which grief runs dry, or goes underground.[116]

When Alice in Wonderland goes underground, falling down the rabbit-hole, she comes to grief in a "pool of tears." Another Eve, she is trying to get "into the garden" but she eats so much of a "very small cake" that she grows too big for the attempt. Then she grows too small, so small that she wishes she "hadn't cried so much. . . . I shall be punished for it now, I suppose, by being drowned in my own tears!" When she climbs out, it is because the pool of tears "was getting quite crowded with the birds and animals that had fallen into it." In *Alice's Adventures in Wonderland* all the birds swim to safety with her.[117] But in "The Flowering of the Rod" they stay in the water, for they "would rather drown, remembering—/ than bask on tropic atolls" (*T* 121). In *Tribute to Freud*, H.D. recalls her own sensation of "drowning" as she struggled to sustain a sequence of visions at Corfu in 1920: "I must hold on here or the picture will blur over and the sequence be lost. In a sense, it seems I am drowning; already half-drowned to the ordinary dimensions of space and time, I know I must drown, as it were, completely in order to come out on the other side of things (like Alice with her looking-glass or Perseus with his mirror)" (*TF* 54).

Who are these visionary birds, "the snow-geese" (*T* 116) who risk drowning as they circle and plunge over the lost island of paradise in the opening sections of "The Flowering"? Alice's? Eve's? Like Eve or like Alice, each bearing a troublesome hunger, "they have known bliss, / the fruit that satisfies" (*T* 120). And like Eve and Alice, each barred from the garden, they rise and reach only to "fall from the innermost centre of the ever-narrowing circle" (*T* 119). But unlike Eve or Alice, their hunger, their grief, opens not onto a scene of punishment but onto a state of grace; yes, it is true

> they fall exhausted, numb, blind
> but in certain ecstasy,
>
> for theirs is the hunger
> for Paradise.   (*T* 120)

Not Eve's, not Alice's (not exactly), these birds are Milton's; they are the gulls he sets squawking over the waste of paradise, "an Island salt and

bare, / The haunt of Seals and Orcs, and Sea-mews' clang."[118] Their par-
adise, the paradise Eve lost, is now a sea garden, salted, infertile, ruined
beyond all hope of retrieval. But H.D. tends to put more store in sea gar-
dens than Milton did. As Eileen Gregory writes of *Sea Garden* itself, "in
H.D.'s poems the garden is still the place of love, but love washed with
salt. It is a *sea* garden, inimical to all but the most enduring. The sea rep-
resents here the harsh power of elemental life, to which the soul must open
itself, and by which it must be transformed or die." Maybe, Gregory sug-
gests further, the garden, the "rocky island," is Sappho herself.[119] And "if
the islands are lost?" (*T* 120). The sea, the pool of tears, is still there: for
basking or drowning or sea-change, for opening oneself to the dead.

So the dead are also unalterably part of the picture. With their "hun-
ger / for Paradise," these geese draw from Freud's life instinct the urge for
nourishment, for self-preservation. Yet they also draw from Freud's death
instinct the urge to "to restore an earlier state of things" (*Beyond the Plea-
sure Principle* 36). "Seeking what we once knew," they "would rather
drown remembering"—they would rather kill themselves than forget (*T*
117, 121). Freud, like Milton, equates the scene of return with the scene
of death, lacing the garden with salt. The action of the returning repressed
is the action of dying. Freud goes on to argue that remembering, working
through, can replace repetition, substitute understanding for return, and
keep death at bay. But for H.D. memory doesn't replace return; it guar-
antees it. Then again, what memory returns is "washed with salt." It's
been grieved over, and if grieving feels a little too much like dying, like
drowning, so be it. There are worse things in the world of "The Flow-
ering" than death by drowning.

For instance, there is "the steel sharpened on the stone" and "the pyr-
amid of skulls" (*T* 121–22); there is killing. Or there is "this duality, this
double nostalgia," "the insatiable longing / in winter, for palm-shadow"
(*T* 118), or in heat for the snow:

> this is the eternal urge,
> this is the despair, the desire to equilibrate
>
> the eternal variant.   (*T* 119)

It is the desire for loss to cease ("I would cry out, stay, stay" [*T* 118]), the
desire to keep everything you ever had, stacked up, balanced, a weight in
your arms. In sections 4 and 5, H.D. acknowledges the strength of this
"insatiable longing," but she has already given notice, in section 1, that
the time for crying "stay, stay" is over. "Having given all, let us leave all"
(*T* 114), she advises, emptying her pockets of pity and self-pity. For emp-
tying, leaving, are actions not of betrayal but of grace, even "resurrec-

tion" (*T* 123). Like Eve, expelled from the garden, Christ, escaped from the tomb, is himself a wanderer: "He journeys back and forth / between the poles of heaven and earth forever" (*T* 128). And it is to "an outcast and a vagabond"—another sinner, another Eve—that he links leaving and emptying with plenty, with return: *"to-day shalt thou be with me in Paradise"* (*T* 128).

When H.D. turns from the story of the snow-geese to that of Mary Magdalene in section 12, the birds' "ecstasy" reappears in yet another outcast and wanderer, a woman "naturally reviled for having left home / and not caring for housework . . . or was that Mary of Bethany?" (*T* 125, 129; H.D.'s ellipses). And their spiraling flight reappears in one of those "twisted or . . . tortured individuals / out of line, out of step with world so-called progress" (*T* 129). The geese confer on the narrative that follows a pattern of fall, flight, and return that is itself divine. Placed at the center of this pattern, Mary Magdalene repeats it in her own body. "An unpredictable woman" (*T* 159), she is the site of crossed thresholds, leaky jars, and disappearing acts:

> she knew how to detach herself,
> another unforgivable sin,
>
> and when stones were hurled,
> she simply wasn't there;
>
> she wasn't there and then she appeared,
> not a beautiful woman really—would you say?
>
> certainly not pretty.   (*T* 131)

Certainly not pretty, Mary commands instead a physical presence that makes men uncomfortable. Freud traces the source of such discomfort (as well as women's impulse to beautify themselves with ornament) to the young boy's (mis-)recognition that women are castrated. The possibility of their own castration held out by this fantasy of the castrated woman prompts an anxiety that, according to Freud, men seek to contain in fetishes. The fetish adorning the woman's body simultaneously assuages and incites male anxiety, insofar as it represents both the missing penis and its frightening detachability ("Fetishism" 156). A repentant sinner in the biblical tradition, the Magdalene appears in H.D.'s sequence with an undiminished and unabashed sexuality that is clearly fetishistic. Unloosing "her extraordinary hair" before strangers, she uses it to wipe her tears from Christ's feet before anointing them with ointment (*T* 141).[120] In the eyes of Judas Iscariot, this gesture is "Extravagant" (*T* 141), wandering outside permissible limits, exceeding all bounds of decorum; and Simon, her host, concurs:

> things had gone excellently till now,
> but this was embarrassing;
>
> she was actually kissing His feet.   (*T* 143)

Freud tells us, more calmly, that "both the feet and the hair are objects with a strong smell which have been exalted into fetishes after the olfactory sensation has become unpleasurable and been abandoned" "owing to repression" (*Three Essays* 155). Feet, hair, fragrance: the Magdalene knows "how to detach herself," yes, but she also has a way of holding onto things—"objects with a strong smell," for instance—which others would prefer she repress or abandon.

As we have seen, this exalting of odors, this wash of scent and sensation, became for St. Thérèse a favorite metaphor for her own devotion to Christ. "Pouring out on Him the odorous ointment of our lives" in "imitat[ion] . . . of Magdalen," she figures life lived in his memory as a joyous giving and receiving of perfumes: "Since Our Lord is in Heaven I can only follow Him by the traces full of light and fragrance which He has left behind Him. But as soon as I open the Holy Gospels, I breathe the perfume exhaled by the life of Jesus, and I know which way to run."[121] These lives, these bodies, steeped in perfume, also recall the frightening detachability of the castrated, castrating woman; they too let things go (poured out, exhaled) and leave traces of themselves behind. But St. Thérèse figures such spilling or spending as an act not of depletion but of divine infusion, profusion, and exchange. Merging Mary and Christ with perfume, she prepares the way for H.D.'s own metaphoric mergers in Mary's speech to Kaspar—"(though I am Mara, bitter) I shall be Mary-myrrh"—and Kaspar's final vision of the Christ Child as "a bundle of myrrh" in his mother's arms (*T* 135, 172).

The Saint also helps to underline what H.D. herself makes clear: myrrh, like the Magdalene, is strongly aligned with the sexual body, both in that it adorns and in that it expresses that body, or rather the body's forbidden sexuality, its pleasurable odors. Both myrrh and the Magdalene evoke departure, escape, and the transgression of boundaries: "though the jars were sealed, / the fragrance got out somehow" (*T* 132).[122] Finally, both evoke unknowableness. Simon says of Mary, "I do not know her," and of Christ that he does not *"know / who and what manner of woman this is"* (*T* 142, 143), while of myrrh we learn:

> no one could of course, actually know
>
> what was or was-not in those alabaster boxes
> of the Princesses of the Hyksos Kings.   (*T* 132)

Yet these grounds of resemblance might also constitute a riddling definition of the contents of Freud's unconscious: contents which mysteriously escape their bounds to manifest in conscious thinking or action; which represent the body's sexual and destructive instincts in the field of language; and whose precise nature and location remain unknowable. (These links between Mary, myrrh, and the unconscious gain additional strength from the reported rumors that "this distillation, this attar // lasted literally forever" [*T* 132], which call up Freud's and H.D.'s long-standing equation of the unconscious and the eternal.)[123] One of Freud's own stories suggests a partial explanation for H.D.'s links here between "an unpredictable woman," a leaking fragrance, and the unconscious. His story also serves as a possible source for H.D.'s account of Kaspar's ancestral alibi for passing on "the sacred processes" of the distillation of myrrh in whispering secrecy: "it was never written, not even in symbols, for this they knew— / no secret was safe with a woman" (*T* 133).[124] Freud makes a similar claim in his famous case history of Dora, another woman whose movements prove to be unpredictable, and who chooses in the end to keep her own counsel.

Boasting very much after the fact (Dora has left analysis, and her sudden departure continues to ripple the comprehensive account he would give of her), Freud dilates upon the implications of Dora's idle play with a "reticule" she wears at her waist: "He that has eyes to see and ears to hear may convince himself that no mortal can keep a secret. If his lips are silent, he chatters with his finger-tips; betrayal oozes out of him at every pore. And thus the task of making conscious the most hidden recesses of the mind is one which it is quite possible to accomplish" ("Fragment" 77–78). Freud here refers to his sense that Dora's toying with her purse serves as an unconscious confession that she masturbates. But his elaborate figures seem to verbalize an unacknowledged fear of his own, prompted by the memory of the "reticule, which came apart at the top in the usual way" ("Fragment" 77).

Revising his conviction that "no mortal can keep a secret" for "betrayal oozes out of him at every pore" as Kaspar's knowledge that "no secret was safe with a woman," H.D. makes plain what Freud's generic "he" would disguise. His imagery of the oozing body, repeated in the jar of myrrh whose fragrance escapes its seal, gives voice to his own phobic fantasies of the castrated woman, or perhaps simply the woman who menstruates, casting her body as a leaky vessel singularly unable to control or contain its fluids.[125] In contrast to the open, oozing body of the hysterical woman/patient, Freud himself remains admirably self-contained. Indeed, in *Tribute to Freud*, H.D. describes him as a "guardian at the gate," a die-hard rationalist who "slam[s] the door on visions of the future, of the after-life" (pp. 103, 102). But this is hardly a compliment, for in such a role Freud descends to the level of the cautious mollusk in "The Walls," who unlocks its "portals / at stated intervals" (*T* 8), giving its life over to the anxious and hopeless—if civilized—task of regulating its body's boundaries, defending its gates equally against the risk of loss and the promise of eternity.

H.D. defines Kaspar too as a doorkeeper, or maybe (again like Freud) a keeper of Dora. Indeed, Mary's entire visit to the marketplace is dominated by Kaspar's (and the narrator's) comic fascination with a door. While Kaspar's obsessive focus on the door during Mary's visit signals his resistance to the vision she will offer him (*T* 134), his obsessive memory of the door after her departure seems to signal exactly the reverse. Even as an old man, he lingers over the moment long ago when

> Mary lifted the latch and the door half-parted,
> and the door shut, and there was the flat door
>
> at which he stared and stared.   (*T* 163–64)

Kaspar's undying interest in a door elevates it too to the status of a fetish, not of the penis but of the vagina[126]—or, if not a vagina, then at least a reticule. For Dora, like Mary, has caused a wise man to suffer the memory of her leavetaking and to linger over a protracted moment of "parting." In this sense, Freud's lengthy account of Dora's toying with her reticule— "opening it, putting a finger into it, shutting it again, and so on" ("Fragment" 76)—"betrays" more than her pleasure in masturbating. It also betrays his own chagrined inability to control the term of "her visit" ("Fragment" 122): "opening it" and "shutting it again," Dora plays out with her reticule what she will shortly play out with her analysis.

Just as Freud, left holding the bag after Dora's sudden departure, must read back to her much missed presence through the text of her absence, H.D.'s Kaspar reads the door Mary shuts in his face

> as if the line of wood, the rough edge
>
> or the polished surface or plain,
> were each significant, as if each scratch and mark
>
> were hieroglyph, a parchment of incredible worth
> or a mariner's map.   (*T* 164)

Here, both Kaspar and Freud attempt to command a woman's movements by recalling them. Yet this fused act of remembering and revoking becomes only a more sophisticated version of the game of *fort-da* Freud's grandson plays with a spool in a magical attempt to supervise his mother's comings and goings. Freud attributes his grandson's actions to an urge for mastery, just as he claims that Dora broke off her analysis because he "did not succeed in mastering the transference in good time" ("Fragment" 118). Similarly, H.D.'s Simon questions Christ's status as "Master" by claiming that he doesn't know *"who and what manner of woman"* Mary is (*T* 143). Insofar as Simon takes Mary for a prostitute, his claim comes down to the accusation that she circulates, gets around, and comes and goes as she pleases. As we shall see, all three would-be masters' obsessions with a woman's movements reveal their aversion not so much to female promiscuity or even to female lack, but to loss itself; the loose woman, like the oozing body, absorbs into her incalculable movements the threat of death, that singular form of departure that defies all men's attempts to recall it.[127]

Like Dora, like Christ, Mary Magdalene is a "Guest," a visitor, someone who's just passing through (*T* 142). But like "dora," like Christ, she's also a gift, something that leaves "increase" in its wake. She is a gift of myrrh, precious and bitter, a gift the recipient is fated to lose. Adalaide Morris has argued persuasively for H.D.'s lifelong participation in a sacred gift economy inherited from the Moravian communities of her ancestors. This economy demands the passage, not the accumulation, of goods: "if boundaries are unbreached, no one is richer or poorer, no change occurs." "Not to return the gift poisons the recipient and destroys the life-sustaining gift cycle." Moreover, "in the interval between the moment a gift comes to us and the moment we release and forward it, we suffer what Hyde calls 'the labor of gratitude,' the struggle to rise to the level of the gift and integrate it with our own vision so that we can give it away again."[128]

Morris places in this economy H.D.'s gift of gardenias to "greet the return of the gods" upon the safe arrival of Freud's antiquities collection in England during the war. These sweet-smelling flowers (as opposed to the scentless orchids other people send him) embody that spiritual "increase" or *hau* insured by the exchange of gifts.[129] By the writing of "The Flowering," however, H.D. merges the gift of flowers with the gift of tears, a surplus of grief that is also created when we give what we love away. Flowers greet the return of the gods but they also mark the passing of the dead.

When St. Thérèse dies, a series of miracles replace the smell of her corpse with the smell of flowers. At her funeral bier, "a child of ten . . . perceived a strong perfume of lilies, a fact which could not be naturally explained since only artificial lilies adorned the remains." Later, at the removal of the Saint's relics, when "the vault was opened, a delicious fragrance of roses filled the air."[130] The miracle of St. Thérèse's fragrant remains stands in for the miracle of Christ's resurrection, asserting on a smaller scale the victory of life over death. Yet insofar as the miraculous sign of rebirth—the "delicious fragrance" of flowers—derives through negation from the sign of death—the stinking corpse—it absorbs the contradictory logic of the fetish, which represents the very fears it disavows. In passing from St. Thérèse's autobiography to H.D.'s poem, these uncomfortable links between Mary's fragrant myrrh and the body in death no longer require hiding. In fact, they are foregrounded.

Thus, where Kaspar and Freud, like the mollusk, seek to master the body's tides, its leakages and leave-takings, Mary Magdalene claims them as central to her own masterless identity. She vows to Kaspar before leaving his booth, "(though I am Mara, bitter) I shall be Mary-myrrh" (*T* 135). Her self-identification with the leaking fragrance depends on two further identifications: with the Greek princess Myrrha, mother of Adonis, and the Phrygian goddess Cybele, mother of Attis. Linked through the composite identity of their sons, "Attis-Adonis-Tammuz" (*T* 135), Cybele and Myrrha also share a common association with sexualized violence which they initiate and which leads to the tragic spilling of the body's essences. "The Mother of Mutilations" (*T* 135), Cybele annually sends her son and lover into a religious frenzy from which he emerges self-castrated, his blood let to fertilize the summer crops. Myrrha, on the other hand, conceives a child by her unwitting father; like Eve, cursed for touching forbidden fruit, she is condemned to labor in sorrow. Thus, her story mythologizes the swollen bark of the myrrh tree (harvested for its sap) not only as Myrrha's guilty womb, which brings forth Adonis, but also as a womb that brings forth tears. The Naiads use the bitter resin of these tears to wash and anoint the newborn Adonis, who later becomes the lover of Venus and suffers a boar wound in the groin.[131] Both these women who spill forbidden blood, seed, and tears revive rather than suppress the frightening image of the destructive mother on display in earlier parts of *Trilogy*. Yet, as their myths insist, such spilling is holy, its trauma redemptive.

When Mary Magdalene cements her identification with Myrrha by claiming, "I am Mary, I will weep bitterly, / bitterly . . . bitterly," she foretells the tears she will spill at Golgotha where Christ spills his blood to save mankind (*T* 135; H.D.'s ellipses). But this allusion to Christ's death also links her more uncomfortably with Simon Peter, who denied Christ three times before the cock crowed and "went out, and wept bitterly."[132] Then again, her own treatment at the hands of Simon the host links her with Christ himself, and it is this last identification that proves to be definitive. Where Simon Peter tells the chief priests and elders, "I do not know the man,"[133] H.D.'s Simon the host observes Mary kissing Christ's feet and bends

> to whisper
>
> into the ear of his Guest,
> I do not know her.   (*T* 142)

In this early substitution of Mary Magdalene for the messiah, H.D. recasts Simon's denial of her as a betrayal, which, like Simon Peter's, is inevitably a self-betrayal as well. Just as Freud suggests that his patients' acts of "negation" or disavowal are attempts to deny their own unconscious thoughts ("Negation" 239), Simon's denial that he knows Mary (like his subsequent attempts to "eject" her from his house)[134] suggests that he does in fact know her, even that she is wrapped up in his self-knowledge. Indeed, just before his denial of Mary, Simon reveals that he has "seen something like this" before "in a heathen picture" of mermaids and sirens, and has learned that "wrecks followed the wake of such hair" (*T* 142).

Simon's thoughts here once again recall de Rougemont's account of the troubadours' mystical lady as a lure to death, as well as wider wartime associations of war with a dangerous femininity. Yet despite the fact that *Trilogy* as a whole has evoked these associations in order to dismantle them, Simon is right. Christ's death *will* follow in the wake of such hair; though his other followers would avoid the thought, displacing the central issue off onto insincere quibbles about poverty and unnecessary expense, Christ recognizes Mary's actions with the words: "For ye have the poor always with you; but me ye have not always. For in that she hath poured this ointment on my body, she did it for my burial."[135] What Simon the host and Simon Peter so violently deny is the premonition that they are about to lose Christ, that his resurrection depends on his mortality. Yet Christ's insistence "but me you have not always" is itself contradicted by the mystical "secret" that H.D.'s Moravian grandmother, Mamalie, speaks to the child Hilda in *The Gift*: "Mamalie said, 'My Christian [Mamalie's husband] explained the secret to me; it seemed very simple to me. It was simply belief in what was said—*and, lo, I am with you alway, even unto the end of the world*. You see, those words were taken literally'" (p. 84).

"But me ye have not always." "And, lo, I am with you alway." This is the language of the unconscious, where contradictions abide, where no truth rules out another. And it is the language of memory and dream; "the dead were living," H.D. writes in *Tribute to Freud*, "in so far as they lived in memory or were recalled in dream" (p. 14). No wonder Simon, a man who believes "we must draw the line somewhere" (*T* 142), prefers the postures of ignorance to this knowledge of nonsense. Ironically playing up to Simon's penchant for rational distinctions in a sequence well on its way to overturning reasonable argument for the greater truths of the unconscious and of religious faith, H.D. assures us,

> but it is not fair to compare
> Kaspar with Simon;
>
> this Simon is not Simon Peter, of course.   (*T* 146)

But if Simon is more like Simon Peter than he knows, Kaspar is also a lot like Simon himself. He too justifies his wish to eject Mary from his hut in the marketplace on the grounds that she is indecorous. As she drops her veil before turning to go, Kaspar thinks:

> it was unseemly that a woman
> appear disordered, dishevelled;
>
> it was unseemly that a woman
> appear at all.   (*T* 137)

This account of Kaspar's initial rejection of Mary precedes and prefigures Simon's more densely allusive denial of her. On the other side of Simon's denial, however, H.D. returns to this moment in the marketplace in order to revise it. In the interim, she has produced as the enabling condition of Kaspar's vision his "heathen" knowledge of the mother goddesses who possess Mary's body in "*daemon*" form (*T* 145). These mothers—Isis, Cyprus, Demeter—all lose precious lovers or children, and Kaspar too will become a losing, grieving mother as well as a lost child before his vision is over.

Kaspar receives his vision after stooping to pick up Mary's fallen veil and before remarking on the unseemliness of her appearance. In the brief moment framed by these acts, Mary reveals her fragrant hair. Her "dishevelled" appearance (*T* 137) links her once again to Milton's Eve, who "her unadorned golden tresses wore / Dishevell'd."[136] Likewise, the "disorder" of her hair represents the psychic or spiritual disorder she calls on Christ to cure: her possession by the newly demonized mother goddesses of the pre-Christian era. Milton's "On the Morning of Christ's Nativity" describes these pagan goddesses turning back in horrified flight from the one god who, though a child, "to show his Godhead true, / Can in his swaddling bands control the damned crew."[137] H.D. conflates Christ's birth with his later exorcism of Mary to reverse Milton's argument; not like their Miltonic counterparts, but rather like the Magi themselves, Mary's demons in

> crossing the threshold
> of this not un-lovely temple,
>
> . . . intended perhaps to pay homage,
> even as Kaspar had done,
>
> and Melchior
> and Balthasar.   (*T* 147)

In "crossing the threshold" of her body, Mary's demons supply the penultimate terms of her representation as a leaky vessel, and confirm that her sins, her trespasses, inhere in the fact that she allows her body's boundaries to be trespassed. This casting out itself becomes a demonized form of the labor of birth, a bringing forth from the body women need not occupy singly. But if this form of passage or trespass is the most forbidden, the most demonized, H.D. also argues that it is the most sacred. Susan Schweik has noted that as a barterer in myrrh, Mary enters the act of exchange as a subject; as a prostitute passing between men, she becomes the object exchanged (p. 272). But as a woman possessed of demons, she stands as the site or the medium of exchange, the ground on which the dead do business with the living, the lost with those who lose, the remembered with those who remember. Only through this placement in the gift economy can one exchange the boundedness of one's own body for that larger infusion or profusion of scent and sensation, that give-and-take of perfumes, that "infectious" "reality" mystics call "ecstasy" (*T* 125).

Freud follows Charcot in asserting that states of daemonic "possession and ecstasy" are "manifestations of hysteria" ("Seventeenth-Century" 72).[138] On their authority, then, we might identify this "twisted," "unbalanced, neurotic woman" as a hysteric (*T* 129), whose somatic "disorder" typically encodes repressed fantasies of sexual struggle, ecstasy, and the labor of birth. In Freud's own professional life the question of hysteria was wrapped up in the question of mastery, of the body's precinct of (self-)control. As noted earlier, he defines his failure to master the transference between his hysterical patient Dora and himself as the cause of her humiliating departure. In contrast, H.D. reconstitutes that failure of mastery as the very condition of transference, the transference of grief and of vision. As Kaspar bows before Mary at the door, he reacts to his hysterical visitor hysterically. Like hysterics who "suffer mainly from reminiscences" (*Studies on Hysteria* 7), he suffers with a memory. And like hysterics who acquire each other's symptoms through "psychical infection" (*Interpretation of Dreams* 150), he catches Mary's demon pregnancy, experiencing a visionary act of labor and rebirth that "mirror[s]" the "exalted ecstasy" of her own outcast status (*T* 150). For

though Kaspar, like Simon, "did not at first know her," when Mary
dropped her veil and

> he saw the light on her hair
> like moonlight on a lost river,

> Kaspar
> remembered   (*T* 148)

> he saw as in a mirror, clearly, O very clearly,
> a circlet of square-cut stones on the head of a lady,

> and what he saw made his heart so glad
> that it was as if he suffered,

> his heart laboured so
> with his ecstasy.   (*T* 150)

Refusing to keep grief shut up in the body of a woman, Mary com-
municates the demonized memory of lost paradise to Kaspar, whose own
hysterically maternalized heart provides the laboring beat behind the
"rhythmically" "stressed" echo of his vision (*T* 156). In this vision, as in
the man who must "drown, as it were, completely" to sustain it, the op-
positions between male and female, losers and lost, time and eternity, at
last rest in balanced unity. At the same time, Kaspar's vision redeems one
of H.D.'s own hysterical fantasies which could well stand behind the trou-
bling associations between women, repetition, return, and death that
preoccupy her in *Trilogy* as a whole. Writing to Bryher from London dur-
ing the Blitz, H.D. places her current depressions in the context of two
past pregnancies, the first of which ended in the birth of her stillborn
daughter shortly after the sinking of the *Lusitania*, and the second in a la-
bor complicated by pneumonia that, against all odds, resulted in the
(re-)birth of Perdita ("the lost one") and H.D.'s own recovery. Thus,
H.D. reports across a running series of letters:

> May 30, 1940: I imagine my chief trouble may be going to be, to "be sick"
> at the sound of the sirens. I wake and imagine them at night. I have no actual
> fear, am remarkably strong, but apparently having had the first infant while
> threat of air raids was on, I may go through sort of hysterical symptoms. . . .
> it is all "hysterical" in the sheer text book sense.

> June 2, 1940: The sort of emotional-paralysis comes in waves. One feels very
> alert and alive, then something snaps, everyone is the same. One almost
> "times" these seizures of mental weakness and despair, like birth-pains.

> June 3, 1940: I hope my last letter did not give you the impression I was down
> in the mouth, but I feel it is the world-travail in the Biblical sense, and not
> only does "war" connote the two bad confinements I had during the last one,

but other people have these same symptoms, a blank, black depression that comes down over ones head. I am sure we are all "travailing" together for this birth of a new era, and now I have faced it, I simply rush about between "pains" and tell a few (not many) of this, my theory.[139]

While H.D. here openly aligns her symptoms of "sick[ness]" and "blank, black depression" with "text book" hysteria, we might further read them as an inverted enactment of Klein's depressive position, in which the child works through its grief for the loss of the loved mother. Indeed, we might describe these symptoms as a mother's "mourning sickness" for the loss of her first daughter, but a mourning sickness that, as the pun suggests, successfully transforms loss into rebirth along Kleinian lines. Kaspar's vision delivers the promise of new life already contained in H.D.'s account of her "birth-pains," equating the birth of a new era with the return of a lost paradise, and reuniting the grieving mother and the lost child in the body of the visionary seeker. For if Kaspar's heart takes over the maternal agony of birthing, in the vision that ensues his eyes take on the joy of the newly born.

Refiguring her negative associations between the successive waves that sank the *Lusitania*, the pains that birthed her dead child, and the "waves" of bombing over London at the same time that she lifts depression into ecstasy, H.D. reconstitutes her own "two bad confinements" as Kaspar's free passage through the birth canal of time, with its echoing "sound as of many waters, / rivers flowing and fountains and sea-waves washing the sea-rocks" (*T* 155). Tears and flowers merge in the vision's rush of waters and "circle" of "petal[s]," as its spiraling birth canal opens not onto the world, but onto "infinity" (*T* 153). Like the snow geese who dive into the sea to learn that *"many waters can not quench love's fire"* (*T* 122), Kaspar sees "before he was lost, / out-of-time completely" "the drowned cities of pre-history" which harbor "the Hearth-stone / and the very fire on the Great-hearth" of the lost Atlantis (*T* 153, 156, 155). For it is not just H.D.'s history as a mother that Kaspar redeems here: with the mediation of Mary, Eve—expelled from the garden and condemned to bring forth children in sorrow—also passes into Kaspar, whose laboring heart brings forth the return of the sea garden Eve lost.[140]

Lost in memory's "pre-history," Kaspar suffers another loss as Mary Magdalene departs from the marketplace, leaving behind the text of her absence, the gift of a door. When we see him next, Kaspar is an old man tending his flock and "griev[ing] as always, / when a single twin of one of his many goats was lost" (*T* 162). In memory, it seems, Mary Magdalene herself has become the lost twin of god's lamb; for as with the two jars of myrrh that Kaspar gives to Christ and Mary in turn—about which "it was

always maintained / that one jar was better than the other"—Kaspar
himself

> grumbled and shook his head,

> no one can tell which is which,
> now your great-grandfather is dead.   (*T* 168)

Closer now to his own death, Kaspar plays back the past in thought;
it is through the returning action of his memory that we witness the Child
return in the final epiphany of the poem, though which Child it is "no one
can tell." For, as many others have noted, this Child is no infant in swad-
dling clothes, but a "bundle" of bitter myrrh with "a most beautiful fra-
grance, / as of all things flowering together" (*T* 172). As such, the Child's
return in the text stands as the site of yet another return of the text within
itself—a "flowering," perhaps, of the lines "irony is bitter truth / wrapped
up in a little joke" associated with Hatshepsut's cartouche in section 9 of
"The Walls Do Not Fall" (*T* 16). Anticipating Klein's account of the role
symbols play in the child's phantasies of reparation, Freud defines joking
itself a site of retrieval. In *Jokes and Their Relation to the Unconscious*, he
argues that jokes "retriev[e]" "primary possibilities of enjoyment" that
have been "lost to us" through "the repressive activity of civilization" (p.
101). Freud further credits the innocent "facade" of jokes—their "Janus-
like, two-way-facing character"—for their ability "to conceal not only
what they have to say but also the fact that they have something—forbid-
den—to say" (pp. 155, 106). Using the guise of nonsense or innocence to
smuggle forbidden pleasures into consciousness, jokes allow the energy
usually allotted to inhibiting these pleasures to "be discharged *in statu na-
scendi* by laughter" (p. 151).

Any number of "primary possibilities of enjoyment" gain represen-
tation *in statu nascendi* through H.D.'s retelling of the divine birth of Christ
as a comic moment of baby-swapping. At first take, the "bundle of
myrrh" the Virgin "held in her arms" is a simple transposition of Mary
Magdalene for the Christ Child. It is also the metaphor, however, for the
bridegroom, Christ's prototype in the Song of Solomon: "A bundle of
myrrh is my well-beloved unto me; he shall lie all night betwixt my
breasts."[141] As such, it suggests that the new messiah is the Virgin's lesbian
lover as well as her child. With this possibility, H.D.'s joke retrieves from
obscurity an older, "renounced" order of divinely eroticized mother-
daughter pairs—Demeter and Persephone, Artemis with her band of les-
bian daughters, and the alluring Venus-daughter of H.D.'s dream-life—
who were "lost to us" with the injunctions of Christian monotheism. In
doing so, the joke also reverses the conventional schema of war poetry,

which would portray all the losers as women, all the lost as men. Casting Kaspar as the maternalized onlooker on the edge of a scene of sorrow and rejoicing, H.D. reserves for the central action of her winter's tale the divine comedy of the lost daughter's return.

Reading back to H.D.'s earlier formulation that "gods always face two-ways" (*T* 5) through Freud's description of the "Janus-like two-way-facing character of jokes," we might describe the relationship between the male and female referents of this "bundle of myrrh" as one of deliberate confusion. On one level, H.D.'s final figure of the messiah, or "anointed one," simply substitutes the tabooed lesbian mother, daughter, and lover for the orthodox son of god. On another level, however, the figure exploits the unconscious logic of condensation to enact the syncretic doubling or "twinning" of mother and child, daughter and son, bridegroom and lesbian, and thus yields a conception of divinity in which any number of sexual and familial designations are invoked simultaneously.[142] At this level, the figure's very figurality, in refusing to fix its meaning, prevents any one meaning from subordinating or canceling out the rest; bundled from view like the unconscious, the myrrh with its invisibly escaping scent sets multiple and contradictory definitions of god's sexual identity flashing and fading upon one another.[143]

Yet while the oblique revelation of Mary Magdalene as the divine mother, daughter, and lover of the Virgin goes a long way in explaining the surprising force of the Child's return, it does not account for H.D.'s repeated designations of the Magdalene herself as a site of loss and return. Nor, for that matter, does it account for H.D.'s sudden departure from the Magdalene's story in sections 36 and 37 to present the image of snow falling on a desert to bring forth "over-night, a million-million tiny plants" (*T* 161). This miraculous snowfall, recalling the "mist / of snow: white, little flowers" of Osiris's reviving breath in "The Walls" (*T* 56), also bodies forth a vision of eternity articulated by H.D.'s Greek persona, Day-Star, in "The Sword Went Out to Sea." In this vision, a loose federation of living particles gather together to form god's perfect and immortal body:

> They told us that the snow-flakes were the same but different, so we were all the same but different. That is why we went up on the mountain, it was to celebrate our sameness and our difference. It was the mountain of Zeus, of God. . . .
>
> You melted, you went back to the mountain. The Cloud took you and the others and you were God. The snow fell, you danced on the mountain. We danced on the mountain in the snow and were God.[144]

Like the rain that lies "in the furrow" only to "return to the cloud," like Christ who "journeys back and forth / between the poles of heaven and earth forever" (*T* 115, 128), or like the Magdalene herself, the desert snowfall embodies a model of everlasting life based not on unity and permanence but on multiplicity, loss, and return. A mystical precipitation whose recurring cycles guarantee the land's fragrant flowering, this snowfall seems to revise Freud's memorably bizarre discussion of the history of human sexuality in *Civilization and Its Discontents*, where he accounts for the "organic repression" of just such an order of periodicity in favor of an order of permanence. Freud founds the origin of families on a moment "when the need for genital satisfaction no longer made its appearance like a guest who drops in suddenly, and, after his departure, is heard of no more for a long time, but instead took up its quarters as a permanent lodger. When this happened, the male acquired a motive for keeping the female, or, speaking more generally, his sexual objects, near him" (p. 99). In an accompanying footnote, he elaborates on his idea that human sexual desire was originally a nomadic "guest," and only gradually came to be "a permanent lodger":

> The organic periodicity of the sexual process has persisted, it is true, but its effect on psychical excitation has rather been reversed. This change seems most likely to be connected with the diminution of the olfactory stimuli by means of which the menstrual process produced an effect on the male psyche. Their role was taken over by visual excitations, which, in contrast to the intermittent olfactory stimuli, were able to maintain a permanent effect. The taboo on menstruation is derived from this "organic repression," as a defence against a phase of development that has been surmounted. . . . This process is repeated on another level when the gods of a superseded period of civilization turn into demons. (*Civilization* 99)

Like Freud himself, frustrated by Dora's ability to come and go as she pleases, or like Simon, who would deny the words of "his Guest" (*T* 142)—"but me ye have not always"—early man here appears as a mortal creature who would construct his sexuality around an illusion of permanence, and ban from it all reminders of life's discontinuities, losses, and sudden departures. With this primordial ban on the body's testimonies to its own mortality, humankind is also said to have lost its chief source of erotic pleasure, as the sexual odors of the mother's body, like the old gods demonized under a new order, gave up their former attractiveness and power to become "diminished" and displeasing. But the Magdalene reverses the original reversal of Freud's "organic repression"; through her joint action of redeeming the demonized mother goddesses "of a superseded period of civilization" and retrieving the lost possibility of the oozing womb's erotic odor, she offers the reader access to pleasures history has taught us to do without.[145] Further reversing the Freudian male's phobic apprehension of the female genitals as a castration wound signaling irreparable loss, "Mary-myrrh" insists on the womb's (self-)restorative properties; thus, she detects in the maternal precipitations of bitter weeping and fragrant bloodshed not only the "bitter truth" of our mortality, but also our repeated "flowering" in recurring cycles of birth and rebirth, loss and return. For within the logic of H.D.'s faith, it is not death that returns with the lifting of man's oldest "organic repression," but life. Resurrection follows the womb in offering

> remuneration,
>
> food, shelter, fragrance
> of myrrh and balm.   (*T* 123)

If, then, one of the referents for the bundle of myrrh is the menstruating womb, we might take the womb itself as a figure for the bundle of myrrh's own proliferation of meanings, its ability to body forth several distinct and yet finally indeterminate genderings of divinity; for like the bundle of myrrh, a baby in the womb is sexed but has no fixed gender. Such a reading recalls Kloepfer's identification of the bundle of myrrh as a symbol for "the semiotic subtext of language," associated with Kristeva's *chora* and the child's presymbolic and unbroken relation to the mother (p. 139). By linking the bundle of myrrh with its hidden referent, the pregnant womb, H.D. transfers to the body itself—specifically the divine body—that logic of "doubleness" and "shifting" which is more properly the domain of language.[146] Throughout *Trilogy*, she has relished her power to reveal "the meanings that words hide," but here she celebrates and deifies their opacity, their pregnant ability both to mean and to hide what they mean, to say one thing and mean another.

In this sense, H.D.'s bundle of myrrh recalls a remark made by Walter Schmideberg "that J.C. [Jesus Christ] was a bi-sexual image, as the genitals were always couvered." It also recalls H.D.'s own remark to Bryher that she is "that all-but extinct phenomina, the perfect bi-," after Freud tells her that "you had two things to hide, one that you were a girl, the other that you were a boy." H.D. goes on to explain to Bryher that her current writing block or "conflict consists partly that what I write commits me—to one sex, or the other, I no longer HIDE."[147] In contrast to her previous figures for the object of bisexual longing—the planet Venus moving between male and female aspects or the earthly geese endlessly migrating between the mutually exclusive poles of cold and heat[148]—the bisexual seeker here finds both sexes in a single, mercurial body, whose genitals, by remaining hidden, can remain in flux. Thus, if H.D. initially condemns words for forcing her "to commit—to one sex or the other," by the writing of "The Flowering" she has discovered a way to recruit words to convey the syncretic logic of noncommitment—of having it both ways. Hiding the body within the womb and the womb within the word, she comes to witness god's "bi-sexuality" in the Janus-face of irony, of jokes, and of figures, and to witness eternity in "the store-room" of language's returns (*T* 123).[149]

Stealing from "muddies body" her figures for everlasting life, H.D. translates (back) into religious terms Klein's faith that the act of grieving can itself restore both the lost mother and those the mother has lost. Moreover, with her claim that *"this has happened before somewhere else"* and *"will happen again"* (*T* 167), she once again rebukes John for his presumption in offering the final word on Christ's second coming; H.D. herself presumes to stage neither the first nor the last but merely the newest manifestation of an eternal being who forgoes the masculine order of permanence to immortalize the feminine order of periodicity. In this latter order, female sexuality, female aggression, and female mourning unite with the unconscious and eternity as common forces of repetition, reversal, and return. Through their own successful transfiguration from agents of madness and death to agents of ecstasy and rebirth, however, these combined forces insure not life's vanquishing but its resurgence, and with it the resurgence of sexual love, of appetite, and of vision.

But Only If I Say Alice

Writing to Bryher on October 26, 1934, as she prepares to return to analysis with Freud, H.D. presents a marvellous plan for evading censorship should she decide to discuss the Nazi presence in Vienna and the prospects of another war:

> Now IF I want to imply anything political in any letter, I will begin ALICE SAYS: or Alice thinks—and will follow [with] talk of gardens, innocent roots, bulbs, transplanting from mts. etc. etc. If I say, she wants to make a WILD rock garden or use the word WILD flowers and so on, it will mean things are WILD or difficult. . . . If I talk about magnificent roses or what-not, it will mean things are VERY good, but that I could write outright, anyhow. But only if I say ALICE.

Here, H.D. turns once again to our agent in wonderland to advertise her entry into that "political" underground which censorship inevitably creates. If, in this letter, H.D. suspects that the disclosure that "things are VERY good" is something "that I could write outright," by the early 1940's she composes her war *Trilogy* with full awareness that narratives of affirmation can be censored right along with narratives of protest. Devising another "language of flowers"[150] in order to explore the socially volatile topics of female aggression, lesbian incest and orgasm, maternalized loss and mourning, and bisexual godhead, she adopts the strategies of wit and joking to evade political censorship of a different kind. Nor should we necessarily count ourselves out in enumerating who is likely to reject the forms those strategies take. For the success of H.D.'s rhetorical figurations often depends on assumptions that many feminists would oppose.

H.D.'s equation between the manifestations of the unconscious and those of eternity directly counters ongoing feminist attempts to historicize the workings of the Freudian unconscious.[151] Where secular feminists engage this project out of the belief that the terms of resolution to historical conflicts must and will be found in history, H.D.'s visionary poetry comes out of a different set of givens entirely. She assumes that such resolutions cannot be found in history and must be located in eternity: as she writes in *Tribute to Freud*, "For the time being, I leave my conflicts, trusting they will be solved or resolved in the dream" (p. 153). Adalaide Morris notes that "feminists who have examined *Trilogy*'s visionary moments tend to mute the mysticism of H.D.'s practice by turning it back to the material realm and using it to reshape social definitions of gender."[152] In such acts of muting and mutation, we sidestep the resistance of H.D.'s poetry to its own recruitment as a model for a feminist politics conceived in secular terms. To take only one example: when H.D. redeems women's rhetorical association with loss by placing both women and loss in a wider context of spiritual return or resurrection, she takes the terms of such redemption literally. Substantiating this argument would require raising the dead, a turn of events that secular feminists cannot hope to supply.

But to argue that H.D.'s visionary resolutions, which held a literal, practical value for her, cannot be implemented in a political sphere defined in secular and historical terms is not to say that these resolutions have no rhetorical purchase in such a sphere. This, in fact, is part of the problem. When read from a secular rather than a religious or mystical perspective, H.D.'s visionary resolutions are not in fact eternal, but instead draw freely and often inconsistently on a wide spectrum of historically situated political stances. Furthermore, her bid to discover the truth of both the unconscious and eternity in what remains historically constant ("the Holy Ghost" or "the Dream" "explains symbols of the past / in to-day's imagery," and "merges the distant future / with most distant antiquity" [*T* 29]) often tips these political stances decidedly to the right.

In a move Julia Kristeva has made familiar to us, *Trilogy* repairs the association of maternity, inadequacy, and loss within the order of language and history by first positing an order outside history (if not, in the end, outside language) where all that is missing returns, and then aligning women (and maternalized men) with this same nonhistory or "prehistory." At the same time, however, this ostensibly ahistorical order of maternal plenitude derives its redemptive status from its ascribed power to represent badly needed resolutions to current historical conflicts or problems. In other words, the value of eternity in *Trilogy* depends on its power to be of value to a historical world.[153] In response both to cultural fantasies linking war with a threatening maternity and/or death-dealing femininity and to the ironic replication of those fantasies in Melitta Schmideberg's hostile attacks on her mother's work, H.D. stages redemptive dramas in which grievance flowers into ecstasy and maternalized mourners retrieve the lost Child. At the same time, H.D.'s insistence on the mysterious bisexuality of that Child, like Klein's lack of interest in the child's assumption of sexual difference, confounds the polarizing logic of a war rhetoric that would pit men against women in yet another fruitless narrative of injury and accusation. The otherworldiness of these resolutions constitutes part of their historical appeal; the end of hostilities between mother and daughter or between men and women occurs not through compromise, negotiation, or treaty, but through internal conversion, a change of heart:

> the way of inspiration
> is always open,
>
> and open to everyone   (*T* 29)

"In resurrection, there is simple affirmation" (*T* 116).

Fair enough. But what exactly are we saying yes to? Critics have long charged Melanie Klein with reviving Christian doctrine on original sin and atonement in her models of infant development.[154] While such a parallel makes H.D.'s syncretic project in *Trilogy* that much easier, readers who do not feel that the aggrieved acknowledgment of past wrongdoing is a necessary condition for healing have legitimate cause to doubt that H.D.'s reparations to the Lady or her story of Eve's "forgiven[ess]" fully forgoes the teachings of "the old-church" for "the unwritten volume of the new" (*T* 157, 63, 103). Of potentially greater concern to feminists is Klein's sense that infantile patterns of unconscious phantasy can explain all forms of human behavior, from the fear of long division to colonial conquest.[155] The shortcomings of such an approach are startlingly evident in Walter Schmideberg's reduction of the complex history behind the personification of Britain as a woman on the war posters to a local outcropping of the universal phantasm of the "bad mother." And yet in taking the scenes of bitter anger and loss within the mother-child dyad as her interpretive models for the global violence of World War II, H.D. too mythologizes history by maternalizing it, and—however much she works against it—incurs the same risk of holding mothers responsible for all of history's ills.

Female aggression constitutes one of Klein's most daring and welcome areas of theoretical and clinical inquiry, though here, too, it is important to point out that Klein's almost exclusive focus on the infant's psychic life restricts the agency of the mother to the realm of fantasy. This move has mixed implications for feminists. On the one hand, as Janice Doane and Devon Hodges argue, Klein's refusal to theorize maternal agency directly implies "a refusal to regulate motherhood" that is "wonderfully subversive" (pp. 2–3); indeed, in Klein's account, it is not the mother but the one making demands on her whose "grossly distorted" "concepts" of motherhood are in need of (internal) regulation (*DPA* 135). On the other hand, Klein's theories both replicate and anticipate a wider psychoanalytic indifference to the mother's own psychic and social experience.[156] To be sure, Klein eloquently describes the psychic field the mother shares with the child: a field marked out on one side by delusions of the mother's omnipotence and on the other by demands for her total submission to another's will; but while Klein has much to say about how the child learns to plot a course of legitimate and productive action within that field, she has little or nothing to say about how the mother does so. To manufacture such an account from the guidelines Klein provides us, we must be willing to make the daughter's experience a model for the mother's and hence to declare those experiences interchangeable.

This is the compromise H.D. seems to make in the latter two sequences of *Trilogy*, where the mother's and daughter's fantasies of reparation and erotic contact mirror one another. But while we might welcome H.D.'s own attempts to stake out a productive and life-affirming ground for female aggression and lesbian desire within the mother-daughter dyad, we must also note that the constraints of Klein's model confine H.D. to an account in which the mother's power, though ostensibly greater than the daughter's, takes on "cool beneficence" (*T* 96) only when it fulfills the daughter's desire; there is still no voicing of the possibility of a beneficent maternal power that operates in contradiction to, or independent of, the daughter's demands. Thus, while the Kleinian daughter's acts of reparation to the mother form her point of entry to a larger world of language and community, Kaspar's maternalized mourning for the lost Child in H.D.'s poem initially embraces "the whole scope and plan // of . . . civilization" only to end up circling in on "the Hearthstone / and the very fire on the Great-Hearth" of the lost Atlantis (*T* 154, 155).

In this sense, Kaspar's vision recapitulates a privatizing logic at work throughout H.D.'s poem and Kleinian theory. According to this logic, the problems women (including mothers) face when we try to make authoritative and socially productive use of our aggression in the public sphere find their proper origin and solution in the private sphere. (Klein thus locates the widespread cultural intolerance of mothers who exceed or defy their roles as nurturers in the hungry infant's early grievances against the absent breast, while H.D. locates the immortalizing ecstasy of reunited mother and daughter in the private time told by a "little clock" at her bedside.) To their credit, both Klein and H.D. articulate specifically for women the wider social question, raised more recently by Jacqueline Rose, "of how, or where, violence should be placed."[157] To take up this question at all is to resist the powerful cultural fantasy that women should be or can be free of all violence, that female aggression "goes against nature." But their answers to this question—in direct contradiction to the example of their own lives—seem to conform to the conservative idea that women's capacity for aggression is best understood and best served when confined to a purely sexual and/or familial field of expression and explanation.

This brings us to the difficult task of evaluating H.D.'s celebration of women's powers of reproduction and mothering in the concluding epiphany of *Trilogy*. Susan Schweik notes H.D.'s consistently metaphorical representations of—or substitutions for—"the infant male god" in her nativity scenes (in this poem and elsewhere), and argues that such scenes offer the reader "images of fertility without maternity, nativities opposed to pronatalism" (p. 269). But the poem's debts to Kleinian theory, as well as its coded or uncoded images of menstruation, labor, and the inhabited womb, make it impossible to maintain the already fragile distinctions between Schweik's juxtaposed terms. We might instead follow Schweik's own lead back to the work of Denise Riley, whose account of the conservative politics of pronatalism in postwar Britain motivates Schweik's distinctions in the first place.

Riley argues that despite its ostensible responsiveness to "the needs of mothers," pronatalism's "prominent rhetoric of the 'value of motherhood' blurred the needs of mothers with the essence of maternity in a way that was fatal for any real approach to the meeting of need." She then moves from this historical account to the much larger claim that "there can be no version of 'motherhood' *as such* which can be deployed to construct a radical politics. The apparent validation of 'motherhood' by a particular psychoanalytic tendency, Kleinian or other, cannot be hailed as a guarantee of that tendency's kinship to feminism, in the name of respecting female creativity, or female 'power'" (p. 196). As Riley ably demonstrates, celebrations of the abstract value of motherhood can easily backfire, particularly on women eager to increase their power outside the family. This is, in fact, exactly what happened to H.D. in her analysis with Schmideberg, where her persistent efforts to secure time away from her daughter in order to recover her health, travel, and write got translated into an unconscious maternal "guilt that I did not feed Puss." As we shall see in the next chapter, H.D. returns to the figures of the grieving mother and the Freudian hysteric in *Helen in Egypt*, as well as to a Kleinian model of mourning as a means of reparation. She also returns to the scene of a mother's regretted independence and to a definition of maternal power that feminists can only protest.

But as *Trilogy* so magnificently demonstrates, there is a politics to be had in pleasure as well as protest, and a poem that takes such a lively interest in opening up avenues of enjoyment for and between women is a hard thing to denounce. Perhaps then, for the time being, H.D.'s success in creating epiphanies that reward her readers with such a large "yield of pleasure . . . from words" should outweigh even our feminist objections as to how we come by it.

"I read the writing when he seized my throat"

Hysteria, Montage, and Revolution in *Helen in Egypt*

Whose Egypt?

My Egypt of Karnak and the Tomb of 1923 is not this Egypt, as I tried to explain in the snow, on that memorable trip.

—H.D., "Compassionate Friendship"

Between 1952 and 1955, H.D. wrote her montage poem, *Helen in Egypt*, which returns to Stesichorus's *Palinode* and Euripides' *Helen* to resurrect the argument that a phantom Helen presided over the Trojan War while her real counterpart was held captive by the gods in Egypt. Yet where Euripides' play is a marriage comedy in which Helen proves her innocence and wins back her husband, H.D.'s poem is a more somber meditation on the trauma of war, in which Helen and her three male lovers, Achilles, Paris, and Theseus, gather in Egypt and Leuke to brood over their parts in the killing at Troy. The poem has strong autobiographical underpinnings. Modeling Helen after herself and her mother, Helen Wolle Doolittle, H.D. takes Lord Hugh Dowding, Air Chief Marshal during the Battle of Britain and a fellow Spiritualist, as her model for Achilles; her friend Erich Heydt, a young psychiatrist at the Küsnacht sanatorium, as the model for Paris; and Sigmund Freud as the model for Theseus. H.D.'s trip to Egypt with her mother and Bryher in 1923, which included a visit to Tutankhamen's newly opened tomb, informs the poem's setting in ancient Egypt. And, as Susan Stanford Friedman has argued, H.D.'s experiences during the London Blitz inform both the poem's representation of war as

an inevitable effect of patriarchy and its attempts to recover a lost matriar-
chal and pacifist tradition in ancient myth.[1]

In reading *Helen in Egypt* as a retrospective condemnation of the vi-
olence of World War II, Friedman aligns the poem with *Trilogy* and pre-
sents as equivalent acts H.D.'s attempts in both poems to set up a re-
demptive relationship between ancient myth and her contemporary mo-
ment.[2] But events of the postwar period change the significance of
otherwise similar acts of mythic correlation. During this period, African
colonies, only recently called upon to aid Allied nations in the fight against
Nazi imperialism, now confronted their own imperial overlords with new
expectations and renewed resistance.[3] The increasingly hostile relations
between Egypt and imperial Britain played a prominent part in this wider
confrontation; as a result, H.D.'s two acts of returning to ancient Egyptian
myth for models of peace, first in 1942 and then in 1952, carried different
contemporary historical burdens. For instance, throughout 1942, as H.D.
was recording in "The Walls Do Not Fall" a dream in which the Egyptian
god Amen appeared to her in "the *House of Friends*," Allied forces fought
unsuccessfully to stem German advances on Egyptian soil until a crucial
victory finally fell to them in October.[4] By the time the war was over, the
British owed a huge war debt to their colonial charges. But most Egyp-
tians felt little loyalty to the British during this war,[5] and by September
1952, when H.D. began *Helen in Egypt*, they were taking violent means
to secure their full independence.

Indeed, 1952 began with the January 26 mob uprising and burning of
Cairo after Egyptians refused to cooperate with a British plan to occupy
the city. On July 23 of the same year, roughly a month before H.D. began
her poem, the Free Officers staged a coup in the Egyptian Army, wresting
control of the military away from British sympathizer King Farouk; three
days later they forced him off the throne. On June 18, 1953, the Revolu-
tion Command Council declared Egypt a republic and General Naguib
took office as President; shortly thereafter, in "late summer 1953," H.D.
began "Leuke," her poem's second part. The poem's last part, "Eidolon,"
begun in January 1954, "was put aside and continued again, September in
Lugano"; during this time, Egyptians forged an agreement with Britain
for the final evacuation of British troops. The last British troops left Egypt
the following June, a few months before H.D. assembled the prose cap-
tions for *Helen in Egypt* in the autumn of 1955.[6]

There are several indications that these events in Egypt caused Bryher
acute distress, which she repeatedly tried to convey to H.D. In letters to
H.D. during a 1954 trip to India and Pakistan, Bryher repeatedly com-
pares the "picturesque" people she sees there to "the Egypt of my child-
hood." In contrast, on her return through Cairo, she notes "how Egypt

has changed," and complains that "the Egyptians were as difficult as they could possibly be, unlike our dear Pakistanis."[7] In an entry for September 18, 1955, in "Compassionate Friendship," H.D. records Bryher's alarmed response upon learning of Erich Heydt's fanciful proposal to move to Egypt with her, extended in the winter of 1954–55:

> Bryher sent me a book about modern Egypt, *The Picnic at Sakkara* by P. H. Newby. I remember Erich's talks about Egypt, last winter—my Egypt of Karnak and the Tomb of 1923 is not this Egypt, as I tried to explain in the snow, on that memorable trip. "I had no illusions," I had said to Bryher, when I told her all this, at Lugano, last summer. But she seems to have sent me this story, all the same, to stress her own "but this [proposal] is dangerous."[8]

H.D. does not declare her own position on recent events in Egypt here. She does, however, indicate a familiarity with postwar Egyptian nationalism, which, if we take Bryher's letters into account, would date from at least the early months of 1954 (though it seems likely that she would have learned of such dramatic events as the 1952 burning of Cairo as they were happening). And she clearly suggests her nostalgic preference for the ancient dynastic Egypt, which she associated with prewar Egypt and Carter's discoveries outside Karnak.

In Friedman's analysis, H.D.'s conflation of the Trojan War and World War II allows her to move beyond an account of specific historical conflicts to a more general and radical account of the contrasting ethos of matriarchal and patriarchal traditions.[9] But the nostalgic evocation in *Helen in Egypt*, of an Egypt laid bare by British excavators during the final years of the Egyptian Revolution, reasserts the poem's historical embeddedness in the contemporary politics of colonial dismantlement, and complicates the terms both of its pacifism and of its critique of patriarchy. Given this embeddedness, we need to ask what declared political purposes, feminist or otherwise, are served by the poem's use of an ancient Egyptian setting and mythology; and what relationship obtains between the poem's evocation of ancient Egypt and the rapid changes in modern Egypt that stand behind it.

Deferring a consideration of the second question until the end of my argument, I approach the first by proposing that H.D. grounds her poem's project of social reconstruction in a return to the model of familial peace offered by the ancient Egyptian myth of Isis. Here I build on Rachel Blau DuPlessis's analysis of Helen's efforts to construct a "sufficient family" that nurtures women's abilities, but I want to locate Freud's model of the destructive oedipal family, rather than DuPlessis's paradigm of "romantic thralldom," as the target of Helen's reforms.[10] I argue that Helen's political project to reconstruct society coincides with a literary project to "reconstruct the legend" of Troy, in which she attempts to convert the Greek oedipal "legend of murder and lust" back into an earlier, and pre-oedipal, Egyptian legend of familial reparation and reunification (*HE* 11, 88). Here my argument parallels the argument of Deborah Kelly Kloepfer, who proposes that Helen's project is "to fundamentally reformulate the oedipal story" through "a return to the preoedipal." Using a Kristevan approach, Kloepfer contends that such a return forces "the son to confront the 'too intense primary experience' ([*HE*] 162) of the mother," and opens up "a way of access to the mother which allows a space for the daughter as well as the son and for an increase in language jarred free from the symbolic" (pp. 165, 171, 169). Yet despite its intermediate points of contact with Kloepfer's reading of the poem, my argument proceeds from different critical premises and reaches opposing conclusions.

Working with psychoanalytic and psycholinguistic concepts available to H.D., but outside the later theories of Lacan and Kristeva, I come to the poem with an interest not in the semiotic's eruptions within the symbolic register of language, but rather in Helen's own deep investment in visual and verbal signification. I read Helen herself as a reader, and a reviser, of inherited texts. Recovering forgotten traces of Egyptian writing within later Greek drama, she "transpose[s] or translate[s]" the myth of Oedipus back into the earlier myth of Isis (*HE* 1). This peculiarly literary revision of the Western family romance, as Freud conceived it, depends on Helen's visionary act of "reading" a lily whose hallucinatory image organizes her promotion of a series of marginal, faintly Egyptian details in Euripides' Helen plays and in Homer's *Iliad* to central, and revelatory, positions within H.D.'s own montage narrative. Assigning unanticipated value to fragments of an earlier literary tradition that has been "forgotten," "lost or left over" (*HE* 282, 281) in celebrated Greek texts at the supposed origin of the Western literary canon, *Helen in Egypt* accomplishes the cultural "reinstate[ment]" (*HE* 1) of its heroine, the wanton and wandering woman, through its structural reinstatement of the mislaid linguistic detail.[11]

In forging the terms of Helen's visionary acts of reading and their power to reconstruct Western society, H.D. draws heavily on two earlier bodies of work that feminize the art of vision: Freud's accounts of hysteria and Eisenstein's accounts of "intellectual cinema."[12] Freud identifies the typically female hysteric's practice of registering repressed memories on the body's surface and in hallucinations, her inability to compose coherent life histories, and her appropriation of other peoples' bodily traits and symptoms as debilitating manifestations of a neurotic disorder. In H.D.'s hands, however, these same symptoms of hysteria function as effective strategies of visionary reform.[13] As such, they align Helen with Eisenstein's "creating spectator," whose acts of organizing and interpreting disjunctive filmic images simultaneously prompt his or her own political awakening and commitment to social change. Indeed, Helen is able to draw on, and play off, the legacies of both Freud's hysteric and Eisenstein's creating spectator because of striking parallels as well as significant distinctions between the two figures.

Freud posits that the hysteric's somatic and/or hallucinatory symptoms literalize verbal figures associated with repressed memories of trauma; in turn, the analyst must recover the verbal symptoms behind these figures in order to effect a cure. Similarly, Eisenstein argues that the literalized images of filmic metaphors should "embody" the overarching themes of a montage film; in turn, the creating spectator uses these images to make sense of the film. Yet where Freud pathologizes "embodied thinking," Eisenstein endows it with revolutionary power.[14] Likewise, where Freud pathologizes hysterical fantasy, which scrambles and distorts the contents of the actual past, Eisenstein celebrates something he calls the creating spectator's "womb of fantasy" as the crucible of social change. Behind Freud's distrust of fantasy and Eisenstein's regard for it lie two parallel but opposed views of reordering. Where Freud condemns hysterical fantasy's multiple ways of rearranging the "proper order" of past events, Eisenstein rejoices in the power of montage to create new visions of society through its reordering of profilmic events. Finally, Freud posits that the unconscious attempts to evade censorship by displacing volatile emotions onto innocuous details only distantly related to the ideas and events that first roused these strong reactions. Similarly, Eisenstein displaces the spectator's attention onto details that might otherwise pass unobserved through his use of the close-up shot. But where Freud regards such relocations of attention and affect as antagonistic to the ends of truth and mental health, Eisenstein relishes the ease with which cinema can alter the value and import of events by altering their visual scale.

Each of these strategies—the visual literalization of verbal figures, the use of fantasy to reshape the past, the reordering of previous narrative sequences, and the revaluing of narrative import through the promotion of peripheral details—finds a place in Helen's visionary project to reform the family. Allowing Helen and her male lovers to recover the culturally suppressed "memory forgotten" (*HE* 304) of an earlier, redemptive past in Egypt within their personal memories of a traumatic Greek past, these strategies also provide a way to grant that ancient memory material expression in the present. Yet while H.D.'s pairing of Freud with Eisenstein allows her to recuperate the female visionary (whom Freud would pathologize) as a powerful agent of social change, it is important to point out that her heroine's project to reconstruct the family, however radical, is not necessarily revolutionary. Indeed, the poem's plot eventually turns on a surprisingly conservative application of Melanie Klein's theories of reparation and the good and bad mother, one that diverts blame from the oedipally conflicted fathers and sons who occupy the battlefield at Troy to the very mothers and daughters who are most insistently absent from it. Furthermore, Helen's very project to render the peace-loving family of ancient Egypt present again constitutes the revolutionary present of modern Egypt as a new "memory forgotten" that must be buried from view. Like any memory forgotten, however, this contemporary scene has the power to return at the surface of a narrative that would enforce its suppression.

Phantasmagorias of Troy

He was part of my dream, of course—but then I was part of his dream, too! *Was* it the Red King, Kitty?

   —Lewis Carroll, *Through the Looking-Glass*

and Troy-gates broken
in memory of the Body,

wounded, stricken
   —H.D., "Pallinode"

As critics before me have noted, *Helen in Egypt* is a long and difficult poem: even a matter as simple as establishing the plot is rendered complex by the confusion H.D. creates around the ordinarily stable narrative elements of character, setting, and event. Susan Stanford Friedman remarks that "external action is fragmentary, emerging suddenly and briefly out of extended periods of reflection when Helen is alone with her thoughts," and again: "narrative based on identifiable action is scanty and often like a dream sequence in its shifting time and locale."[15] Characters float ambiguously between the categories of living and dead, "phantom and reality" (*HE* 3). In their tenuous and ambiguous relationship to material bodies, their tendency to manifest as images and/or voices, the poem's cast evokes the cinema, and indeed, we might just as aptly ascribe to *Helen in Egypt* Kenneth Macpherson's 1930 description of *Borderline* as a journey "into the labyrinth of the human mind, with its queer impulses and tricks, its unreliability, its stresses and obsessions, its half-formed deductions, its glibness, its occasional amnesia, its fantasy, suppressions and desires."[16] Characters in H.D.'s poem enter each other's dreams and fantasies, read each other's thoughts, forget key moments in their pasts, and yet can also "remember" events that took place in their absence or have yet to take place (*HE* 225, 218, 70).

Moreover, Jeanne Larsen notes that Helen displays "shifting, multiple identities," frequently merging with other characters (p. 93). Helen repeatedly signifies her identification with others through her changing image, but, as Thomas Whitaker suggests, the voice also serves as an important juncture for the fusion and splitting of identity.[17] Friedman points out that H.D. divides her own voice in the poem between the poetic sections and "the prose insets . . . written after the lyrics were completed," which "do not provide authoritative readings of the lyrics, but rather, in their rhetoric of indeterminacy, emphasize the Penelopean endlessness of (re)interpretation and inscription."[18] Similarly, Helen twice hears a "voice within" herself—first "an heroic," Spartan Helen and then "a lyric" Helen—that speaks for otherwise silenced parts of herself (*HE* 175, 176, 178). And Clytaemnestra's voice is so subversive that it can be admitted into the poem only indirectly, through the speech of Paris (*HE* 219). If the poem's multiple voices at least share an insistence on the life of human speech, elsewhere H.D. aligns Helen with the sacred writing of the gods and the dead; as Elizabeth A. Hirsh points out, she occupies a "status as nothing more nor less than a textual effect. . . . 'She herself is the writing,' we are told and told again, her identity palimpsestically inscribed by several hands in several variant narratives" (p. 6).

The course of time turns back in its bed, and spaces tumble over one another, allowing Helen's lover to become her son, and Helen herself to travel to the island of Leuke without leaving Egypt (*HE* 209). Rachel Blau DuPlessis comments on "the mingling of backward-moving memory and forward-moving quest in the structure of the poem."[19] Just as the last sequence of *Trilogy* repeatedly returns to rehearse and open out the encounter between Mary Magdalene and Kaspar in the marketplace, *Helen in Egypt* constantly returns to a handful of crucial encounters: between Helen and Achilles on an Egyptian beach, and across the battlefield at Troy, and between Helen and Paris at Troy's fall. With each return, new information emerges that in turn supports new hypotheses about these encounters' import. Reinforcing and elaborating this yearning for return at the level of the plot, the poem's many recurring phrases, images, and questions load the narrative with familiar sounds, giving it a motionless quality that works against a sense of localized motivation, causality, and progress.

All of these factors make the task of summarizing the poem's contents as thankless as it is necessary: more so than usual, any synopsis of this poem must also be an interpretation and a compromise. Furthermore, because I am proposing that part of H.D.'s project here is to reconceive the relationship between central action and peripheral detail in her source texts, the very act of deciding which narrative elements in her poem are crucial and which can be ignored is rendered suspect by the poem's own organizational premises. In the following synopsis of the poem's contents, I have tried to give an exact account of the order in which events transpire, since ordering will be one of my critical preoccupations. But the account I give is only a crude working model of the plot, to be filled in with finer detail later in the argument.

In "Pallinode," Helen reviews her first night with Achilles in Egypt, hears out his memories of Troy, and fantasizes about the day of Iphigenia's sacrifice at Aulis. Her running meditations introduce questions about the relationship between love and death, illusion and desire, and male heroism and female sacrifice, which will become increasingly pronounced in the course of the poem. As the poem begins, the solitary Helen addresses the Greek host who died at Troy from within the temple of her Egyptian father, "Amen-Zeus" (*HE* 34). She proposes that "Love's arrow" (*HE* 9) killed their leader, Achilles, at Troy, and recounts her first meeting with him on a "desolate coast" in Egypt (*HE* 16). In that meeting, when Helen pronounced the name of Achilles' mother, he tried to strangle her. But desire overcame him and they made love under his cloak. In the temple, Helen wonders why Achilles attacked her, and remembers the vision of a lotus that came to her in Achilles' stranglehold.[20] Achilles joins her in the temple and introduces the recurring question: "Helena, which was the dream, / which was the veil of Cytheraea?" (*HE* 36). Helen associates the veil with the ghosts of the war dead and with the Horus child, while she equates the dream with their fiery "kiss in the night" (*HE* 37). She ponders the relationship between love and death, and questions Achilles about her own identity. He recalls the Greeks' bitter hatred of Helen at Troy, and a fatal epiphany in which his eyes met hers across the battlefield as the arrow pierced his heel. He then recalls his journey in the death-ship of Osiris, and marvels over the power of "Another," feminine force to upset the patrilinear and hierarchical social structure of the Greek "Command" (*HE* 61).

Helen sees her relationships with Achilles and Clytaemnestra reflected in temple pictures of Isis with her wicked brother Typhon and her loyal sister Nephthys (*HE* 66, 68). She equates her own child, Hermione, with her niece Iphigenia and recalls how the girl, lured to Aulis to marry Achilles, was sacrificed to Artemis instead. She sees her sister and niece together at the altar, and relates Clytaemnestra's later violence to her anger and grief at the loss of her daughter. She first blames and then excuses Achilles from responsibility for this death. Vowing to "find a place" for Egyptian "enchantment" in Greece (*HE* 90), she awaits the return of Achilles and Orestes by the sacred lotus pool. At this juncture, the eidolon of Thetis instructs Helen to leave her violent sister to another fate, announces Helen's own deification along with her brothers, the Dioscuri, and calls her "home" to the white island of Leuke (*HE* 108).

In "Leuke," Helen shifts ground, putting distance between herself and Achilles as she explores the past with her other lovers, Paris and Theseus. While this book introduces the story of Oedipus as a central concern, it also repeatedly returns to the question of Achilles' deadly relations with women. Newly arrived on the island of Leuke, Helen recalls the "suppressed memory" of Paris, the Trojan prince banished at birth (*HE* 109). She suggests that Paris shot the arrow that killed Achilles and rejoices in this second escape with him from the Greeks. Paris speaks, recounting how his lover Oenone tried to make him give up the memory of Helen. He remembers Helen at the fall of Troy trying to escape down the burning Tower stairs, and argues that she died there with him. Paris then recalls Aphrodite's promise to give him the white island if he will forget Helen, and asks Helen why she persists in "remember[ing] Achilles" (*HE* 142). Finally, he asserts that the Greek hero never loved her, and denounces her for trying to imitate Aphrodite.

Fleeing Paris's anger, Helen takes refuge with Theseus. Her arrival prompts Theseus's memory of his own efforts, long ago, to abduct her as his child bride. He equates her with Athena, Demeter, and Persephone, and notes that her feet are wounded. Helen declares that she now thinks of Paris more as a son than as a lover, but backs away from aligning herself with Hecuba, who "exposed him on Ida, // like Oedipus, to die" (*HE* 156). Theseus views Achilles and Paris as hostile rivals. After he recalls his own mythic past, he points to the many women sacrificed to Achilles. Within Helen, a voice emerges that loves violence. Helen then tries to "reconcile" "the slayer" with "the slain" (*HE* 178, 184) by equating Paris, who killed Achilles, with Achilles' son, conceived under his cloak on the Egyptian beach. She also equates Achilles and Theseus, but still balks at playing the mother in this new familial configuration, declaring "I am only a daughter" (*HE* 195). Aligning Thetis with Artemis, she aligns herself and Achilles with Persephone and Dis, and remembers his stranglehold on the beach as a moment of contact with the Absolute. But she resists the fatal purity of this moment and, clinging to life, tries to bring time and eternity together. As the sequence ends, she prays that Achilles might "find the way" (*HE* 207).

In "Eidolon," Helen breaks through her own resistance to memory and recovers the repressed history of the mother's importance to the child. At the same time, her thoughts on love and death gain in intensity, prompting her penultimate choice between rival lovers and a final, cryptic moment of revelation. At the book's opening, the eidolon of Achilles greets Helen, who rests on a bier in an Egyptian temple. Paris protests this reunion, and threatens Helen with the memory of his own mother's banishment of him in infancy. He too rehearses the names of women sacrificed to Achilles and urges Helen to "*remember Iphigenia*" (*HE* 219). Helen awakes, as if from a dream, rejecting the words of Paris and denying that she was ever in Troy. She again wonders if her encounter with Achilles was fatal, and suddenly remembers leaving her daughter to set out for Troy with Paris. Next she recalls her narrow escape down the Tower stairs just after she learns of Achilles' death and just as Paris, too, is shot with a fatal arrow. Helen returns to Achilles' question, equating the veil and the dream of Cytheraea and relating both to the sail of Achilles' warship. She decides that his attack on the desolate beach was prompted by a memory of the Thetis figurehead on his ship's prow at Aulis, and recalls her own fear that he would sacrifice her to his mother. She then recalls Achilles' return to the battle at Troy, his journey in the death-ship of Osiris, and the time his mother bathed him in the river Styx. She realizes that Achilles must have seen the "slant" of his mother's eyes in her own face as he stared at her on the desolate beach (*HE* 253, 254).

Helen imagines Achilles "numb with a memory" of Thetis, and realizes how bitterly he felt his mother's absence as a child (*HE* 256). She relates this to the memory of her own desolation when no one was willing to ferry her to the land of the dead. She recalls Achilles' fear at hearing her pronounce his mother's "secret . . . name" as they stood amid a circle of spirits on the beach (*HE* 279). She remembers how he adored a wooden eidolon of his mother as a child, and how he forgot both the image and the goddess when he entered the war. Now, Helen is able to identify Euphorion, her child by Achilles, as two children in one, uniting the childhood selves of both its legendary parents. She is also prepared to understand her epiphanic encounter with Achilles as a fused moment of love and death. She notes that Thetis mourned the Trojan as well as the Greek dead, but concludes her own meditations with a rejection of Paris and a partisan commitment to the Greeks. The poem ends with an unidentified eidolon chiding Paris for his ignorance of the sea.

This synopsis should make clear that the bulk of *Helen in Egypt*'s narrative explores the questions, ambiguities, and conflicts that arise between the various accounts of the past offered by Helen and her three lovers. The characters' conscious proceedings, however, are punctuated at four points by repressed memories that abruptly return. This chain of returning memories eventually links the initial moment of a son's inscrutable anger at the sound of his mother's name to the final moment of revelation that he loves her. The first repressed memory returns on the desolate beach early in "Pallinode," when Helen speaks the name of Achilles' mother, "Isis . . . or Thetis" (*HE* 14). As we have seen, this naming prompts Achilles' sudden memory of his ship's Thetis figurehead and his subsequent attack on Helen, although Helen herself does not learn the contents of this memory until well into "Eidolon" (*HE* 239–40). She initially registers its effects only indirectly through her vision of an Egyptian lotus (*HE* 25). This vision turns out to function both as a distorted version of Achilles' memory and as a divine clue to its actual contents. A second "suppressed memory and unspoken name—Paris" returns to Helen at the opening of "Leuke," while the third repressed memory—of abandoning her young daughter to follow Paris to Troy—returns to Helen early in "Eidolon" (*HE* 109, 228). This third memory leads directly to Helen's recovery of Achilles' memory of the Thetis figurehead at Aulis and the concomitant knowledge of his love for his mother.

By the end of the poem, this sequence of repressed memories supplies the components of a hidden logic of recovery, which invokes both Freud's therapeutic program for hysteria and Eisenstein's revolutionary program for film montage, and revises these programs along Kleinian lines. In seeking to understand the logic of this sequence and the redemptive power attributed to it, I will begin with a close analysis of Helen's vision of the lotus. Here, I focus on the vision's puzzling status as an act of "reading" that converts violence into sexual love. I relate Helen's traumatically induced vision of the Egyptian womb-flower to the hysteric's production of symptoms and the creating spectator's acts of interpretation within a "womb of fantasy," and go on to analyze how this single hallucinatory image foreshadows and directs the poem's entire project of familial reconstruction. I then turn to demonstrate the logic behind Helen's attempts to realize the promise of her "transcendental" vision "in material terms" (*HE* 11)—a logic encoded in the series of repressed memories identified above, and one that draws on and transforms both the hysteric's and the montage filmmaker's strategies of reordering. Before we set out on this extended path of interpretation, however, it will be useful to establish with a few broad strokes the parallels between H.D.'s cast of characters in *Helen in Egypt* and Freud's hysterics. In turn, the hysteric, who is said to see remembered scenes "before her, in a plastic form and in their natural colours . . . with all the vividness of reality" (*Studies on Hysteria* 53), will find a ready counterpart in Eisenstein's creating spectator, transfixed and transformed by the art of contemplating the silver screen.

As I noted in my discussion of Mary Magdalene and Kaspar, Breuer and Freud propose in their joint *Studies on Hysteria* that "hysterics suffer mainly from reminiscences" (p. 7). Repressing memories that cause mental conflict and pain, the hysteric experiences partial amnesia and produces bodily symptoms, or "stigmata," which serve as "mnemic symbols" of the memories barred from consciousness. These bodily symptoms, such as tics, spasms, impaired mobility and/or speech, and various kinds of sensory hallucination, *become* the reminiscences from which the hysteric suffers. Relief comes only to those who regain conscious access to their forgotten memories through verbalization, and thus dissolve the symptoms marking their repression.

While in 1895 the population considered most susceptible to hysteria was one of housewives and adolescent girls, Freud notes in 1920 that "the terrible war which has just ended gave rise to a great number of illnesses" among the predominantly male veterans. These illnesses were classified as war neuroses, whose "symptomatic picture . . . approaches that of hysteria in the wealth of its similar motor symptoms" (*Beyond the Pleasure Principle* 12). In the meantime, however, Freud sharply revises the clinical picture of hysteria. First he advances his seduction theory, which traces hysterical suffering back to early scenes of sexual assault, often in the form of father-daughter incest; then he retracts it in favor of a theory of a universal fantasy life, which redefines the scenes of sexual assault that hysterics themselves take to be memories as "phantasies erected on the basis of memories" (*Interpretation of Dreams* 491), and the symptoms of hysteria as the somatic manifestations of these same unconscious fantasies.

This latter move entails its own complications, as Freud was well aware. He writes in 1911 of "the difficulty of distinguishing unconscious phantasies from memories which have become unconscious," when the unconscious itself "equate[s] reality of thought with external actuality, and wishes with their fulfilment—with the event" ("Formulations" 225).[21] In *Helen in Egypt*, characters have a similar difficulty distinguishing between "phantom and reality" (*HE* 3). Unable to prevent each other's hidden wishes from distorting their joint account of the past, they are equally unable to decide whether they possess autonomous bodies in the Egyptian afterlife or merely exist as hallucinated effects of one another's fantasies. Where Freud views such indeterminacy as an obstacle to disinterested and truthful historiography, however, H.D. celebrates it as the condition of her poem's extraordinarily fluid and assertedly redemptive transactions between wish and event, between bodies, memories, and desire.

Cast as a woman badly shaken by the long battle at Troy and the final victory—"Troy-gates broken / in memory of the Body" (*HE* 7)—Helen has lost the desire to remember that continues to drive the limping war veteran, Achilles; thinking back to her encounter with him on the beach, she cries out:

> I would rather forget,
> I would rather forget,
>
> but a phantom pursues him;
> shall a phantom threaten my peace?
> what does it matter,
>
> who won, who lost?
> must the Battle be fought and fought
> in his memory?   (*HE* 35)

While the battle at Troy still raging in Achilles' memory absorbs his conscious attentions, a second battle or conflict besets the warrior at another, unconscious level. His limping gait, a common hysterical complaint that also (not by chance) besets Oedipus of the "swollen foot," will eventually prove to be a somatic symptom encoding the memory of an earlier conflict. Only when this second conflict is discovered and addressed can Helen hope to locate and deactivate the forces of war at Troy. Helen's own hysterical appropriation of Achilles' wounded heel, when she enters the cabin of the Freud figure Theseus with "wounded" "feet" (*HE* 151, 153), turns out to be both a defense against the discovery of this earlier conflict and a necessary stage en route to that same discovery.[22]

Indeed, Helen's very propensity for hysterical identification becomes a crucial condition for her peculiar ability to take over the identities of other characters, as well as her eventual success in reconstructing the legend of the Greek oedipal family romance. As Freud explains, hysterics "catch" each others' symptoms in order to express a shared investment in the events and/or fantasies that lie behind them. Thus, hysterical identification "enables patients to express in their symptoms not only their own experiences but those of a large number of other people; it enables them, as it were, to suffer on behalf of a whole crowd of people and to act all the parts in a play single-handed" (*Interpretation of Dreams* 149). In the logic of H.D.'s poem, Helen's hysterical identification with Achilles underwrites her ability to recover the repressed childhood memories of Thetis that return to Achilles on their first night in Egypt, even though Achilles himself never verbalizes their content. Furthermore, through a series of somatically registered identifications with other women, Helen makes use of the hysteric's ability to "act all the parts in a play single-handed" in order to transfer entire life histories from one set of characters to another via their joint association with herself: identified with Jocasta and Hecuba as well as Thetis and Isis, she stands as the bridge between the oedipal family and the divine Egyptian family, upon whose example her reconstruction of Achilles' personal past and her wider project of social reconstruction will depend.

If Helen's appropriation of Achilles' wounded heel suggests her desire to identify with him, his obsessive memories of past conflict awaken more ambivalent reactions. H.D. sets Helen's wish for the peace of oblivion against an earlier vow to remember, made during the scene of physical and sexual struggle with Achilles "that first night / on the desolate beach" (*HE* 38). On that occasion, Helen reversed a plea for forgetfulness made to her father Zeus-Amen, when Achilles' "attack" turned to lovemaking, praying anew to his sea-mother, Thetis: "*let me remember, let me remember, / forever, this Star in the night*" (*HE* 18, 17). While her vow to remember this night fuels Helen's larger commitment to search her Greek past for the causes of war at Troy, her opposing wish for oblivion will continue to assert itself at crucial moments in her investigations.

Helen's project to "reconstruct the Greek past" (*HE* 112) is further complicated by a number of uncertainties as to whose past, exactly, is being reconstructed by whom and for whose benefit, and whether this reconstruction is an act of responsible historiography or mere wishful thinking. At one point, H.D. inscribes the entire Greek past at Troy within the fantasy of god the father, and at another reinscribes it within the fantasy of his daughter. On the verge of Achilles' attack, Helen cries out in her defense:

> "Zeus be my witness . . .
> it was he, Amen dreamed of all this
> phantasmagoria of Troy,
>
> it was a dream and a phantasy."   (*HE* 17)

At the other end of the poem, H.D. suggests that the heroes of Troy inhabit Helen's fantasy instead ("Yes, Achilles spoke, Paris spoke. Greece and Troy challenged and contradicted each other in her fantasy" [*HE* 225]), but she then retracts this suggestion to reassert the autonomy of Helen's fellow participants in their joint project of recollection.[23] Sharply raising the stakes of this double inscription, H.D. invokes the central scene of the seduction theory in the middle of "Leuke."

When Helen flees a hostile interview with Paris to the snowy refuge of her aging "god-father" (*HE* 156), the Freud figure Theseus, he greets her with the memory of his failed attempts to take her as his child bride. Although Theseus notes that Helen might yet "fear my touch," he persists in pressing his claim, proposing, discreetly enough:

> you must have loved me a little,
> frail maiden that you still were,
> when your brothers found you.   (*HE* 149, 148)[24]

Yet if these remarks seem to identify Helen as a survivor of incestuous sexual assault, Theseus elsewhere doubts the accuracy of his own memories, going so far as to declare his famous battle with the Minotaur

> an idle fancy,
> a dream, a Centaur,
> hallucination of infancy. (*HE* 168)

In light of Helen's own silence on the subject, H.D. leaves open the possibility that the seduction attempt may be merely another idle fancy of an overly fond analyst, and thus foregrounds the distorting effects of the analyst's own counter-transference, which pass unnoticed in Freud's first accounts of hysteria. Yet when placed within the poem's wider frameworks of fantasy, Theseus's memories might record not his own wishes but the contradictory wishes of either Zeus-Amen or Helen that the father seduce the daughter and/or that the father of psychoanalysis be discredited for his wish to seduce the daughter.

H.D.'s attribution of the narrative of *Helen in Egypt* to both Helen's and her father's fantasies raises the possibility of the father's and daughter's complicity as well as of their conflict, a possibility reinforced by the fact that Helen conducts her inquiries into the past on the grounds of her father's temple. In the end, H.D. declares neither for nor against Freud's desire to trace hysteria back to the daughter's fantasies rather than the father's acts of seduction. Instead, she multiplies Freud's own designated alternatives to place the vertiginous question of female complicity and/or resistance with respect to paternal desire and, more loosely, patriarchal designations at the literal and figurative center of *Helen in Egypt*.

As we have seen, for Freud the issue that eventually subsumes the question of the daughter's relationship to paternal desire is the question of whether it is even possible to distinguish memories of the past from fantasies built upon it. It is this latter question that runs right through Helen's project to "reconstruct the Greek past," with its continual equivocation between reconstruction conceived as an act of recovering or restoring the past and as an act of revising and rehabilitating that past. This equivocation receives its first, pivotal expression in Helen's visionary "reading" of the lily, in which the unorthodox nature of Helen's reading blurs the very distinction between textual restoration and textual revision. To follow out the implications of this reading, both as a complex response to Freud's hysteric and Eisenstein's creating spectator and as the foundation of Helen's project to reform the oedipal family romance, it is necessary to go back and offer a more detailed account of the events on the desolate beach.

Out of the Womb of Fantasy

But it was I . . . who was seeing the pictures, who was reading the writing or who was granted the inner vision.

—H.D., *Tribute to Freud*

Creative not only for the author, but creative also for me, the creating spectator.

—Sergei Eisenstein, "Montage in 1938"

When she intuitively identifies the form of "a night-bird" flying overhead—"a carrion creature"—as the hieroglyph of "Isis, . . . or Thetis," Helen rouses Achilles' anger. She quickly tries to avert blame by blackening her face and arms with ash "like the prophetic *femme noire* of antiquity" (*HE* 13–16),[25] but her strategy backfires. Cursing her as "Hecate," "a witch," "envious Isis, / . . . a vulture, a hieroglyph," Achilles accuses Helen of causing the deaths of his Greek warriors at Troy:

> you stole the chosen, the flower
> of all-time, of all-history,
> my children, my legions;
>
> for you were the ships burnt.   (*HE* 16–17)

During the struggle and lovemaking that ensue, Helen has her "vision," whose terms of presentation recall H.D.'s own hallucinatory visions at Corfu in 1920.

In a preliminary headnote, H.D. distinguishes the Greek warships Helen "visualizes" from the "death-ship of Osiris," and insists that "her vision is wholly Greek" (*HE* 24). The story of Osiris's death-ship, however, clearly underwrites Helen's vision. In ancient Egyptian myth, the sun-god, Rā, travels each night by ship through the underworld as a dead Osiris, only to emerge at dawn from a lotus flower as the newborn Horus.[26] Horus, in turn, is the hawk-headed god whom his mother, Isis, conceives after Osiris's death and raises to avenge his father's murder. Horus fights Typhon, his father's brother and murderer, but Isis intervenes to reconcile them. In the nightly rehearsal of Osiris's death and resurrection, Horus and Typhon guard over the Osiris-Rā's journey, protecting him from further harm. In the underworld, Horus assumes Isis's role of reconstituting and reviving his father's dismembered body. He also takes the image of the lotus, the mythic womb-flower of his mother's body from which he is reborn each day, as his hieroglyph. Ancient Egyptians endowed the lotus hieroglyph with the god's own powers of resurrection.[27]

Helen's vision directly recalls this myth cycle when, amid a swirl of wing-feathers, ship sails, and flower petals, she sees "the thousand sails" of the Greek war fleet converge as "the thousand-petalled lily" sacred to Horus (*HE* 25, 29).[28] At the same time, this composite image of Greek sails and lily petals literalizes Achilles' figure of the Greek host as "the flower / of all-time":

> no, I was not instructed, but I "read" the script,
> I read the writing when he seized my throat,
>
> this was his anger,
> they were mine, not his,
> the unnumbered host;
>
> mine, all the ships,
> mine, all the thousand petals of the rose,
> mine, all the lily petals.   (*HE* 25)

As she stands in the Amen-temple, Helen relates this vision to the actual lotus hieroglyphs lining the temple's corridors:

> I have "read" the lily,
>
> I can not "read" the hare, the chick, the bee,
> I would study and decipher
> the indecipherable Amen-script.   (*HE* 2, 21)

There are no walls of writing, however, in the original scene of her vision, which takes place near an open campfire "that first night / on the desolate beach" (*HE* 38): the "writing" she "reads" when Achilles seizes her throat is hallucinatory. Both the hallucinatory status of Helen's vision and the tropes of reading and pictography she invokes to define her relationship to it link this vision to H.D.'s account of her own series of projected images at Corfu in 1920. In *Tribute to Freud,* H.D. describes her visions—which Freud would later declare her "only actually dangerous 'symptom'"—as "picture-writing," and asserts: "it was I . . . who was seeing the pictures, who was reading the writing or who was granted the inner vision" (pp. 41, 48–51).

Similarly, Freud repeatedly invokes tropes of reading and pictography to describe the multiple relations between hysteric patients, their visual symptoms, and their psychoanalytic cure. He compares one hysteric's orderly progress through a series of pictorial memories to "reading a lengthy book of pictures, whose pages were being turned over before her eyes" (*Studies on Hysteria* 153). But he also asserts that the hysteric who "reads" these images aloud dissolves them: "the patient is, as it were, getting rid of it [the memory picture] by turning it into words." After all memories associated with it have been verbalized, "the picture vanishes, like a ghost that has been laid" (*Studies on Hysteria* 280–81). Extending his analogies further, Freud defines even nonvisual hysterical symptoms as a kind of somatic picture-writing. He writes, "We . . . had often compared the symptomatology of hysteria with a pictographic script which has become intelligible after the discovery of a few bilingual inscriptions. In that alphabet being sick means disgust" (*Studies on Hysteria* 129).

As Freud's example here suggests, his "bilingual inscriptions" record the same message not in two different languages—verbal and pictographic—but in two different orders or levels of the same language—figurative and literal. Hysterical symptoms literalize absent verbal figures associated with repressed memories and/or fantasies. Freud goes on to declare, however, that hysteric symptom-formation may bypass verbal figures entirely:

> In taking a verbal expression literally . . . , the hysteric is not taking liberties with words, but is simply reviving once more the sensations to which the verbal expression owes its justification. . . . These [sensations] may now for the most part have become so much weakened that the expression of them in words seems to us only to be a figurative picture of them, whereas in all probability the description was once meant literally; and hysteria is right in restoring the original meaning of the words in depicting its unusually strong innervations. (*Studies on Hysteria* 181)

This explanation makes for clumsy linguistics and clumsy science, and Freud, in fact, immediately provides examples that contradict it. H.D., on the other hand, puts the terms of Freud's discussion to quite skillful poetic use in a reading of Euripides' *Helen* that underwrites Helen's own hysterical "reading" of the lily.

As Menelaus prepares to overthrow the Egyptian crew on the getaway craft passed off as his own death-ship, he addresses his small party of Greeks with Achilles' figure of the "flower / of all-time":

> τί μέλλετ', ὦ γῆς Ἑλλάδος λωτίσματα,
> σφάζειν, φονεύειν βαρβάρους, νεώς τ' ἄπο
> ῥίπτειν ἐς οἶδμα[29]

Here the Greek phrase Ἑλλάδος λωτίσματα, literally meaning "the flower of Hellas," already carries the figurative meaning of "choicest" or "best" for Euripides. Yet the roots of the Greek figure point directly back to Egypt: λώτισμα derives from λωτός, meaning "lotus," or even "Egyptian lotus."[30] Both Euripides' Menelaus and H.D.'s Achilles employ the flower figure to represent the superiority of the Greek host: the former as a means of inciting his men to slaughter, the latter in an elegy for his men's own slaughtering. Thus, in transposing Euripides' figure to a new context, H.D. ironizes it, revealing that strength in arms is never proof against death, but rather its agent. More importantly, however, Helen's response to Achilles' use of the figure indicates that its very figurality is of a piece with its violent associations: in a series of translations and semantic abstractions from the original Egyptian hieroglyph through the Greek to Achilles' English usage of "flower" as a synonym for "chosen," the lotus's magical powers of resurrection have been lost.[31]

Through a reverse translation that exploits Freud's conflation of the verbal and figurative over and against the pictographic and literal, Helen literalizes Achilles' flower figure as the visionary lily with sails for petals. Gathering the lost ships of his dead "children" into the form—and sign— of the lotus hieroglyph, she uses its recovered power to reconstitute

> the scattered host
> (limbs torn asunder)
> . . . the Osiris

as the reborn Horus, "the one name for the thousand lost" (*HE* 27, 41). At the same time, H.D. dislodges the flower figure from its peripheral and ornamental status in Euripides' play and promotes it to a primary and generative place in her own narrative. This intertextual transposition functions simultaneously as a feminist revaluing of female hysterics' powers of vision. For Helen's complex "reading" of the lily marks *Studies on Hysteria* itself as a hysterical text that symptomatically manifests a linguistic "memory" it does not consciously possess. If Breuer thinks to remind his reader that "hysteria" is "derived from the Greek word for 'uterus'" (*Studies on Hysteria* 247), he more absently reports, "The overflowing productivity of their minds has led one of my friends to assert that hysterics are the flower of mankind, as sterile, no doubt, but as beautiful as double flowers" (*Studies on Hysteria* 240).[32]

Where Breuer exalts hysterics as the flower of mankind only to condemn their indubitable sterility, Helen discovers a literally generative and curative power in her visionary "productions" that has been lost in the abstract verbal language Freud would use to remove them. Turning Freud's and Breuer's own verbal figures back into visionary pictures, she revives dead men and dead metaphors alike and raises all the ghosts they would lay to rest. For Helen's visionary conflation of the Greek warships and the Egyptian womb-flower literally resurrects Achilles' "lost legions" as phantom agents of love and peace; "encircl[ing]" and "shelter[ing]" her as she faces Achilles' murderous wrath (*HE* 38), "the invisible host" converts his rage into ardor:

it was they, the veil
that concealed yet revealed,
that reconciled him to me.   (*HE* 40, 44)

As Helen will later reveal, their protection ushers in an actual moment of impregnation under Achilles' cloak, whose fruit will be a savior child (*HE* 17, 185).

Helen's "reading" of the lily closely reproduces the major types of literalization traced by Margaret Homans in nineteenth-century women's writing: it stages a woman's translation of a male text, represents the virgin birth of the Word (of Horus), and occasions the conception of an actual child.[33] Where Homans uses the terms "literal" and "literalized" interchangeably, however, opposing both to the substitutive action of figures, the transformative power of Helen's vision depends on a necessary distinction between these terms. For the hysteric the literalization of a figure does not shake off that figure's tenor to reestablish a prefigural or literal meaning, but acquires the figure's tenor as its own.[34] Likewise, when Helen translates the Euripidean flower figure from English and Greek back into Egyptian, she does not simply restore to the lotus hieroglyph the "original meaning" it had before it was translated into Greek, but instead reassigns to the lotus hieroglyph the tenors of later flower figures. The visionary lily with sails for petals embodies and manifests the life-restoring powers not only of the Egyptian Isis and Horus (to whom these powers are originally and solely attributed), but also of the mentally productive hysteric Helen and the chosen Greek legions. In fact, it is precisely because Helen's vision bestows on both herself and the Greek host the powers of life traditionally ascribed to the Egyptian mother and child that she can hope to reconstruct and redeem, rather than merely replace, the Greek legend of the destructive oedipal family.

Protected from Achilles' violence by the phantom presence of the Greek host that she has raised through "reading," Helen would seem to defend herself against Achilles' accusation that she has caused the deaths of his warriors with the very proof of its injustice: after all, she has just caused not their destruction but their rebirth. Yet her invigorating response to Achilles' mysterious show of aggression turns out to tell only half the story of "that first night / on the desolate beach," and a misleading half at that. Helen's vision does not stand as a simple reminder to a misogynist male companion of women's neglected powers for good, but as a complex moment of social criticism in which men and women alike are called to account. Far from repudiating Achilles' anger, Helen spends the rest of the poem justifying it, and comes to regard her vision of the lily not as a palinode, or self-defense, but rather as a scene of conversion.

Whereas a purely hysterical "conversion" of memories and/or fantasies into somatic symptoms serves to evade the frequently erotic conflicts standing behind them, the conversion Helen undergoes uses her eroticized struggle with Achilles to stimulate personal and social reform.

In this sense, her vision aligns Helen with Eisenstein's "creating spectator," whose sexualized act of viewing doubles as an act of political awakening. Indeed, as I suggested in the first part of this chapter, Eisenstein's account of the creating spectator offers a number of arresting parallels to and inversions of Freud's account of hysteria, parallels and inversions that bear directly on Helen's "reading" of the lily. Like the mentally productive hysteric, Eisenstein's creating spectator is said actively to engender the images he beholds on screen in a "womb of fantasy." Like hysterical symptoms, these filmic images stand as literalizations of absent verbal figures, which the creating spectator, like the hysteric's analyst, must decode if he is to ascertain the film's message. And like the hysteric who embodies repressed ideas in somatic symptoms, the creating spectator engages in "embodied thinking" in order to imbue the abstract ideas literalized on screen with material efficacy in the real world. But where for Freud hysterical literalizations function as signs of repression—the conscious mind's refusal to acknowledge irresolvable psychic conflicts—for Eisenstein filmic literalizations function as signs and agents of revolution, prompting the creating spectator to acknowledge irresolvable political conflicts and to join the fight for a visionary new society. Thus, when read against Eisenstein's account rather than Freud's, the literalized terms of Helen's vision of the lily cease to mark her hysterical amnesia, her passionate desire to forget the trauma of war, and instead mark a coming to consciousness, a willingness to remember the conflict-ridden past in order to revise it.

While he has insisted on the spectator's active engagement of the montage film all along, Eisenstein's explicit discussion of the creating spectator develops out of his new attitude toward "intellectual cinema," discussed in "Film Form, 1935—New Problems" which ran in *Life and Letters Today* during the fall of 1935.[35] In this essay, Eisenstein reviews the original goal of intellectual cinema, which was to achieve "an effective materialisation of ideas" by "transmuting to screen form the abstract concept . . . without intermediary. Without recourse to story, or invented plot, in fact directly—by agency of the image-composed elements shot."[36] He now argues for the need to reinstate sustained characters and story lines in his films, but remains committed to the hope that intellectual cinema will "restor[e] emotional fullness to the intellectual process."[37] First claiming interior monologue as the successor to intellectual cinema, he then proposes to use the peculiar logic of unspoken thought or "inner speech" as the model for a kind of artistic composition that can engage its viewers at emotional and visceral as well as intellectual levels.

Eisenstein borrows the concept of inner speech from the Russian theorist Lev Vygotsky's accounts of sociolinguistic development rather than from Freud's theories of the unconscious. Inner speech, however, displays the same principles of irrational or syncretic logic that characterize Freud's unconscious.[38] Moreover, both Freud and Eisenstein consistently associate syncretic thinking with ancient and/or primitive societies, people of color, women, the visual image, and the body. Eisenstein identifies inner speech with "sensual and image thought processes," "sensual, prelogical thinking," "embodied thinking," and "early thought processes," and finds manifestations of its logic in ethnographic accounts of Bushmen, Bororo Indians, Polynesians, and—for a little variety—Catherine de' Medici, who, "aided by her court magician, wished ill to her foes by transfixing with pins their miniature wax images."[39] While he specifically insists that inner speech is present in all social stages of thinking (and that even "so-called 'Primitive' peoples"[40] employ rational logic to some degree), he argues that artists intuitively foreground these "early thought processes," which accounts for the greater emotional impact of their work.

Eisenstein first proposes to make the film spectator an artist in his own right in "Montage in 1938," published in *Life and Letters Today* during the summer and autumn of 1939. This proposal falls neatly into line with his previous associations among inner speech, visual images, women, and the body. Here Eisenstein's early figures of dialectical conflict and *Aufhebung* for montage juxtaposition give way to new figures of sexual reproduction and embodiment. In 1930, he had seized upon what he called the Japanese "hieroglyph" to illustrate the montage principle that "from the collision of two given factors *arises* a concept."[41] On the basis of this principle, he had proposed that maximizing visual conflict between successive shots would shake the spectator out of a passive engagement of the film and into a "higher dimension" of thought, capable of combining antithetical images into new conceptual syntheses. Compelled by the dialectical construction of the film to think dialectically, Eisenstein's spectator was thus to begin in the cinema hall the mental and political awakening necessary to take part in the Russian Socialist Revolution. In 1938, this "higher dimension" of dialectical thinking becomes a "womb of fantasy," while the spectator himself becomes "the creating spectator."

Eisenstein's "womb of fantasy," though merely a figurative term, is weirdly reminiscent of H.D.'s 1919 notion of the "vision of the womb," which ascribes visionary powers to the womb as a second "centre of consciousness."[42] Neither Eisenstein nor H.D. are at all original in yoking mental creativity to the womb. In his use of the figure to insist that the act of viewing is "dynamic" and productive rather than passive or possessive, however, and in the positive value he assigns to the spectator's "personal creative" contribution to the images viewed[43] (what Freud would call projection—and would value negatively), Eisenstein both breaks with tradition and anticipates H.D.'s portrayal of Helen's acts of visionary "reading" in *Helen in Egypt*. For Eisenstein, the "womb of fantasy" syncretically unites abstract meanings, visual images, and emotional impressions drawn from the montage film into a single *obraz*—the "global image" or "generalized *image*, wherein the creator [filmmaker], and following him the spectator, experiences the given theme" of the film.[44] This global image, a product of the irrational thought patterns of inner speech, becomes a kind of baby that the act of interpretive viewing calls to life. Easing out his earlier figures of conflict, Eisenstein asserts that two montage shots "in juxtaposition give birth to the [global] image in which the content of the theme is most clearly incarnated."[45] In more extravagant applications of the same rhetoric, he writes: "out of the womb of his fantasy, out of the warp and weft of his associations, conditioned by the premises of his character, habits, and social appurtenances, [every spectator] creates a [global] image in accordance with the precise guiding representations suggested to him by the author"; and, again: "the [global] image invented by the author has become flesh of the flesh of the spectator's [global] image. . . . By one—the spectator—engendered, in one, born and emerging. Creative not only for the author, but creative also for me, the creating spectator" (Eisenstein's ellipses).[46]

Ostensibly chosen to emphasize the creativity of viewing, these figures of virgin birth for an act of spectatorship Eisenstein nevertheless imagines as generically male also call on stereotypes of female intuition and maternal instinct to evoke the strong emotional, visceral, and irrational components of viewing that it is the business of intellectual cinema to promote. The association of the global image with figures of parturition and embodiment persists in later, less polemical attempts to characterize it: Eisenstein's recent critic Jacques Aumont defines the global image as a "generalization which incorporates all of the diverse metaphors produced in the course of the work of representation" (p. 178). Aumont's extended discussion of relationship between the global image and filmic "metaphoricity" confirms what Eisenstein's own examples make clear, and points to the source of this persistent emphasis on embodiment. Due to the materiality they acquire both within the fictive space of the film's narrative and the actual space of the film frame, film "metaphors" function as literalizations of the absent verbal figures they thus seem to embody: it is these verbal figures that Eisenstein's spectator, like the hysteric's psychoanalyst, must recover and combine into one global image in order to apprehend the film's themes.[47]

Both Macpherson's film *Borderline* and H.D.'s writing about it indicate H.D.'s own familiarity and fascination with filmic literalization. Anne Friedberg notes the literalization of the common figure "overflowing joy" in *Borderline*, achieved by quick intercuts between Paul Robeson's joyous face and a waterfall.[48] H.D. seems to comment on this moment directly in her 1930 promotional pamphlet for the film, where she links the cinema's revitalizing treatment of dead metaphors to "the famous 'picture' writing" of ancient times; to illustrate the power of film to "bring words back" to their original strength or "'virtue,'" she cites a scene in Pabst's *Pandora's Box* where we literally "'fly' upstairs with Lulu," and adds, "So we can 'swim' in ecstasy and 'drown' actually in happiness."[49] In a 1928 *Close Up* article entitled "Film Imagery: Eisenstein," Robert Herring explicitly links this practice of filmic literalization back to Eisenstein's own early experiments with the global image; focusing on the Odessa steps scene in the 1925 film *Potemkin*, Herring argues that "if you state a thing vividly enough by a succession of images, those you have chosen come to condense the meaning of the whole and to contain it" (p. 26).[50]

Eisenstein's scene at Odessa, picked out by Robert Herring for special commentary, encodes one of his most famous and interesting examples of a global image, even as it supplies a literal baby to match the figurative one whose fate will become so closely tied up with that of the global image itself. The scene may well anticipate Helen's vision of the lily in *Helen in Egypt*. In a 1939 essay, "The Structure of the Film," Eisenstein explains how he constructed this scene, in which Cossacks open fire on a milling crowd at Odessa, to transmit its revolutionary message directly to the spectator.[51] In the crowd's terrified stampede down to the sea where mutinying sailors have laid anchor, the camera returns repeatedly to a baby's carriage propelled down the steps by its mother's dying fall. This carriage "propels the idea of [the crowd's] rushing downward into the next dimension—*from rolling, as understood "figuratively," into the physical fact of rolling.* . . . This is . . . a *leap in display method* from the figurative to the physical, taking place within the representation of rolling."[52]

According to Eisenstein, this "leap in display method" communicates to the spectator a further "leap 'out of oneself'" which is simultaneously the leap of "ecstasy" and of revolution.[53] At the center of his organization of the sequence, the galloping course of the baby carriage's revolving wheels stands as a polyvalent literalization of the crowd's political break with the *status quo* and mobilization toward revolution. By investing the carriage with its thematic import even as he responds passionately to the baby's plight, the creating spectator performs an act of interpretation in a state of ecstasy powerful enough to transform his own political affiliations.[54]

The plunging baby carriage in *Potemkin* helps to underline several parallels between the creating spectator's womb of fantasy and Helen's vision of the lily.[55] The spectator's production of a global image "out of the womb of his fantasy" anticipates Helen's visionary lily, which fuses a visual configuration with its figurative meanings. Similarly, the goal of intellectual cinema—to achieve "an effective materialisation of ideas" on film—anticipates Helen's desire to "realize the transcendental in material terms" in the aftermath of her vision, as well as that vision's own strategy of literalization (*HE* 11). The state of ecstasy in which the creating spectator apprehends the global image in *Potemkin* anticipates the "ecstatic or semi-trance state" in which Helen regards and reviews her vision (*HE* 109). And the very ambiguity of the creating spectator's production of a global image—at once an act of personal creation and an act of recovering the global image previously invented by the filmmaker—parallels the "intuitive or emotional knowledge" through which Helen rediscovers the ancient hieroglyph behind Achilles' figure of speech (*HE* 13, 22).

Like the spectator's womb of fantasy, Helen's vision of Isis's womb-flower will prove to embody the entire course of her project to reconstruct the Greek past. And like the hurtling baby carriage in *Potemkin*, imbued with revolutionary import, the lily encodes a new model of society and prompts Helen to bring that model into being. Yet where Eisenstein locates social revolution at the point where a baby flies loose from its dying mother's grasp, H.D. locates her reconstruction of the family at the point where mother and child join forces. Helen's vision of the lotus hieroglyph holds the clue to the particular terms of this project in its peculiar conjunction of word and picture: conflating the sign of the child with the image of its mother's womb, it testifies to the redemptive force of their enduring attachment.

Helen the Egyptian

> How could I hide my eyes?
> how could I veil my face?
> with ash or charcoal from the embers?
>
> I drew out a blackened stick
>
> —H.D., "Pallinode"

Like Eisenstein's spectator, politicized by his or her visceral engagement with the film, Helen registers the impact of her vision directly on her body. Yet where Eisenstein merely likens "embodied thinking" to the thinking of the "racially" distinct "so-called 'Primitive' peoples," H.D. stages Helen's response to her vision as a moment of actual racial conversion. Recalling how Achilles cursed her as an "envious Isis," Helen speculates:

> in the dark, I must have looked
> an inked-in shadow; but with his anger,
> that ember, I became
>
> what his accusation made me,
> Isis, forever with that Child,
> the Hawk Horus.   (*HE* 17, 23)

As the emphasis on her darkness suggests, Helen becomes a black woman in becoming Isis.[56] This change of race initially appears to be cosmetic: she blackens her face and arms with charcoal after sighting the "night-bird" of Isis and just before Achilles' attack. As she later reviews this moment of assuming blackface, she laments, "I could not hide my eyes" (*HE* 38), as if to mourn the limits of her disguise. In an echo of Freud's unorthodox claim that Moses was an Egyptian rather than a Semite, however, Achilles later recalls this moment, describing Helen as "another / whose eyes slant in the old way," and asking: "is she Greek or Egyptian?" (*HE* 254).[57]

For Achilles, Helen's slanting eyes render her race ambiguous. Because he never decides this issue definitively, we too are left to wonder whether Helen's work with "a blackened stick" actually transforms her into, or reveals her to have always been, an Egyptian Isis, or only indicates her impersonation of the goddess (*HE* 16). In passing, H.D. hints that Achilles' attack on Helen may have been prompted by this very threat of impersonation, the possibility of deceit or fraud lurking at the bottom of representation. For, just as Achilles recognizes in Helen's slanting eyes a disturbing copy of his mother's gaze, Paris too eventually cries out:

> are you that other
>
> or do you dare impersonate Her?
>   . . .
>
> do not repeat
> Aphrodite's inimitable gesture   (*HE* 146)

before his own sudden rage forces Helen to flee. The possibility that she is masquerading in another's image keeps returning as a kind of local outcropping of the larger, unanswerable question of the relationship between Helen's actual self and her phantom likeness presiding over the killing at Troy.[58] This trace of falseness and imitation that besets Helen's self-representation aligns her with that infamous fraud, the hysteric, who recklessly acquires the traits, gestures, and symptoms of other people in an effort to signal an alignment with, or appropriation of, their life histories. Along these lines, Helen's sudden manufacturing of a dark complexion can be read as a sign of her hysterical identification with the Egyptian mother-goddess, an identification poised ambiguously between a maligned woman's attempt to steal the esteem accorded to Isis and the more candid impulse to confess a hidden sympathy with, or longing for, Isis's own situation or story. Yet, as the connections between Helen's physical transformations and Eisenstein's concept of embodied thinking would suggest, her proposed change of race goes deeper than a particular identification with Isis, indicating a radical change in Helen's own modes of thought and experience.

Thus, the Spartan and "reputedly fair-haired" Helen's surprising claim to have "become" the dark Egyptian "Isis, forever with that Child, / the Hawk Horus" (*HE* 9, 23) also resembles the "strange and unusual" claims of Eisenstein's Bororo Indians who "maintain that, while human beings, they are none the less at the same time also a special kind of red parrot very common in Brazil."[59] Eisenstein immediately cites the actor's ability to get in character as a familiar parallel to this exotic "Bororo idea concerning simultaneous double existence of two completely different and separate and, none the less, real images,"[60] thus offsetting the impulse to identify such ideas exclusively with "so-called primitives" or people of color. Indeed, although he repeatedly chooses to illustrate "the sensual, prelogical thinking" of intellectual cinema with examples drawn from the thought patterns of Polynesians, Bororo Indians, and Bushmen, he explicitly resists identifying such thinking as an inherent characteristic of people of color, explaining:

> Usually the construction of so-called early thought-processes is treated as a form of thinking fixed in itself once and for all, characteristic of the so-called "Primitive" peoples, racially inseparable from them and not susceptible to any modification whatsoever. In this guise it serves as scientific apologia for the methods of enslavement to which such people are subjected by white colonisers, inasmuch as, by inference, such peoples are "after all hopeless" for culture and cultural influence.[61]

Yet Helen's change in skin color at the time of her vision suggests that H.D. does characterize "embodied thinking" as a racial trait, at least for the purposes of her narrative: Helen's blackened face and arms serve as a somatic expression of the "depth of her racial inheritance" from which, by the headnotes' account, she initially "invokes . . . the symbol or the 'letter' that represents or recalls the protective mother-goddess" (*HE* 13).

In turn, this "enchanted" recognition of the mother's sign in the body of a flying bird—a recognition that the headnotes derive from "intuitive or emotional knowledge, rather than intellectual" (*HE* 13)—anticipates the magical, sensual, and antirational terms of Helen's subsequent vision of the lily. Yet if H.D. here seems to assert a direct correspondence between race and mode of thought that Eisenstein would reject, it may well be due to the influence of Freud, whose similar associations between women, people of color, ancient and/or primitive societies, and unconscious thinking are usually passed on to the reader without Eisenstein's important qualifications. In fact, the only exception to this general trend is Freud's concerted effort to historicize his links between pictorial thinking,[62] the mother's body, and Egypt in *Moses and Monotheism*, whose argument, as we have seen, haunts this whole question of Helen's race. Starting with this assertedly historical argument, and moving back to the unhistoricized analogies that underlie it in Freud's earlier essays, we can begin to track down the complex associations between ancient Egypt and the unconscious that inform Helen's provocative racial transformation.

In his unorthodox revision of sacred history, Freud attributes the originality and civilizing power of Jewish monotheism to "a victory of intellectuality over sensuality." He traces this victory to three historical occasions on which "sense perception" was subordinated to "the higher intellectual processes—that is, memories, reflections and inferences": the Hebraic injunction against Egyptian image-making (with its concomitant injunction against hieroglyphs), the discovery of the father's role in procreation, and the related transition from a matriarchal to a patriarchal society (*Moses and Monotheism* 43, 112–15, 117–18). Thus, Freud posits that Moses was an Egyptian only to celebrate his exodus from Egypt's matriarchal and idolatrous culture. This physical and spiritual exodus becomes the condition for the Mosaic foundation of an abstract, monotheistic form of father-worship (originally derived from the short-lived and unpopular worship of Aten in Egypt), which itself supports the entire Western intellectual tradition, culminating in modern science. As we have seen, H.D. follows Freud in positing that Helen of Troy may have been an Egyptian, but does so in order to critique Western abstraction, which Freud celebrates, as an unwitting source of violence,[63] and to recover the lost matriarchal religion of Egypt that he denigrates.

The "racial inheritance" Helen calls upon in identifying the flying night-bird as a sign of "the protective mother-goddess" closely parallels Freud's notion of a group member's "archaic heritage," which includes "not only dispositions but also subject-matter—memory traces of the experience of earlier generations" (*Moses and Monotheism* 99). But Helen's racial inheritance harbors a radically different content or history than

Freud would assign it. For Freud, the Semites' archaic heritage consists of the sons' guilt over their father's murder; he comes up with the notion in *Moses and Monotheism* to explain the unconscious transmission of this guilt from actual patricides to their descendants several generations down the line. In contrast, for Helen there appears to be no guilty memory of the father's death lurking in "the depth of her racial inheritance." Despite Achilles' accusations that she caused the deaths of the Greek host at Troy ("the scattered host / [limbs torn asunder] / was the Osiris"), the "carrion creature," perhaps a vulture, that she sees on the desolate beach "is no death-symbol but a life-symbol" (*HE* 27, 13). Helen's recovery of the vulture and lily as signs of the life-giving mother's body in acts of reading that variously exalt "sense perception" over intellectual abstraction would thus signal her regression on a historical time line laid out by Freud. In this regression, she moves away from a Western (Hebraic and Greek) culture in which "intellectuality" triumphs over "sensuality" and the insensate body of the father cries out for retribution, and moves toward an earlier culture in which the mother, ground of the senses and origin of images, triumphs through her power to awaken the father's corpse to second life.⁶⁴

Before we follow Freud in assigning this earlier culture an actual place and time in history, however, it is important to point out that Helen's "Egypt," like her vision of the lily, is a literary synthesis conflating several literalizations of earlier Freudian figures. In his case histories of the Wolf Man and Leonardo da Vinci, Freud compares unconscious syncretic thinking to the ancient "Egyptian pantheon" which manifests a parallel tendency to fuse the identities of its various gods (*Leonardo da Vinci* 93; "From the History of an Infantile Neurosis" 119). Mental derivatives of the unconscious posing as conscious thoughts remind him of "individuals of mixed race who . . . betray their coloured descent by some striking feature or other, and on that account are excluded from society" ("The Unconscious" 191). He calls adult female sexuality "a 'dark continent' for psychology" (*The Question of Lay Analysis* 212), and compares the surprising discovery of a pre-oedipal period of female sexuality (which he claims is "especially intimately related to the aetiology of hysteria") to "the discovery . . . of the Minoan-Mycenean civilization behind the civilization of Greece" ("Female Sexuality" 227, 226).

Against this background of Freudian analogies, H.D. adjusts her long-standing poetic use of ancient geography to superimpose a map of the mind onto the map of the ancient world.⁶⁵ In *Helen in Egypt*, Parnassus and Athens are equated with "reality," "Greek creative thought," and "the delight of the intellect," while Egypt, Crete, and Eleusis become common strongholds of "dream," "magic," and the "Mysteries" of the mother-goddesses Demeter and Isis (*HE* 168–69, 209, 212, 89). In this strangely

literal landscape of the mind, Egypt *becomes* the ground of the uncon-
scious, of female sexuality and hysteria, and of the pre-oedipal phase, and
thus enables Helen to realize her vision "in material terms" (*HE* 11). As
the unconscious itself, Egypt equates "wishes with their fulfilment—with
the event," while as the "dark continent" of female sexuality and the pre-
oedipal phase, it stands as antecedent and antidote to the oedipal family,
target of Helen's project of reconstruction. The plethora of Freudian as-
sociations between women, people of color, ancient societies, and irratio-
nal thinking thus overshadows Eisenstein's own interest in art's debt to the
"earlier thought processes" of inner speech, and constitutes a surer source
for H.D.'s portrayal of ancient Egypt as the ground of the unconscious.[66]
When H.D. links her heroine's unconscious thought processes to the ends
of social reconstruction, however, Eisenstein's program for leashing "sen-
sual, prelogical thinking" to the ends of Russian Socialism resurfaces in
terms that no one would mistake for Freud's.

In becoming "Isis, forever with that Child, / the Hawk Horus"
through her vision on the desolate beach, Helen completes the first step in
"transpos[ing] or translat[ing]" the Greek oedipal "legend of murder and
lust" into the Egyptian legend of Isis. Yet the very possibility of this trans-
lation precedes any act of reading on Helen's part, lying instead in a num-
ber of striking continuities and variations in these two cultures' accounts
of the nuclear family. Thus, Oedipus's identity as a son who kills his father
and commits incest with his mother is split between two characters in the
Isis legend: Horus, the son of Osiris and Isis, and Typhon, who kills his
brother Osiris and attempts to have sex with his sister Isis.[67] The allocation
of Oedipus's crimes to the brother rather than the son spares Horus from
blame; conceiving Horus after his father's death, as if to emphasize the
impossibility of his role in it, Isis raises her son to defeat his murderous
uncle and eventually gives him the words of power used to reunite and
revive Osiris's dismembered body. Upon his return to life, Osiris becomes
lord of the kingdom of the dead, while Horus rules on earth with his
mother's help.[68]

This allocation of the oedipal son's crimes to the brother in the Isis
myth has one important effect, of which H.D. takes full advantage: in an-
cient Egypt, the alliance between mother and son, far from being the
source of the family's ruin, becomes the source of its salvation. Thus, like
Jocasta, Isis forms an alliance with her son in the aftermath of her hus-
band's murder. But where for Jocasta this alliance only compounds Oe-
dipus's crimes against Laius, for Isis it becomes a means of reprisal and
reparation. From this perspective, the Isis myth plays out the ever-
appealing fantasy of having it both ways: exploiting a convenient lacuna
in the reign of the father, Isis and her son pair up in order to bring Osiris

back, while enjoying the freedom of having him gone. Indeed, the source of Isis's tremendous power can be attributed to her ability to maintain peaceful relations between the several male relatives competing for her attentions simultaneously. Throughout the various cycles of the myth, she intervenes to prevent further killing and to consolidate a family that, like Osiris himself, seems bent on fragmentation.

Situated at the crossroads between Greece and Egypt, Helen comes to view the hostility between her two lovers, the youthful Paris and the fatherly Achilles, as a version of the oedipal struggle: her question "how reconcile Trojan and Greek?" reappears as the question "must youth and maturity quarrel . . . ?" (*HE* 157, 181). Her solution will be an act of "subtle genealogy" whereby the oedipal Paris is reconstituted as a Horus who comes not to destroy but to restore the life of his new father, Achilles (*HE* 184–85). Helen approaches her project to "reconstruct the legend" of Oedipus through the strategy of reordering, applying this single strategy at multiple points. Within the specific terms of her project, reordering governs her transposition of key events in the story of Oedipus to comply with the dictates of the story of Isis: where the Oedipus myth proceeds rationally, narrating the son's conception and birth before his murder of his father, the Isis myth calls for an irrational or magical reversal of this order, narrating the father's murder before the son's conception. When Helen attempts to "transpose or translate" her Trojan lover, Paris, from a family structure constructed on the oedipal model to one constructed on the model of Isis, she conflates the two myths' story lines while preserving the irrational reversal of normative genealogy that characterizes the Isis myth. In her discussions with Theseus on the island of Leuke, Helen claims that it was "Paris whose swift arrow / (O Wolf-slayer) pierced the Achilles-heel" at the same time that she links Paris to the Greek host who lost their lives at Troy:

> alike but different, apart from the heroes slain,
>
> but one, one other, *the* other,
> incarnate, manifest Egypt;
> he, the fire-brand, was born of the Star,
>
> was engendered under the cloak
> of the new-mortal Achilles.   (*HE* 185)[69]

Achilles' and Helen's act of conceiving Paris on the desolate beach after Achilles himself had died at Troy parallels Isis's conception of Horus after the death of Osiris. Then again, Helen's identification of Paris as the son who slays his father follows the pattern laid out by Oedipus. Using both stories simultaneously, she comes up with a further genealogical contradiction—"this is no easy thing / to explain, this subtle genealogy" (*HE* 184). While Oedipus's destiny decrees that he will become the slayer of Laius because he is his son, in Helen's version Paris becomes the son of Achilles precisely because he is already his slayer: "the slayer becomes the son of the slain" (*HE* 184). Here, the prior example of the Isis myth frees Helen from the rigors of a logical chronology, allowing her to reorder generations and lines of descent, as well as the prescribed order of mythic events, at will.

If these irrational acts of reordering stand at the center of Helen's project to reconstruct the legend, they do not constitute the only acts of this kind. Indeed, toward the end of *Helen in Egypt*, Helen defines her lovers' and her own entire project to remember the past as a species of montage reordering. Reviewing the shape of her own meditations, she recalls

> the million personal things,
> things remembered, forgotten,
>
> remembered again, assembled
> and re-assembled in different order
> as thoughts and emotions.   (*HE* 289)[70]

This description closely echoes one of Freud's definitions of the relationship between the hysteric's unconscious fantasies and the childhood memories from which they derive: "If we examine [such fantasies'] structure, we shall perceive the way in which the wishful purpose that is at work in their production has mixed up the material of which they are built, has rearranged it and has formed it into a new whole" (*Interpretation of Dreams* 492). Freud argues that hysterical fantasies reorder memories of past events in order to express wishes unfulfilled in the actual past; when viewed against this model, both the characters' meditative reorderings of their personal pasts and H.D.'s own montage reorderings of her epic and mythic source materials can be read as a strategy for realizing alluring narrative possibilities that have been passed over in the extant literary tradition.[71] Freud himself, however, views the hysteric's unconscious strategies of reordering as a source not of artistic possibility but of social menace.

In the early part of his career, Freud links such reorderings to the hysteric's assault on the father's reputation, his or her fantastic charges of paternal seduction or rape. By the time he writes *Moses and Monotheism*, the stakes increase: textual reordering becomes no less than an analogy for patricide, a crime of composition as heinous as, and tainted with, the sons' oedipal crimes against the father. In this regard, Eisenstein's own discussions of the reorderings at the heart of montage film only confirm the murderous power Freud assigns to the otherwise meek business of composition. When we recover the full arguments behind this surprising narrative freight that both Freud and Eisenstein attach to the formal strategy of reordering, the contours, and limits, of Helen's own project to reconstruct the legend of Oedipus become clearer.

H.D.'s very attempt to make positive use of the strategy of reordering sharply revises the relationship that Freud promotes between hysteria and its cure. For Freud, hysterics' pathological reorderings of memory occur at two levels. Just as their unconscious fantasies rearrange memories for the purposes of wish-fulfillment, hysterics' repression of certain events in the past impair their conscious memory, forcing them to patch over lost links between events with "false connections." As Freud argues in his case history of Dora, these "connections—even the ostensible ones—are for the most part incoherent, and the sequence of different events" in the hysteric's self-reported life-histories "is uncertain" (*Studies on Hysteria* 67, 294; "Fragment" 16). Beneath the fraudulent and disturbed surface of the hysteric's account, Freud insists that a repressed history "in some fashion lies ready to hand and in correct and proper order" (*Studies on Hysteria* 287). It rests with the analyst to restore this "proper order" to consciousness, so as to dissolve the bodily symptoms that symbolize the repressed parts of the hysteric's past, and thus cure her or his suffering.[72]

Yet Freud's distinction between the hysteric's pathological reorderings of memories and the psychoanalyst's therapeutic efforts to set matters straight is undermined by his own make-do procedure in writing up the case history of Dora. When she abruptly breaks off treatment and thus leaves Freud himself holding an incomplete story, he is forced to "restore what is missing" with educated guesses based on other cases, and to rearrange the order of his recollections "for the sake of presenting the case in a more connected form" ("Fragment" 10). Freud attempts to minimize the margin of inaccuracy incurred by such a procedure in order to make a case for his own scientific objectivity: in reordering his case history, he insists "nothing of any importance has been altered," while in restoring "what is missing," he claims merely "to follow the example of those discoverers" who reconstruct the original forms of "the priceless though mutilated relics of antiquity" they unearth ("Fragment" 10, 12). But here, Freud's choice of an analogy is unfortunate. For in *The Interpretation of Dreams* he argues that hysterical fantasies "stand in much the same relation to the childhood memories from which they are derived as do some of the Baroque palaces of Rome to the ancient ruins whose pavements and columns have provided the material for the more recent structures" (p. 492). The uncomfortably similar methodologies of the archaeologist who tries to reconstruct the original forms of ancient fragments and the Baroque architect who combines those fragments into new wholes carry across their respective analogies to suggest how much the psychoanalytic cure of hysteria resembles the very dissimulating structures of fantasy it would dislodge. H.D. underlines this isomorphism when she traces the Freud figure Theseus's memories of his own mythic exploits back to "idle fancy" and "hallucination of infancy" (*HE* 168). In doing so, she strips Freud's charges against hysterics' fantasies of their uniqueness: if everyone's fantasies make Baroque palaces out of the relics of antiquity, the hysteric's account of the past is not necessarily any less credible than the historian's or the analyst's.[73]

While H.D. thus allows the hysteric's assault on the father's reputation to stand, neither proved nor disproved, she balks at the chance Freud offers her to use hysterical reordering as a weapon against the father's life. In *Moses and Monotheism*, Freud attributes the paucity of evidence for his theory that Moses was killed by his own people to a textual "murder" that both replicates Moses' own murder and quashes all rumor about it:

> In its implications the distortion of a text resembles a murder: the difficulty is not in perpetrating the deed, but in getting rid of its traces. We might well lend the word "*Entstellung*" [distortion] the double meaning to which it has a claim. . . . It should mean not only "to change the appearance of something" but also "to put something in another place, to displace." Accordingly, in many instances of textual distortion, we may nevertheless count upon finding what has been suppressed and disavowed hidden away somewhere else, though changed and torn from its context. Only it will not always be easy to recognize it. (p. 43)

In a strikingly similar description of montage editing, which seems to assign aggressive agency to the filmmaker's cuts and shot variations themselves as a man struggles for his life on screen, Eisenstein asks the reader if filmmakers do not cause

> a monstrous disproportion of the elements of a normally flowing event, dismembering it suddenly into "gripping hands, large," "medium shots of struggle," and "bulging eyes, filling screen," in making the "montage" disintegration of an event into shots? In making an eye twice as large as a man's full height? By the combination of these monstrous incongruities we gather up the disintegrated event once more into one whole, but in *our* aspect. According to our treatment in relation to the event.[74]

Here, Eisenstein's discussion of the montage method's twin capacities to reorder the sequence of profilmic events and to alter the proportions of the various parts parallels Freud's discussion of textual distortion, in which unsavory details are both relocated and deemphasized in order to escape detection; if Eisenstein rejoices in the very violence Freud decries, both assume that these textual practices are murderous. H.D.'s own interest in the cinematic close-up as an emotionally fraught textual practice can be traced back to the years of her greatest involvement in film viewing, production, and criticism. In *HERmione*, composed between 1926 and 1930, the adolescent Her imagines that "writing had to do with the underside of a peony petal that covered the whole of a house like a nutshell housing woodgnats." For a young woman bent on the agonizing tasks of leaving home and decoding her family romance, a style of writing that would so greatly diminish the size of the family house while reducing its occupants to "woodgnats" itself betrays a certain amount of aggressive wish-fulfillment.[75]

By the writing of *Helen in Egypt*, the patricidal threat at work in textual distortion becomes even more pronounced, lending H.D.'s purportedly life-affirming promotion of a peripheral detail in Euripides' *Helen* play to a central position in her own poem a troubling ambiguity. This ambiguity is only compounded by the fact that Freud's immediate referent for "what has been suppressed and disavowed" and "hidden away somewhere else" in acts of textual murder is not the mislaid evidence of Moses' own murder, but rather "every trace of Egyptian influence" in the Pentateuch's account of Judaic custom and belief (*Moses and Monotheism* 44). In tracing Achilles' Greek flower figure back to an Egyptian hieroglyph, is Helen, like Freud, discovering a crime performed against an earlier, Egyptian heritage, and restoring the lotus figure to its rightful pedigree and import in a historiographic rescue operation? Or is she, like Eisenstein, committing patricide against the integrity of Euripides' play and other canonical source texts, in order to replace the face of the actual past with a face made over "in her aspect," just as she may have made over her own face to impersonate the aspect of Isis?

The question is undecidable, but it is also, in some sense, inadequate to the terms of Helen's project. Like Freud in his Moses essays and like Eisenstein in his historical films, H.D.'s Helen ponders received history in order to revise it. But where Freud and Eisenstein understand history in secular and rational terms, Helen's history, like that of Moses, is a sacred history where the truths of time are subject to the administrations of a higher truth: the truth of eternity. In eternity, past and future coincide, and so Helen's project can be at once an act of recovering a lost past and an act of creating a new face for the future. The rational impossibility of this is no deterrent. Long used to conflating the manifestations of eternity with the manifestations of the unconscious, H.D. grants sacred authority to the very irrationality of the methods Helen employs and the contradictory aims of restoration and revision she hopes to satisfy simultaneously.[76] But with Helen's commitment to the truth of eternity comes a commitment to the truth of second life and a corresponding limit on the kinds of changes she is willing to make in the oedipal family narrative.

For Freud, the death of the father makes way for a new "social contract" in which the surviving sons (or brothers) band together to protect themselves from the very crimes they have committed (*Moses and Monotheism* 82); for Eisenstein, the murderous violence of revolution is also a necessary component in the overthrow of hierarchical government and the institution of that same band of brothers advocated by Russian Socialism. But for Helen, the death of the father is only the temporary nadir in a story of salvation rooted in the triangle of the nuclear family; in this story, Isis's sacred commitment to conserving the father's life underlies a second commitment to conserving the social order.

Thus Isis's and her son's magical acts of gathering and reassembling Osiris's scattered limbs perform the work of reordering as a method not for covering up the father's death, but for reviving and reinstating him as lord of the kingdom of the dead and of eternity. As such, their efforts allow Helen to rid the very strategy of reordering of the taint of patricide it carries for Freud, just as the reordering of the rational sequence of life and death in the Isis myth has allowed her to undo the deaths of the Greek host with resurrection and to exchange the Mosaic piety of guilty sons for an Egyptian faith in family loyalty. Yet, while Helen's transposition or translation of the oedipal legend into the legend of Isis permits her to reclaim the alliance between mother and son as a force of familial solidarity, the terms of such solidarity should give feminists pause. For in identifying with Isis's maternal and magical powers of life, Helen also identifies with a program of family reunification in which the bond between mother and child, far from threatening the father's lordly place, preserves it.

The Fault of Thetis

she fought for the Greeks, they said,
Achilles' mother, but Thetis mourned
like Hecuba, for Hector dead.
    —H.D., "Eidolon"

As we have seen, Helen's attempts to search out the causes of war at Troy initially lead back to the hostility between father and son; in order to "reconcile Trojan and Greek," she must, like Isis, resolve the "quarrel" between youth and maturity and restore peaceful relations in the family. The terms of her proposed reconstruction of the legend—an alliance between mother and child that honors rather than excludes the father—are bodied forth in her vision of the lily that conflates the sign of the child with the image of its mother's womb. Yet when she attempts to realize the promise of this vision, she immediately meets with resistance from her fellow Greeks. In fact, the first to resist is Helen herself. Following Achilles' soliloquy delineating the patriarchal power structure of the Achaeans ("The Command was bequest from the past, / from father to son"), she impulsively takes to "living in fantasy, the story of her sister," Clytaemnestra, whose alliance with her child does cause her to threaten the father's reign—in fact, to rule in his stead and murder him when he returns home (*HE* 61, 85). Clytaemnestra's loyalty to Iphigenia also prompts the poem's only fantasy of an all-female family, like the one in which H.D. and Bryher raised Perdita: equating her daughter Hermione with Iphigenia, Helen reads her own relationship with Clytaemnestra into the Amen temple's depiction of "Isis with Nephthys, / the Child's other mother," while Helen's homoerotic fantasy of Iphigenia's wedding day, in which daughter and mother stand "together / as one, before the altar," evokes the text of Christian matrimony to describe what might otherwise pass as a moment of identification (*HE* 68, 74).

But the story of her sister proves incompatible with the vision of the lily that Helen reviews from her father's temple. In a remarkably thorough rejection of the lesbian eroticism and maternal aggression redeemed and celebrated in the figures of the Lady and Mary Magdalene in *Trilogy*, H.D. here narrates Proteus's delivery of a bribe to Helen through his own daughter Thetis; he offers her deification if she agrees to forget her sister:

> seek not to know
>
> too much; . . .
>
> . . .
>
> grieve not for Clytaemnestra.   (*HE* 105)[77]

She accepts. While "Pallinode" thus ends with the calculated suppression of the sororial bond in favor of paternal endorsement, "Leuke" begins with Helen's involuntary retrieval of "the so far suppressed memory and unspoken name—Paris" (*HE* 109). Banished from "Pallinode," Paris returns, symptomatically, in the memory of an even earlier banishment, inflicted at birth because Hecuba dreamed he would bring war to his father's city (*HE* 109–10). In this prenatal prophecy that "Hecuba's second son would undo / the work of his father, Priam" (*HE* 112), Paris takes after Oedipus, who was also destined to bring about the fall of his father's house. Priam's and Hecuba's decision to banish their infant son in order to evade this prophecy provides a second parallel to Oedipus's story, which Freud overlooks in devising the oedipal complex. Linked to Achilles' accusation that Helen caused the deaths of his "children" by a common theme of maternal violence, this memory of Paris's early banishment will continue to trouble Helen's attempts to realize her vision of the lotus and its promise of family reunification long after she leaves Paris himself behind. When she considers her Trojan lover for the part of Horus during her visit with Theseus, she wonders:

> did he hate Hecuba?
> she exposed him on Ida,
>
> like Oedipus, to die;
> tell me, god-father,
> how can I be his mother?   (*HE* 156)[78]

Like Hecuba and unlike Clytaemnestra, Jocasta values her husband's power over her child's life and agrees to destroy the son destined to overcome his father. Thus, the early period of maternal attachment that stands at the center of the Freudian child's oedipal complex never materializes for Oedipus himself. Yet when Helen finally goes through with her plan to convert Paris into another Horus—the "new Euphorion" "engendered under the cloak" of Achilles during her vision of the Greek host as lily— she focuses exclusively on extirpating the son's crimes against the father by converting the slaying son, Oedipus, into the savior of the slain father, Horus (*HE* 217, 185). What Helen leaves out of her reconstruction of the family here is the anxious memory of the mother's complicity in the father's crimes against the son.[79]

Nor is Paris the first son in *Helen in Egypt* to take after Oedipus. Achilles, too, was a son destined to be greater than his father—a destiny that prompted Zeus to hand Thetis over to her rapist, Peleus, an insignificant mortal. Moreover, Achilles drags Oedipus's "swollen foot" with him to Egypt as the somatic "token" of "his mortality" (*HE* 9).[80] Yet as Helen remembers it, Achilles' wounded heel takes on unmistakably erotic characteristics in a fantasy not of death but of female sexuality:

> though the Achilles-heel treads lightly,
> still I feel the tightening muscles,
> the taut sinews quiver,
>
> as if I, Helen, had withdrawn
> from the bruised and swollen flesh,
> the arrow from its wound.   (*HE* 8)

Under the lens of Helen's fantasy, Achilles' wound functions as a vagina (or more loosely, a womb) thrilling not to a touch, but to its withdrawal. As such, it becomes, quite literally, a hysterical "stigma," marking the male body with the sign both of "woman" and of her withdrawal, in accord with Freud's late work on hysteria, which traces symptoms to fantasies that perform "contradictory actions" simultaneously and have "a bisexual meaning" ("Hysterical Phantasies" 166).[81] Preserving the memory of his stay on Scyros, when his mother dressed him "in woman's robe and ornament" to hide him from the Greek war faction, his wound also recalls the time when Thetis

> had forgotten to dip the heel
> of the infant Achilles
>
> into the bitter water.   (*HE* 214, 253)

Where Oedipus's pierced ankles mark his body with his parents' unambiguous intent to destroy him, Achilles' vulnerable heel, like the fatal wound to follow, poses a contradiction: as the place on his body where his mother held him over the immortalizing waters, it testifies both to her literal attachment to her child and to the limits of that attachment, to her forgetfulness, her "careless, unspeakable" detachment (*HE* 253).

Achilles' ambivalent somatic memory of maternal detachment thus acts as the antithetical condition of Helen's vision: it is both what the lotus hieroglyph, conflating womb and child, tries to deny, and what Helen must eventually admit to consciousness if the promise of family reunification embodied in the lotus is to be fulfilled. In the meantime, Helen's body remembers what her mind cannot; approaching Theseus's fireside in "Leuke" with "wounded" feet (*HE* 151), she appropriates the oedipal stigmata from Achilles in order to signal her hysterical identification with his grievances against Thetis. This identification with the banished son, however, like her earlier hysterical identification with the Egyptian mother-goddess, also rests on Helen's desire to repress her own, uncomfortably Greek history as a mother.

Near the end of her stay with Theseus, Helen insists "I am only a daughter" (*HE* 191), in an attempt to ward off both the anger of all the mothers threatened by her claims on their grown sons' affections and the memory of her former intimacy with her own daughter, Hermione. When Paris returns in "Eidolon" to question Helen's visionary reform of the family, his insistent enumeration of the children betrayed by their parents' loyalty to "the old story" prompts the return of the last, painful "memory forgotten" of how Helen abandoned her daughter for a new life with Paris himself (*HE* 217, 304). Staring after a mother who "never looked back," Hermione upsets her mother's "nest"-like "workbasket." As

> the reels rolled to the floor
> and she did not stoop to pick up
>
> the scattered spools   (*HE* 228),

she signals both her mother's "over-turning" of her maternal role and her
own abrupt relinquishment of a *fort-da* game which Freud's grandson also
played with "a wooden reel" in an attempt to supervise his mother's com-
ings and goings; Hermione's gesture embodies the hysterical knowledge
that *her* mother is not coming back (*Beyond the Pleasure Principle* 15).[82]

While this memory's very painfulness would, in Freudian terms, reg-
ister a conflict between Helen's desires and her daughter's, the rest of the
poem will play out that pain as simple regret and use Helen's revised sense
of her maternal duties to resolve the conflicts building up in its previous
books. Helen's acknowledgment of her daughter's anger and grief at los-
ing her mother allows her to trace Achilles' opening attack to the same
cause. Thus, if H. D. initially appears to follow Homer in linking Achilles'
heroic anger before the gates of Troy to the "memory of the Body" of
Patroclus, she eventually uncovers the more distant memories of a lost
maternal body that lie behind the force of Achilles' grief for his male lover
on the Scamander plains (*HE* 7).

Midway through "Eidolon," Helen retrieves the memory of a mo-
ment between her naming of Thetis and Achilles' attack during their first
night on the beach:

> I think he remembered everything
> in an instantaneous flash,
>
>   . . .
>
> but he only saw the ships
> assembled at Aulis,
> he only remembered his own ship
>
> that would lead them all,
> he only saw an image, a wooden image,
> a mermaid, Thetis upon the prow.   (*HE* 239–40)

Underwriting this vicarious memory of Achilles' Nereid sea-mother, a
chorus of women in Euripides' *Iphigenia at Aulis* look out over the Greek
fleet at Aulis and report:

> These are Achilles' ships.
> On the prow of each
> A goddess sheds gold:
> Sea-spirits are cut in tiers of gold.[83]

Here, Helen's vision of the Greek ships as lotus resolves down to a single ship whose figurehead embodies Achilles' memories of Thetis. Relating the Thetis figurehead to an earlier, childhood eidolon of Thetis, Helen "reads" the Thetis effigies as mnemic symbols that both replace and represent Achilles' absent mother, in order to learn "the bitterness of his loss" and the fact that "he loved" (*HE* 260).[84]

Helen's vicarious recollection of Achilles' "bitterness" over the loss of his mother resurrects Melanie Klein's theory—so central to the "bitter jewel" sequence in "Tribute to the Angels"—of the sources of adult "bitterness of feeling" in the young child's reactions of "frustrated greed, resentment and hatred" toward its parents. In *Love, Hate and Reparation*, we recall, Klein argues that "bitterness of feeling, be it towards people or towards fate . . . is fundamentally established in childhood and may become strengthened or intensified in later life." To "prevent bitterness of feeling," we must be "able, deep in our unconscious minds, to clear our feelings to some extent towards our parents of grievances" and to forgive. Only then are we "able to love others in the true sense of the word" (*LHR* 118, 116, 119). It is important to reiterate here that the Kleinian child's grievances against its parents are often unjust when evaluated by adult standards. For the nursing infant, "the absence of satisfaction is felt as a positive evil" (*DPA* 97). As a result, the infant attributes the pain of its own hunger for its mother's milk, or its longing for her care, to the mother's active attempts to injure it.

In *Helen in Egypt*, the Kleinian child's frustrated longing for maternal nurturance gains representation in the figure of the hated, banishing mother: a Jocasta or a Hecuba who is not merely late for a feeding or preoccupied with another task, but actively wills her child's abandonment and ruin. Even Thetis, elsewhere so solicitous for her son's welfare, merges with this figure when she leaves the young Achilles to be raised by Chiron. In a carefully deployed series of repetitions, H.D. consistently links the young child's "bitter" feeling toward its absent mother, and its related experiences of endless "waiting" and of "nothingness," to all subsequent episodes of neglect or abandonment by a woman, and so traces a direct connection between Achilles' frustrated childhood attachment to Thetis and the wider Greek hatred of Helen.[85]

Focusing on the poem's first scene, where Achilles' attack on Helen follows her identification of the night-bird as sign of the goddess, Deborah Kloepfer describes *Helen in Egypt* as "the story of the confrontation between the daughter's attempt to speak the mother and the son's attempt to banish her" (p. 161). Yet the poem eventually reveals that the son's attempts to banish the mother proceed from his bitter memories of her own willingness to banish, or abandon, him. In this way, *Helen in Egypt* follows a hidden thread from the ostensible cause of war in male rivalry and violence to its secret cause in maternal neglect.[86] Save for Clytaemnestra and Demeter, who bitterly pit themselves against patriarchal rule when they lose their daughters to male treachery and death, all other women in the Greek world comply with adult male desire only to be condemned as bad mothers. Hecuba and Jocasta abandon their unlucky sons. Helen abandons Hermione in Sparta. Thetis leaves Achilles to be raised by Chiron and, at her father's bequest, instructs Helen to abandon her sister, ungrieved, to "a different story" (*HE* 97). Thus, early in "Leuke," when Helen must decide "who caused the war" at Troy, she makes a surprising accusation that is only apparently misplaced: "She [herself] has been blamed, Paris has been blamed but, fundamentally, it was the fault of Thetis, the mother of Achilles" (*HE* 111). Why? At the arranged marriage of Thetis and Peleus,

> the banquet, the wedding-feast
> lacked nothing, only one uninvited guest,
> Eris; so the apple was cast.   (*HE* 111)

Helen quickly drops this line of reasoning, but it comes back to haunt her, as the uninvited guest Eris returns as the banished son Paris, whose

> mother dreamed
> that he . . . would cause war,
> and war came.   (HE 110)

This displacement of blame from the son who apparently causes war to the mother who originally abandoned him informs still another layer of incident and imagery in the poem: the random but persistent collection of broken things. This collection begins with Thetis's promise of eternal life to Achilles, a promise she breaks when she allows him to die at Troy; it goes on to include the "severed" and "broken" weapons of war that mock Achilles' faith in the "unbreakable" "iron-ring" of the Greek leadership (*HE* 39, 243, 51); the "broken strap" on Achilles' sandal that fails to protect his vulnerable heel (*HE* 54, 59–60); a second "broken sandal" that the limping Helen bends to fix on the burning stairs of Troy (*HE* 123); and finally the "broken rung" of the ladder that hinders Helen's solitary efforts to pull herself from the river Styx (*HE* 267).

All of these memories of a failed hold or bond point back to a flaw or fracture in the mother's pre-oedipal bond with her child, that inevitable moment of separation and differentiation that the lotus hieroglyph, merging child and womb, attempts to deny. The child's reluctant recognition of this inevitability lies behind the peculiar power of the sea-mother, Thetis, who is worshipped with a devotion strengthened by poverty and want. Where Aphrodite commands the world's riches, Thetis is

> the richer for poorer worshippers,
> for meaner offerings,
> a filigree ring of no worth,
>
> a broken oar, a snapped anchor-chain.   (*HE* 281)

As if trying to return to her the small child left behind by its powerful mother, her worshippers offer her "grains / left in an emptied sack," "scattered shreds of the sandal-bark": "the simple magic coming / from something lost or left over" (*HE* 280–81). And while the exact repetition in the Isis-name suggests an unbroken flow, the "secret, / unpronounceable name" of Thetis is

> two syllables, yes, like the Isis-name,
> but broken, not quite the same,
> breathed differently

by the "sleepless child" who crouches alone in "Chiron's cave" (*HE* 279).

When Helen speaks this secret name on the desolate beach, she unwittingly awakens in Achilles the "memory forgotten" of his broken attachment to his mother and of the eidolons that commemorate his love for her. With the recovery of her own "memory forgotten" of Hermione's abandonment, Helen can finally afford to acknowledge the depth of Achilles' repressed longing for Thetis. Yet this knowledge, rather than exposing the wrongs or failures of women in an irrevocable past, becomes the occasion for a restoration of the pre-oedipal bond itself and a magical mending of all divisions within the family. For evidence that the broken ties of the Greek oedipal family have indeed been mended, Helen points to the mother's own ability to grieve for the past sufferings of her children. In doing so, she returns to the example of Mary Magdalene in "The Flowering of the Rod," reassigning the Kleinian child's acts of reparation—in which mourning for the lost mother miraculously restores her—to the mother herself.

The Magdalene who vows to "weep bitterly, / bitterly" (*T* 135) finds a precursor in Isis, who signals her abundant love for her brother and lover by the abundant tears she pours out at his death. As they flood the Nile, these tears water the new crops and set in motion the rebirth of the lost Osiris as a newborn Horus.[87] At the start of *Helen in Egypt*, grief sets Helen's own work of reconstructing the legend in motion.[88] Achilles remembers the dead—"my children, my legions" (*HE* 17)—by sorrowing over them, and his intense anger at Helen over the loss of his men seems to stem, in part, from the fear that these losses mean so little to her that she can simply "forget" them (*HE* 20). But the act that most incites Achilles to fury—Helen's attempt to blacken her face with ash from the fire—turns out to signal her assumption not of the witch's guise, as he suspects at the time, but rather the guise of grief (*HE* 16). In *The Iliad*, Achilles blackens his own face in mourning when he learns of Patroclus's death:

> A black stormcloud of pain shrouded Akhilleus,
> On his bowed head he scattered dust and ash
> in handfuls and befouled his beautiful face,
> letting black ash sift on his fragrant khiton.[89]

Once again, H.D. suggests that ancient Greek culture unwittingly preserves a knowledge of the Egyptian afterlife in figurative signs that must be literalized if their magical powers of resurrection are to be restored. For just as Helen's vision of the Greek ships in lily formation literalizes Achilles' Euripidean figure of the slain Greek host as the "flower / of all time," her transformation into "an inked-in shadow," "Isis, forever with that Child, / the Hawk Horus" (*HE* 23), literalizes this Homeric scene of mourning, making the Greek woman in blackface into an actual Egyptian. Helen's darkened visage then serves as a second global image that "incarnates" the poem's project to reconstruct the oedipal family. With this finely condensed gesture, Helen comes into her "racial inheritance" of ancestral memories, where to remember, to mourn, and to become a black woman—to become Isis—fuse into a single, redemptive act. For it is Isis, divine peacemaker and re-memberer, who in mourning restores the dead to life. By the end of the poem, Helen realizes that Thetis's grief for lost sons also spills over enemy lines:

> she fought for the Greeks, they said,
> Achilles' mother, but Thetis mourned
> like Hecuba, for Hector dead.   (*HE* 296)

This grief for Achilles' greatest foe repeats and justifies Achilles' own mourning for Patroclus and his other "children," and performs the final transformation of the destructive oedipal mother, Hecuba, into a grieving Isis.

With the mending force of Thetis's grief, the bitterness of Achilles' loss can at once be retrieved *from* history and negated *as* history, as the stories of abandoned children give way to the recovery of an eternal attachment between mother and child. Once the memory of this bond is restored to consciousness, the social bonds between men ("sworn brother and lover" [*HE* 4]), which underwrite Freud's and Eisenstein's ideal of a new society, dissolve before the prior claims of the mother. Thus, Thetis lets Achilles die avenging his male lover at Troy only to resurrect him in Egypt as a heterosexual pacifist newly committed to the reconstituted nuclear family.[90] In this way, the lotus of Helen's vision on the beach finally serves as the transcendental guarantee of a maternal love that both abrogates and appeases the "bitterness" of Achilles' martial and mortal experience.[91]

Combing the Desolate Beach

and Crete inherited the Labyrinth,
and Crete-Egypt must be slain,

conquered or overthrown
    —H.D., "Leuke"

Where Isis and Horus search out the dismembered limbs of the father's body, H.D. reads ancient Greek texts for dispersed traces of the mother's presence. Like the survivor "on a beach" who searches

for a pearl, a bead,

a comb, a cup, a bowl
half-filled with sand,
after a wreck,

H.D. "remember[s] these small reliques" in an act of mourning for the lost mother that brings about her miraculous recovery (*HE* 164). Once brought into significant juxtaposition in her own montage narrative, Euripides' images of the lotus flower and golden sea-goddesses and Homer's image of the blackened face of grief release the "memory forgotten" (*HE* 304) of the mother's own powers of mourning, resurrection, and reconciliation, a memory grounded in Egyptian myth and retained in marginalized and distorted forms throughout the Western literary tradition. Assigning "forgotten," "lost or left over" traces of the appeasing mother their proper place and value in Western memory, H.D. conflates Freud's reading strategy, which searches out "what has been suppressed and disavowed" in an obscured past; Eisenstein's strategy of montage reordering, which "gather[s] up the disintegrated event once more into one whole, but in *our* aspect"; and Klein's strategy of reparation, in which the child "may soon build up phantasies that he is putting the bits together again and repairing" his mother's body (*LHR* 61). Using all three strategies simultaneously, she creates a version of Helen's own story that is simultaneously the restoration of a lost original and a revision of all its extant derivatives.[92]

Yet before we take this celebration of the mother's power as evidence of a feminist agenda, we might remember Denise Riley's suspicion that "there can be no version of 'motherhood' *as such* which can be deployed to construct a radical politics" (p. 196). Close inspection of the terms on which H.D. "reinstates" mothers in her poem confirms Riley's point: appeals to the abstract value of motherhood tend to work against mothers' own complex interests and needs. Indeed, in the case of *Helen in Egypt*, the very appeal to the value of motherhood is inseparable from the charges laid against actual mothers. In her evolving accounts of infant development, Melanie Klein consistently states that her discussions of the persecuting mother pertain to the infant's psychotic phantasy life, and not to actual atrocities on the mother's part. H.D. preserves this qualification in her focus on ways in which unconscious fantasies distort her characters' perceptions of the past. Despite their quarrels in other areas, however, the poem's characters reach surprising unanimity in their willingness to blame the Trojan war on maternal negligence. Even if we are to attribute the recurring figure of the hated, banishing mother to the infant's irrational sense of abandonment, why does no character emerge to tell the mother's story: her regret at forced separation or inadequate resources, or her anger at the constant claims on her attention, the curtailment of her independence, the culturally enforced expectations that she alone do the work of mothering and that her own desires never outweigh those of her children?

A trace of this story can be found in the poem. In fact, we might tentatively cite it as the poem's very occasion. For Helen's decision to leave Hermione for Paris's company and Thetis's decision to leave Achilles to return to the sea parallel H.D.'s own decision to secure time for travel and writing by handing over many of the duties of raising Perdita to friends, relatives, and professional caretakers.[93] But it is the very fact that H.D. chooses to "reinstate" or rehabilitate mothers so like herself, and on terms that close off their independence for the renewal of pre-oedipal bonds, which makes her poem's "reconstruction of the legend" so alarming. For if Helen and Thetis begin the poem as hated outlaw and forgotten outcast, they end up being "reinstated" on terms that glorify the very roles they initially rejected. In this regard, the poem's undeclared project to bring all wandering mothers home to roost is disturbingly akin to the ancient Egyptians' cure for hysteria—in an etiology and therapy for the complaint that the Greeks would later copy, ancient Egyptians ascribed hysterical suffering to the unhappy migrations of the womb, which, dissatisfied with its place in the body, seeks out other ports. The cure entailed luring it back to the pelvic region with the "precious and sweet-smelling substances" it craved.[94]

In the unbending symmetry between the womb that wanders from its proper place, the Egyptian flower figure that wanders from its proper meaning, and the mother who wanders from her proper function—a symmetry met and matched by the poem's project to restore all strays to the tether—the deeply conservative contours of Helen's reconstruction of the legend emerge. Thus, the Thetis we are finally asked to celebrate is a mother by rape who caters to her adult son's wishes, executes her father's will, and censors the memory of the rebel queen Clytaemnestra. This modern-day goddess presents little challenge to the Victorian white middle-class norms of ideal womanhood with which H.D. was raised,[95] and we might well complain with Paris that "this is the old story, / no new Euphorion" were it not for a final twist suggestively marking the poem as a work of the 1950's (*HE* 217).

Concluding *Helen in Egypt* with Achilles' lonely thoughts of Thetis before a Homeric sea, H.D. forcibly excludes the characters most consistently linked with Egypt from the final picture of Greek mother-love that it has taken Egypt to make visible and legible. Just before Helen herself disappears from the poem, she aggressively dissolves her bond with Paris. H.D.'s unsatisfying explanation for Helen's late show of hostility—"in this last phase or mood, it seems inevitable and perhaps wholly human for Helen to turn on her Trojan lover" (*HE* 299)—begs the question of Paris's "inevitable" dismissal. What has he done—or undone—to deserve it? Paris, the son newly celebrated as "incarnate, manifest Egypt," was, we recall, originally the son who "would undo / the work of his father, Priam" (*HE* 185, 112). Banished from the family and from memory for this very reason, he returns to consciousness when Helen agrees to suppress her sister's memory at the end of "Pallinode." Paris is also the last to invoke Clytaemnestra's name, bidding Helen in "Eidolon" to

> remember Clytaemnestra's
> last words to Orestes,
>
> *remember Iphigenia.*   (*HE* 219)

His warning comes after Helen herself fails to answer Theseus's parting query in "Leuke":

> you sought
> (do you still seek?)
> Clytaemnestra in Egypt.   (*HE* 188)

And it is Clytaemnestra, "child of darkness" and "shadow of us all" (*HE* 187, 2), whose angry violence to her king and lord the poem as a whole must struggle to remember and forget.

Linked to each other and to Egypt throughout the poem, Paris and Clytaemnestra pose threats to the father's life and power that contradict the terms of Helen's visionary reform of the oedipal family. Yet while their crimes against the Crown evince a resistance to ancient Egypt's promise of familial peace, such violence also evinces the resistance of modern Egypt, which was to secure its full independence from Britain while H.D. was writing her poem. Jane Marcus reminds us that Virginia Woolf's grandfather, James K. Stephen, was

> the architect of an ideology of oppression that used the model of patriarchal domestic tyranny as a basis for colonial imperialism. . . . The press called him "Mr. Mother-Country Stephen," for it was he who coined the phrase "the mother country." It was he who made the policies that bound the British colonies in a domestic metaphor that was to determine their relations for more than a hundred years, to yoke whole nations in a position from which to rebel was to insult sacred motherhood itself. The rebel was then a moral outcast, a bad son.[96]

In the long reach of James Stephen's rhetoric, Egypt's efforts to secure national autonomy in the years following World War II (efforts spearheaded, in significant part, by the Moslem Brotherhood) function as an extratextual version of Paris's and Clytaemnestra's own roles as "bad son" and treacherous wife who work to bring down the father's house. Moreover, the very threat of hostile or severed relations between the "mother country" of the British Empire and her colonial children replays at the level of global politics the disintegration of pre-oedipal bonds that Helen seeks to repair in H.D.'s poem. Where Helen is committed to recovering the memory of Egypt as an eternally gentle and conciliatory land, which welcomes the opportunity to foster its Western guests and works tirelessly to promote familial peace, Paris and Clytaemnestra give voice to an Egypt at once wronged and rebellious, whose story parallels Egypt's modern history of successful revolution, the inauguration of an independent government, and the mandated evacuation of British troops. When read against these contemporary challenges to the British Empire's long "family" history, H.D.'s repeated need to ban Paris and Clytaemnestra from the poem's project of familial redemption begins to look like a displaced attempt to "banish the memory" of modern Egypt (*HE* 13).

At one point in the poem, however, H.D.'s portrayal of a gentler, kinder Egypt itself breaks down, and Egypt emerges as "an enemy to be conquered" (*HE* 181). Near the end of her stay with Theseus, Helen abruptly announces that

> Crete inherited the Labyrinth,
> and Crete-Egypt must be slain,
>
> conquered or overthrown. (*HE* 182)

In an accompanying headnote, H.D. instructs us to take Helen's surprisingly violent remark figuratively. Recalling Theseus's earlier equation of Egypt with the Cretan Minotaur and with "Death," the headnote identifies the "enemy to be conquered" in the guise of "Crete-Egypt" as "Death" (*HE* 168–69, 181–82). This explicit link between Egypt and death gives voice to a fantasy of Egypt sharply opposed to the peaceful land associated with Isis's and Horus's powers of life that has preoccupied us for most of this chapter. Yet in doing so, it makes audible a deep equivocation as to Egypt's symbolic status running right through the poem.

This equivocation can be attributed to Egypt's dual status in ancient myth as a land of plenty, associated with the life-giving mother, Isis, and a land of the dead, associated with the returning father, Osiris. At first glance, H.D. seems to replicate these associations in her poem when she aligns Helen with Isis while assigning to Achilles Osiris's role as lord of the dead and Pluto's more malevolent role as leader of "a death-cult" that drags its initiates "further and further underground" (*HE* 28, 196, 216). But Helen's constant ascription of Achilles' violence to his role as a Greek "war-Lord" (*HE* 74) would seem to establish Greece, rather than Egypt, as the prior source of his murderous aggression. In this line-up, Greece takes over the associations of patriarchal violence, treachery, and "desolation," while Egypt reasserts itself as a place of maternal "enchantment" (a version of the "sea-enchantment" associated with Thetis) and rebirth. Standing in the Amen-temple, Helen hopes to

> take our treasure,
>
> the wisdom of Amen and Thoth,
> back to the islands,
> that enchantment may find a place
>
> where desolation ruled,
> and a warrior race,
> Agamemnon and Menelaus.   (*HE* 89–90)

Yet just as Helen wakes up in "Eidolon" to the possibility that "the script was a snare" (*HE* 220), the patness of this last opposition, so complimentary to women, turns out to be a trap luring the flattered mother back to a scene of past wrongdoing. For "desolation" derives from the Latin *desolare*—"to abandon, desert"—and so, once again, points past the desolation of male rule to the oedipal mother's forgotten crimes against her abandoned son.[97] Arriving on Egypt's own "desolate beach," Achilles charges Isis herself with the crimes of the oedipal mother when he suspects her emblematic bird of being "a carrion creature" (*HE* 13, 66). Despite Helen's protest that the sacred vulture is "no death-symbol but a life-

symbol," she too later speculates that Achilles may have "strangled her /
and flung her to the vultures" during their first night on the beach (*HE*
13, 19). This lurid possibility underlies Helen's identification with her sis-
ter's daughter, Iphigenia; just as Artemis had demanded the "white
throat" of the young girl at Aulis, Helen repeatedly suspects Achilles of
"promis[ing]" her own throat to his mother, Thetis (*HE* 244, 270).[98]

Helen's fear that Thetis wants her dead is puzzling in a poem so ready
to celebrate the mother's powers of life. With this fear creeps in the sug-
gestion that H.D. cultivates the loving and bountiful Isis as a magical an-
tidote to the daughter's, rather than the son's, experience of maternal
aggression and neglect, much as she cultivates the Isis myth as a whole as
a magical antidote to the oedipal conflict between father and son.[99] Al-
though the story of the daughter's desolation over the loss or failure of the
mother-daughter bond is directly told only intermittently, it makes good
on the poem's wider insistence that grief propels Helen's attempts to re-
member the legends of the nuclear family in a way that charges of the
mother's inadequate ministrations to her sons probably cannot. For unlike
the son, whose early demands on the mother are rarely countered by the
later expectation that he assume the mother's place, the daughter must rec-
oncile childhood feelings of frustrated longing for the mother with an
adult appreciation of the mother's own frustration before both the relent-
lessness of her child's needs and the wider cultural insistence that the
child's desires should take precedence over her own. To say that the daugh-
ter must reconcile these competing claims is not to say that she can. This,
then, is where H.D.'s story of Helen—who fears maternal "reject[ion]"
(*HE* 117) but also longs to escape from the pallid pleasures of Spartan mar-
riage and motherhood—takes on the sharp poignancy of a grief that only
deep ambivalence can muster.

We might assign the poem's contradictory portrayals of Egypt as a
benevolent land of life, made rich and peaceful through maternal solici-
tude, and as a malevolent land of desolation and death, born of maternal
rejection, to a related ambivalence on the daughter's part, in which she
simultaneously faults the mother with inadequacy and defends her from
this grievance with demonstrations of her abundance.[100] Yet it is curious
that at the only point in the poem in which Helen explicitly revenges her-
self on Egypt's malevolent aspect, it is in the guise of the daughter, rather
than the mother, that she condemns "Crete-Egypt" to death. For when
Helen tells Theseus that

> Crete inherited the Labyrinth,
> and Crete-Egypt must be slain,
>
> conquered or overthrown   (*HE* 182),

she alludes to his own earlier charge that "Crete-Egypt" is guilty of the (god-)daughter's illicit acts of seduction:

> Crete would seduce Greece,
> Crete inherited the Labyrinth from Egypt,
> the ancient Nile would undermine
>
> the fabric of Parnassus.   (*HE* 169)

Lest we mistake the nature of Theseus's charges, another headnote instructs us to take them figuratively as well: "The mountain, the reality, Theseus seems to argue, must recall us from the dream, 'the opiate of non-remembrance.' The magic of Crete was inherited from Egypt. Parnassus, or Greek creative thought, must not be entangled in the Labyrinth or dissolved or washed away by 'the ancient Nile'" (*HE* 169). Yet this patient translation of Helen's and Theseus's intricately figured comments into the advice that the conscious (and creative) mind must resist the fatal attractions of dream seems oddly beside the point, particularly in a poem that sounds the irrational thought processes of unconscious fantasy for its methods of social reform. Moreover, both Theseus's and Helen's choices of metaphor for an abstract struggle between "thought" and "dream" are so highly overdetermined that the figural coding of their remarks tends to overpower the indicated message.

Drawing on a discourse of war, empire, revolution, and the antagonism between West and East, Helen's demand for Greek retribution on a subversive Egypt would seem to recall the very situation in modern Egypt that the rest of the poem buries under fantasies of an eternal land of healing, hospitality, and familial peace. Similarly, the fear that a treacherous Nile will "entangle" Parnassus recalls Clytaemnestra's murderous work with a crimson tapestry, "Asiatic" in its opulence,[101] and Thetis's claim that "a woman's wiles are a net" (*HE* 93). And Theseus's own charge that "Crete would seduce Greece" recalls not only the Athenian hero's desire for the slant-eyed child Helen, but also Freud's conclusion that the "dreams" of female hysterics, and not the "reality" of their fathers' actions, lie behind their childhood memories of incest. In the relay from Theseus's remarks to those of his adulterous god-daughter, the figure of the dangerous seductress herself becomes "an enemy to be conquered," and the malevolent face of Egypt peers forth not as a bad mother but as a bad wife and/or daughter.

As H.D.'s efforts to stave it off suggest, a literal reading of Egypt (rather than "Death") as the seductive enemy who must be conquered cannot be consciously admitted into the poem. In an unconscious or repressed register, however—the register in which Helen's own literalizing readings take place—a wish to defeat or punish modern Egypt for its successful revolution against the British Empire may hereby gain representation. Burying this literal reading under a figurative one, H.D. further obscures its possibility by supplying an imaginary crime to justify Helen's retributive violence, much as the hysteric supplies "false connections" to replace the missing logical links in his or her life story. Thus, Theseus's fantasy of a seductive Crete-Egypt who would "undermine the fabric of Parnassus" functions as a criminal version not of modern Egypt, whose current relations with the British are decidedly noncooperative, but of its more hospitable, ancient counterpart. Indeed, its crime inheres in the fact that it has become *too* hospitable, too inviting. But what kind of seductress proves so dangerous that she "must be slain"? The witch, burnt to death in the United States' own colonial period for reputed crimes of sexual excess and communion with the devil.

The witch enjoys a long history in H.D.'s writing as a figure for the female visionary and/or sexual (often lesbian) pariah.[102] As we have seen in exploring the character of H.D.'s Mary Magdalene, Freud follows Charcot in identifying the women condemned to death in Europe's witch-hunts as hysterics, and the states of daemonical "possession and ecstasy" ascribed to them as hysterical symptoms ("Seventeenth-Century" 72). Achilles, we recall, tries to strangle Helen after she blackens her face with a burnt stick, crying:

> what sort of enchantment is this?
> what art will you wield with a fagot?
> are you Hecate? are you a witch?   (*HE* 16)

In the main action of the poem, Helen successfully counters Achilles' charge by hysterically aligning her blackened face with the redemptive maternal grief of Isis. But that other hysteric—the seductive and/or rebellious daughter who appears as Hecate, malevolent goddess of the night—persists as a threat of what Helen may, again, become. To counter this largely internal threat, Helen attempts to locate it outside herself. Her fantasy of slaying the seductive "Crete-Egypt" not only shifts the blame for the (god-)father's possible sexual crimes against the (god-)daughter, but also indirectly clears Helen herself of the charges of wantonness she faces from the Greek host, as well as the more deeply repressed charge that she desires to follow her dark (and possibly lesbian) sister Clytaemnestra into violent revolt. Instead, H.D. assigns to Helen the role of condemning *another* "wanton" to death—the wanton who is simultaneously "Crete-Egypt" and the "black-Calcutta self" of her own suppressed rebelliousness.[103]

Yet Helen's attempts to distinguish herself from the poem's rebel element must inevitably backfire. Her fantasy of slaying a subversive Egyptian seductress simultaneously returns H.D.'s celebratory representations of hysteria to their violently misogynist antecedents in the witch-hunts of an earlier age, and thus subverts the poem's own narrative strategies for Western (and white) women's "reinstatement." The patent futility of Helen's attempt to assert her own innocence by scapegoating the very Egyptian persona on which her project of social reconstruction depends should alert us to wider problems implicit in H.D.'s use of an ancient Egyptian mythography and setting. In literalizing Freudian figures linking ancient Egyptian and pre-Hellenic civilizations with the unconscious, female sexuality, and the pre-oedipal phase, H.D. maps sites of women's reprieve from and/or resistance to their designated positions in the oedipal family romance onto a land whose current history is one of revolt, even as she denies that there is any cause for unhappiness by restoring in that land all the lost pleasures of the pre-oedipal phase. Yet the ease with which this poetic Egypt splits into a land of maternal plenitude and a land made desolate by maternal neglect suggests that the daughter's attempts to escape from the plot of the father's desire are not likely to be well served by her nostalgic return to an infantile dependency on the mother. Here, the poem's very celebration of maternal nurturance, solicitude, and pacifism does not function as a contented testimony to remembered pleasures so much as it articulates a fantasy of what H.D. herself had yet to receive from the nuclear family[104]—a fantasy that, for all its poignancy, is quickly absorbed into the antifeminist impulse to hold the mother accountable for all the family's ills.

Meanwhile, in the poem's insistence on the adequacy, even virtue, of Helen's reconstruction of the nuclear family, despite the paucity of its provisions for women, two alternatives are lost: contesting the father's position as patriarch and the mother's position as sole nurturer, and exiting the family altogether. H.D. fully explored both these alternatives in setting up the terms of her "menage" with Bryher, Kenneth Macpherson, and Perdita after the collapse of her marriage with Richard Aldington. Why then do they fail to gain a hearing in *Helen in Egypt*? One answer would lie in the possible resurgence of H.D.'s maternal "guilt," like that she experienced in her analysis with Walter Schmideberg. The growing cultivation in postwar Britain of John Bowlby's thoughts on the necessity of "keeping mothers in the home" would provide a context for understanding both the timing and the terms of such a resurgence of maternal guilt in the early 1950's.[105] I would suggest, however, that the contemporary revolution in Egypt provides another possible source for H.D.'s conservatism here. In provoking the rhetorical fusion of the breakup of the traditional nuclear family with the breakup of the British Empire, this revolution may have threatened H.D. with a wider set of implications for her experiments in family living than she was prepared to meet.

On at least some level, her investment in empire was financial. It cost a great deal of money to set up residences in two countries, travel freely, pay for child care, and work without wages during the most active years of H.D.'s dual career as writer and mother. While Friedman points out that H.D. insisted on paying her own way, accepting Bryher's financial aid only in the form of gifts, these gifts could be substantial and the money that paid for them derived from Britain's largest shipping fortune, acquired during the height of its naval power. Furthermore, there is some indication that Bryher either invested or encouraged H.D. to invest gifts of money back into the British Empire.[106] But the larger part of H.D.'s investment in empire may well have been artistic. While her 1927 novel *Palimpsest* critically equates imperial rule with men's sexual possession of women,[107] another long-standing strain in H.D.'s writing uncritically figures artistic ambition as a species of colonial exploration and conquest. Given this figural pattern (which I will outline in Chapter 3), H.D. may have viewed the postwar period of decolonization as a threat not so much to the value of her financial securities as to her status as a modernist epic poet.[108] Perhaps, in the end, it is this threat that lies behind Helen's fantasy that an unruly Egypt will "undermine the fabric of Parnassus"—that lofty home of the Muses at "the center of the world"[109] that H.D. equates with "Greek creative thought."

Nevertheless, while it is possible to establish Bryher's anxiety over the emerging collapse of the British Empire in the early 1950's with a good deal of certainty, my attempts to ascertain H.D.'s response to these events remain speculative, spun like her own narrative from stray hairs of evidence, mislaid details, faint anomalies and enigmas of the plot. At present, there is simply not enough evidence available from this period for us to know in any detail how H.D. viewed the disjunction she clearly recognized between modern Egypt and "my Egypt of Karnak and the Tomb of 1923." By the end of the decade, however, she would revisit this disjunction between modern history and ancient myth as she began to write *Hermetic Definition*. H.D.'s deeply ambivalent attitudes toward empire form a sustained and explicit object of self-inquiry in this last poem, as Lionel Durand's involvement in the Algerian War prompts her to reconsider the relationship between her habitual use of the modernist "mythical method" and her contemporary moment of African decolonization. Chapter 3 takes the changing course and context of this ambivalence as its major focus.

"That Memnon in the desert"

~ Modernism and Decolonization in
Hermetic Definition

Rethinking the Mythical Method

from chaos making order
—Virginia Woolf, *The Waves*

In *Hermetic Definition*, the last poem of a long career, H.D. records her
highly fantasized relationships with two men: Lionel Durand, the French
journalist who interviewed her for *Newsweek* in April of 1960, and St.-
John Perse, the distinguished French poet who was honored along with
H.D. at the award ceremony of the American Academy of Arts and Let-
ters in May of the same year. Critics to date have focused on the poem's
internal features, whether they have studied its figures of artistic creation
and its place in a European tradition of mystical love poetry, or concen-
trated on its politics of race and gender.[1] With the recovery of its historical
context, however, *Hermetic Definition* emerges as a uniquely situated and
deeply self-reflexive account of three writers whose lives were variously
enmeshed in the rise of modernism, the history of European imperialism,
and the contemporary moment of African decolonization. Even brief bio-
graphical sketches of the figures H.D. draws on in her poem emphasize
this point.

To begin with the familiar facts: H.D., born in the United States in
1886 and educated there, became a British citizen in 1913; by 1914, she had
emerged as the leading Imagist in a movement that greatly influenced the
rise of Anglo-American modernism. From 1911 to 1945, she maintained

a series of residences in London and Switzerland and traveled extensively in Europe, the United States, the Mediterranean, and Egypt on a British passport. After World War II she took up residence in Switzerland and in 1958 she reclaimed U.S. citizenship. Her contemporary Alexis St.-Léger Léger, who used the pen name St.-John Perse, was born to French planters on an island off Guadeloupe in 1887. He was educated in France, served as a French diplomat in China for five years and as Secretary General of the French Foreign Office for eight years. T. S. Eliot introduced Perse to an English-speaking audience with his 1930 translation of *Anabase*. In his preface, Eliot describes this poem, which would also strongly influence British and American modernists, as "a series of images of migration, of conquest of vast spaces in Asiatic wastes, of destruction and foundation of cities and civilizations of any races or epochs of the ancient East."[2] Exiled by the Vichy government during World War II, Perse took up residence in the United States. Like H.D., Perse was an accomplished and prolific poet, but unlike her, he enjoyed considerable fame throughout his lifetime. Lionel Durand, the son of a prewar Haitian ambassador to France, was born in Haiti in 1922 and was educated in France, Germany, and England. During World War II he fought in the French Resistance. Accepting news assignments in the United States, France, the Middle East, Africa, and the Soviet Union, he became French Bureau Chief for *Newsweek*, and died while covering the Algerian War before H.D. finished her poem. Durand's own ties to modernism may have influenced his original decision to interview H.D. upon the 1960 publication of *Bid Me to Live*. In his *Newsweek* obituary, Durand is described as "a painter of quality" and a close friend of Pablo Picasso.[3]

The biographies of H.D., Perse, and Durand help to underscore the extreme complexity and diversity of the three historical formations—modernism, imperialism, and decolonization—in which they were each to varying degrees caught up. In drawing on these biographies in her poem, H.D. engages a network of events and attitudes that cannot be explained according to any one analytical system, but instead, as Biddy Martin and Chandra Talpade Mohanty have noted, participate in "multiple, overlapping, intersecting systems or relations . . . that implicate the individual in contradictory ways" (p. 209). In an essay on H.D.'s relationship to the Harlem Renaissance, Susan Stanford Friedman opened up scholarly discussion of H.D.'s attempts to address the "intersecting systems" of race and gender oppression in her literary writing. She argues that H.D. practiced a "modernism of the margins rather than the reactionary center," and that her "personal experience with the Harlem Renaissance played a key role in deepening and broadening her early feminism into a fully progressive modernism based in an identification with all the people who exist as 'the scattered remnant' at the fringes of culture."[4] Friedman carefully grounds this argument in a close examination of H.D.'s letters, fiction, and film work from the late twenties and early thirties. When Rachel DuPlessis applies the terms of Friedman's analysis to a reading of *Hermetic Definition*, however, she fails to provide either textual or historical substantiation for her claims that the poem is "a bold story of sexual desire not incidentally for a black man, a revelation of doubled possibilities for marginality and negotiation with Otherness to suggest a heterodox unification of those *en marge*."[5]

In 1984, two years before these arguments were published, bell hooks published *Feminist Theory from Margin to Center*, in which she attempted to expose and displace white women's self-positioning at the center of U.S. feminism's second wave. Both Friedman and DuPlessis can be understood in these essays to be applying hooks's insights in an admirable attempt to imagine how white women might situate ourselves in a decentering feminism. They in effect close over, however, the very historical moment of black feminist protest which shapes the terms of their argument when they present H.D.'s "modernism of the margins" as the spontaneous and historically prior fulfillment of a political vision that hooks had in fact criticized white feminists for lacking. Furthermore, in setting up margin and center as strict alternatives, they lose hooks's important point that the logic of "rather than," of either/or, governs the relations between margin and center only if one stands exclusively at the center.[6]

Growing up at the margins, hooks asserts that she has learned to look "both from the outside in and from the inside out"—"a mode of seeing unknown to most of our oppressors."[7] Similarly, in *Hermetic Definition*, H.D. plants herself at various points in relation to the literal schemes of center/margin or inside/outside that she repeatedly uses to organize the sexual, racial, mythical, and journalistic strands informing her fantasies of Durand and Perse. hooks pointedly defines her own "oppositional world view"—a redeemed version of W. E. B. Du Bois's "double-consciousness"—as a source not of internal conflict or self-doubt but of a saving "sense of wholeness."[8] In contrast, H.D. portrays the experience of looking in both directions across the inside/outside divide as the scene of an ambivalent recognition that her contemporary moment of decolonization "implicates her in contradictory ways." In doing so, she appears to be staging the realization, articulated by Jacqueline Rose, that "protest . . . is not incompatible with desire" and "being a victim does not stop you from identifying with the aggressor. . . . Wherever it is that subjects find themselves historically, this will not produce any one, unequivocal, identification as its logical effect."[9]

Here, Rose draws directly on Freud's account of the numerous, con-

flicting identifications set in motion by fantasy, a structure of thought that
Jean Laplanche and J.-B. Pontalis define as "a scenario with multiple en-
tries," "not the object of desire, but its setting." Rose departs from Freud,
however, to argue that "fantasy operates inside historical process," taking
historical formations and events as its points of departure and destina-
tion.[10] The inside/outside schemes of *Hermetic Definition* provide a setting
for several scenarios of multiple entry, scenarios we can follow Rose in
characterizing as at once sexual, literary, and, in the widest sense, histor-
ical. Using erotic fantasy to fracture her position vis-à-vis modernism,
imperialism, and decolonization, H.D. exceeds the fixity of political al-
legiance that feminist critics have claimed for her literary writing. Yet in
charting her own variable and contradictory patterns of desire and iden-
tification, she does not abandon political commitment altogether. Rather,
she uses writing to achieve a politically informed self-reflexivity. This self-
reflexivity, in pointing up the features of her ambivalence, also appears to
underwrite H.D.'s final rejection of the epiphanic strategies of resolution
and closure with which she has attempted to transcend conflict and am-
bivalence in her previous modernist poetry.

Among the several conflicts in *Hermetic Definition* that the inside/out-
side scheme articulates is a crisis in method. This crisis emerges from the
struggle between H.D.'s opposing impulses to mythologize her relations
with Durand and Perse, and to provide journalistic accounts of their actual
lives and encounters. Durand's career as a news journalist and Perse's ca-
reer as an epic poet provide obvious points of reference for this struggle.
But in the years leading up to the writing of *Hermetic Definition*, H.D. her-
self repeatedly shifts between journalistic and mythological modes in her
poetry. After the elaborate mythologizing of her personal history in *Helen
in Egypt*, she turns to a hybrid style in *Vale Ave*, weaving together reli-
gious, historical, and biographical characters to tell the story of two lovers
"meeting and parting" through history.[11] In *Sagesse*, she engages in a kind
of spiritual journalism, and wavers over the respective capacities of factual
reporting and reverie to achieve the status of "authentic prayer" (*HD* 35).
She resumes mythic masking in *Winter Love*, calling on the figures of
Odysseus and Helen of Troy to retell the story of her relationship with
Ezra Pound.

In *Hermetic Definition*, H.D. brings her journalistic and mythic modes
into direct competition in her poetry for the first time. Returning to Ei-
senstein's concept of conflictual montage, she organizes much of her
poem around a series of stylistically discordant portraits of Lionel Du-
rand's body and person. Just as Eisenstein uses "montage by conflict" to
generate in the spectator a "higher dimension" of critical consciousness,
H.D.'s discordant portraits of Durand generate a space of inquiry into the

political implications of her conflicting poetic modes. While in *Helen in Egypt* reference to modern revolution rarely disturbs H.D.'s mythic representation of ancient Egypt, in the original draft of *Hermetic Definition* the contemporary facts of war in Africa, recorded in Durand's stories for *Newsweek*, directly and repeatedly impinge on H.D.'s mythological fantasies. At these moments, she seems to struggle with the possibility that her strategies of modernist myth-making may themselves be implicated in the very violence of colonialism and decolonization that she would use such myth-making to resolve or mask.[12]

Nor is it an accident that the dichotomy of inside/outside or center/ margin should provide the terms through which this crisis in method is played out. T. S. Eliot implicitly calls upon the same dichotomy to justify modernism's "mythical method" in his influential essay of 1923, "*Ulysses*, Order, and Myth"; he states, "In using the myth, in manipulating a continuous parallel between contemporaneity and antiquity, Mr. Joyce is pursuing a method which others must pursue after him. . . . [This method] is simply a way of controlling, of ordering, of giving a shape and a significance to the immense panorama of futility and anarchy which is contemporary history."[13] In Eliot's account, contemporary history is a vast, featureless "panorama of . . . anarchy," more evocative of the primeval waters of Genesis than of any landscape of modernity. But both Eliot's terms and his tone are suspiciously akin to British imperialist rhetoric of this period.[14] Virginia Woolf appears to comment on this resemblance directly in her 1931 novel *The Waves*, where the Australian businessman, Louis, reconstitutes Eliot's panorama of history as "the far parts of the world" "ordered" by the self-centering "I, and again I, and again I" of imperial Britain: "I roll the dark before me, spreading commerce where there was chaos in the far parts of the world. If I press on, from chaos making order, I shall find myself where Chatham stood, and Pitt, Burke, and Sir Robert Peel."[15]

Here, Woolf's irony sets her securely outside the faith in a centralized order that underpins Eliot's endorsement of the mythical method. In contrast, H.D.'s use of the inside/outside scheme in *Hermetic Definition* serves not so much to condemn the mythical method as to dramatize a struggle between competing loyalties. Furthermore, at a crucial juncture in this struggle—in her editing of the poem's original draft—H.D. submits her poem to a second logic of exclusion that upholds the mythical method against an opposing impulse to expose its limits. In the poem's final version, she retains fantasies portraying Durand as a Lawrentian "Dark God," "an ordinary man," and a literary critic, but cuts all explicit reference to his work as a political journalist and to the Algerian War.

The Jungle of World Events

Lionel—that lion padded cat of the jungle, the jungle of the world and world events.

—H.D., 1961 Diary, May 30

If we integrate a synopsis of H.D.'s poem with a synopsis of the relevant political events of 1960, the various links between text and context begin to emerge. When Durand failed to return H.D.'s last letter in May of 1960, H.D.'s friend and literary adviser Norman Holmes Pearson proposed that his silence may have been due to "the pressure of affairs: the Congo, with its connection with Belgium etc., all of America's international fumbling, the reactions to the American political conventions."[16] Perhaps spurred by Pearson's explanation, H.D. took a subscription to *Newsweek* beginning the first of August, which not only allowed ready access to Durand's journalism but also supplemented an already full plate of world news sources.[17] During this period, the rapidly changing political landscape of Africa was a recurring focus in the news. Following international outrage over the Sharpeville shootings in March, the news media gave almost weekly coverage to the violent political struggles in the Congo dating from its independence in late June, through the intervention of U.N. "peacekeeping" troops in late July, and into the new year. H.D. began the first part of *Hermetic Definition*, "Red Rose and a Beggar," on August 17, 1960. In this sequence, she juxtaposes factual information about Durand with fantasized encounters, in which she becomes an ecstatic initiate seeking union with a divine lover and son modeled on the Egyptian Horus. Responding to the *Newsweek* coverage of Rafer Johnson's prospects in the upcoming Olympics, H.D. also incorporates the African-American decathlon star into the poem. The sequence, completed on September 24, ends with a vision of demons and a crisis of faith.

On October 24, 1960, one week before H.D. began her poem's second part, "Grove of Academe," Durand resumed coverage of the Algerian War. At this time, the three-way power struggle between Moslem FLN rebels, French *colons*, and de Gaulle's rule by decree had spilled over the battlefield into civilian demonstrations and arrests in France and civilian riots and killings in Algiers. As Patrice Lumumba in the Congo and FLN rebels in Algeria added to the already escalating Western anticommunist panic by publicizing offers of political support and/or military aid from the Soviet Union, H.D. would repeatedly compare current events to the frightening years of World War II.[18] Just days before H.D. began "Grove of Academe," St.-John Perse was awarded the Nobel Prize in literature.[19] The sequence opens with a scene of healing in the Aegina temple. There,

H.D. encounters St.-John Perse and, inspired by specific lines in his poems, undertakes a fantasized journey through the boundless and abundant imperial vistas of his imagination. Returning thoughts of Durand, however, threaten the fantasy; by December 24, when she completes this section, she rejects Perse's "incomparable challenge // to time—time—time" in order to "come back // to ordinary time-sequence" (*HD* 44).

During the latter part of December, Durand was covering the Algerian War from Algiers. Writing to Pearson in early January of 1961, H.D. carefully rehearses Durand's report on the civilian riots in Algiers; she notes, among other details, the "sacred texts from Synagogue shredded on the pavement" when Moslems, denied access to the French *colons* after their Casbah was enclosed in barbed wire, broke out in violence against neighboring Jews.[20] H.D.'s comments on the destruction of books and resurging anti-Semitic violence echo her condemnation of the "burning of the books" in *Trilogy* (*T* 16) and place Durand's report in a personally resonant history of atrocity running back through World War II to the thirteenth-century religious persecution of the Cathars, whose books, towns, and people were burned in the Albigensian crusade.[21] In mid-January, Durand, who had a weak heart to begin with, died of heart failure brought on by exhaustion and the tear gas he had inhaled while reporting in the Casbah. On January 24, 1961, H.D. began her poem's last part, "Star of Day," with the news of Durand's untimely death. In an extraordinary move, H.D. conflates this death with the rebirth of the Star of Day each year at winter solstice; figuring the nine months of their acquaintance as a pregnancy, she boldly lays claim to a maternal rather than sexual possession of Durand, and constitutes her own body and poem as the epiphanic site of his "conception" and delivery into second life (*HD* 54).

While this fantasy of possessing Durand is the most startling in the poem, it is not the first. "Red Rose and a Beggar" introduces H.D.'s desire to enter Durand's body in its second section. Governed by acute investments in the inside/outside scheme, this desire takes oddly ambiguous and reversible forms from the start. In an address to Durand in section 2, H.D. claims:

> I walk into you,
>
>   . . .
>
> I would hide in your mind
> as a child hides in an attic.   (*HD* 4)

This figure can be read as both a protest over and a compensation for H.D.'s intense feelings of abandonment by Durand in the absence of a letter from him. Reversing H.D.'s self-characterization as an "old" woman in her "decline" in section 1, the child who would hide in the attic of Durand's mind fulfills a fantasy of dependency at the same time that it conjures up an image of parental neglect.

But in section 3, the figure changes to reveal more mature fantasies of violent sexual possession. Recalling her second, and last, meeting with Durand the previous May, in which he refused her offer of wine and salted nuts because of his weak heart, H.D. writes:

> because you do not drink our wine,
> nor salt our salt,
> I would enter your senses
>
> through burnt resin and pine-cones.   (*HD* 5)

Through the pine cones, H.D. identifies Durand with the self-castrated Phrygian harvest-god Attis, son of Cybele, and then with the Egyptian "Bar-Isis" or "Par-Isis," the divine "son of Isis" (*HD* 5). While H.D. takes Durand's Paris residence as the declared basis of this latter identification, the hidden basis is surely his race. Dissatisfied with Durand's self-identification as French at their first meeting the previous April, H.D. repeatedly sought out more desirable, if imaginary, national and racial identities for him. She records her first impressions of Durand when he came to interview her in a journal entry: "He looked so dark in the shuttered hall-room downstairs, when he turned to greet me that I thought he might be *Créole*, but he is not, he has possibly a touch of Spanish, there seems Africa, the Moor in him. Is this poor Lawrence's Dark God?"[22]

H.D.'s distant memory of Durand in the "shuttered hall-room downstairs" and his more recent silence and withdrawal from her constitute the biographical sources for her portrayal of him as "a cave-hermit" later in section 3 of "Red Rose and a Beggar." The other sources for this portrayal are mythical. H.D. identifies the cave-hermit with the guardian of the sacred underground crypts of Isis, which were symbolically associated with the earth's own silence, darkness, decay, and fertility.[23] Late in "Grove of Academe," H.D. returns to this cave fantasy to spell out its erotic component more fully; leaving St.-John Perse to recall "Paris, Bar-Isis," she declares:

> I must creep into his cavern,
> beat my hand on his breast,
> wake his heart to this instant . . .
> (*HD* 40; H.D.'s ellipses)

By reconstituting Durand as Trojan lover and Egyptian god, H.D. is able to refigure his silence and poor health as signs not of abandonment and imminent death, but of a hidden promise of sexual contact and divine rebirth. The erotic invasion of his body that she articulates openly in section 3 is paired, more obliquely, with the impregnation of her own body necessary to bring about the sacred renewal of the earth. This fantasy of an aggressive sexual encounter between a white woman and a black man in a sacred cave can be read as a literary afterimage of Miss Quested's purported sexual assault by Dr. Aziz in the Marabar Caves of Forster's 1924 novel *Passage to India*.[24] Yet where Forster leaves open the question of whether Miss Quested was actually attacked—by Dr. Aziz or someone else—or only "hallucinated" such an attack, H.D. clearly represents her cave scenario, in which she plays an active role, as the product of her own fantasy.

To say that H.D. experiences such a scenario as a personal fantasy, however, is not to deny its broad historical and cultural determinants, which range from the myth of the black rapist used as an apology for lynching in the United States of H.D.'s girlhood to the modernist cultivation of primitivism. For H.D., D. H. Lawrence stood at the center of this latter set of associations. Susan Friedman has analyzed H.D.'s "critique of the sexual politics pervading Lawrence's work" in *Bid Me to Live*, whose Lawrence figure, Rico, was named for the impotent husband in *St. Mawr*.[25] In that novella, the black stallion St. Mawr embodies the "spirit of animal man, an intuitive, sexual, mystical being," and comes to stand as "the 'dark god' to which civilization must return to be reborn." Yet if, as Friedman argues, *Bid Me to Live* rejects this Lawrentian vision of women's glad acquiescence to phallic supremacy by insisting on the androgyny or bisexuality of the epiphanic moment of *gloire*,[26] H.D.'s portrayals of Durand in "Thorn Thicket" and "Red Rose and a Beggar" are more ambiguous. Conflating Durand with "poor Lawrence's Dark God," she appears to take his race as the single sign of an overpowering sexual energy otherwise hidden. In the absence of any other indication that he shares her passion, Durand's skin professes in silence what his speech does not.

In reading phallic agency into the silent, absent black male body, H.D. restages the historical crisis of black male agency itself, in which accusatory attributions to black men of excessive and/or transgressive potency and force have been used to deny them a sphere of legitimate action. Yet she also appears to be grappling with the fact that the very proliferation and destabilization of agent positions in her fantasies of Durand—an outcome of fantasy's own status as a "scenario with multiple entries" for identification and desire—must bear precisely this historical burden; taken together, these fantasies starkly expose the process by which one white woman wishfully transposes a black man from the object to the subject of a dangerous passion.

When H.D. represents herself taking the active role in her cave fantasy of Durand, she directly recalls her fantasy of ripping the garments from a bronze statue in her 1931 poem, "Red Roses for Bronze," thought to be addressed to Paul Robeson. Friedman reads this earlier moment, in which H.D. "toy[s] with the image of the woman-artist raping the Lover," as a subversion of the "implicit rape fantasies of . . . the black man-white woman script." The same reading can certainly be applied to the cave scenario in section 14 of "Grove of Academe."[27] But in her earlier identification of the French journalist with Attis, Paris, Bar-Isis, and then a "thundering pack / of steers, bulls" (*HD* 10), H.D. also upholds her links between Durand and the rejuvenating sexual violence of D. H. Lawrence's animalistic dark god.

In section 7, these bulls overwhelm H.D. with

> the rush, the fervour,
> the trampling of lush grass,
>
> the bare foot entanglement,
> the roar of the last desperate charge,
> the non-escape, the enchantment,
>
> the tremor, the earthquake.   (*HD* 9)

As such, they appear to slide between a representation of the force of H.D.'s sexual arousal and a representation of a sexual force, or forcefulness, attributed to Durand. For H.D. clearly uses her own desire to animate in turn the stampeding bulls, the entangled human feet, and the trembling landscape. She goes on to associate the bulls with Durand in section 8:

> is it you?
> is it some thundering pack
> of steers, bulls? is it one?
>
> is it many?   (*HD* 10)

In doing so, she dramatizes the way in which fantasy allows her to stage her violent passion as his in a scenario improvising in contradictory ways on the social myth of black male rape and the modernist myth of the dark god. In a comment particularly apposite to Lawrence's cult of the dark god, James Snead notes that "it came to be suspected in the late nineteenth century that primitive states might possess greater power and energy than sterile nations," and that "western material progress had amounted to spiritual and artistic decadence."[28] Against this backdrop, H.D.'s repetition of her poem's opening declaration to Durand at the close of section 8—

why did you come

to trouble my decline?
I am old,
(I was old till you came)   (*HD* 10, 3)

—can itself be read as an act of superimposing her own life history on the modernist primitivist account of the "decline" and magical rejuvenation of the West through passionate contact with the dark god.

But even after identifying three modernist works—Forster's *Passage to India*, Lawrence's *St. Mawr*, and her own "Red Roses for Bronze"—as literary intertexts of H.D.'s Durand fantasies, we are not done with our source hunting. The principal and declared source book for "Red Rose and a Beggar" is Robert Ambelain's *Dans l'ombre des cathédrales*. In this book, Ambelain derives the architecture and statuary of Notre Dame from the iconography of ancient Egyptian and Near Eastern religions and the cryptic teachings of the alchemists. Tracing St. Anne's scepter, which is capped with a pine cone, back to Cybele's pine tree, he provides H.D. with her links between Durand and Attis; tracing the Virgin's lily back to Isis's lotus, he provides her with the links between Durand and Horus (pp. 162, 72). But Ambelain offers H.D. not only a *set* but also a *method* of correspondences, a way of reading the body cabalistically. In searching out the public face of Notre Dame for evidence of hidden, and forbidden, forms of spiritual knowledge, Ambelain provides a model for H.D.'s own attempts to detect in the prosaic data of Durand's life—his eating habits, his amber eyes, his Paris address—a mystical "double sense" (*HD* 12). At the same time, Ambelain grants spiritual power to this very action of reading, of detection or doubling; for the seeker, reading becomes both a prayer for and an instance of sacred transubstantiation, allowing H.D. to sublimate Durand's recalcitrant and ailing biographical body into the potent and willing mythical body of the dark god.

For instance, Ambelain interprets the inscription of the Latin dedication of Notre Dame on the second day of the ides of February 1257, as a set of coded directions for the alchemist's hermetic work. He deciphers the word *Secondo* in the dedication as an allusion to "*Seconde, aide, favorise l'action de la Nature*," the first line of the alchemical prayer for aiding Nature in her conversion of base metals into gold and mortal bodies into everlasting ones.[29] Incorporating this reading into her poem, H.D. returns to her own argument in *Trilogy* to conflate once again the rhythmical action of alchemical Nature with the resurgence of female desire. The "*action de la Nature*" that she calls on God to serve, aid, and favor in section 10 is the divinely transformative action of her sexual passion for Durand (*HD* 12).

Yet in the very act of investing Durand's body with a mythical past of primitive potency or a medieval past of alchemical promise, H.D.'s fantasies may betray a further investment in more recent historical events. Both her cave fantasy and her identification of Durand with Bar-Isis allude to Ambelain's argument that Notre Dame itself rests on the underground crypt of an ancient sanctuary to Isis, whose worshipers took the name Bar-Isis, or "sons of Isis"; Ambelain derives the French *parisien* from this ancient Egyptian religious title (pp. 71, 78–79). His argument appears to have offered H.D. a mythologized explanation for a black man's self-identification as French that bypassed the increasingly bitter history of French colonialism in Africa and the West Indies. In the face of the current, violently resisted presence of French *colons* in Africa, H.D. follows Ambelain in invoking a much earlier time when travelers bearing a religion born on the African continent established a colony in France, stamping its future capital with their name and that bastion of French national pride, Notre Dame, with the icons of the Egyptian theocracy. Thus, H.D.'s very deification of Durand as an Egyptian god points to urgent questions of colonization and the origins of national identity even as it obscures, by inverting, the current political backdrop to these questions.

H.D.'s discomfort with the idea that Durand was French—and her fantasy that he might be a "Moor" (which again invokes a North African invasion of Europe)—eventually led her to assume that his coverage of the Algerian War caused him a unique crisis of identity. In response to a letter from Pearson in late December, where he proposes that Durand must be going through "hell" "with French Algeria" and "may be pulled in several directions," H.D. writes back in agreement, commenting, "I don't know in how many directions Durant is torn."[30] In this letter, H.D.'s image of Durand's torn body locates the interracial warfare in Algeria inside Durand's own person, turning the anticolonial struggle into a drama of one man's competing loyalties. Given H.D.'s own increasing confusion and distress over events in Algeria, the internal conflicts she comes to associate with Durand (whose actual attitudes toward the war I have been unable to determine) could well have been her own. Yet even before Durand resumed his war coverage, H.D. expressed both her anxiety over violence in Africa and her apparent assumption that one's race might throw one's national identification into question in her portrayal of Rafer Johnson in "Red Rose and a Beggar."

In section 12, H.D. merges Attis's pine cones with the flare of an Olympic torch to connect Durand with Johnson. The deeper, unstated, connection is Africa. Upon learning that H.D. was including the U.S. decathlon star in her poem, Pearson comments: "he is certainly a handsome devil, a little I should think like a black-coffee Durand."[31] And, in fact, the August report on the upcoming Olympics in *Newsweek* describes

Johnson as a UCLA college student, studying "comparative political systems, Marxist theory, and African government," and hoping "to make a career of international relations."[32] Combining Durand's interests in Africa and politics with an interest in diplomacy, Johnson held out for H.D. the possibility of peace in Africa.

In deleted lines that originally began section 13, H.D. addresses Johnson:

> Young hero with the spear,
> there is no war,
> nor ever will be war,
> where you appear;

she then quotes Johnson's own words, which follow her comment on his "goodness" in the poem's finished version: "I like people, / I want to do all I can to help them" (*HD* 15).[33] Here, H.D. alludes to the ancient Greek mandate forbidding warring countries to enter competitors in the games of the Olympian Festival.[34] But her representation of Johnson with spear in hand softly blurs his national identity, evoking as it does not only the American athlete with his "poised javelin," but also a fantasy of an African tribesman. Similarly, her invocation of Johnson's Apollonian power to "slay desperation, as long ago (to-day) / Helios slays the Python" (*HD* 15) both obscures and reveals her investment of Johnson with a homeopathic power to allay the despair roused in her by the current bloodshed in the Congo and Algeria.[35] Through his race, Johnson becomes the bearer of H.D.'s hope not that his own country, the United States, will stay out of war, but that fighting will cease in Africa itself.

In deleting the explicit links between Johnson and war in her poem's first draft, H.D. removes the first of a series of lines that openly discuss the current crises in Africa. The threat of violence and death that she associates with Africa, however, continues to affect her treatment of Johnson and Durand in the poem's final version. Thinking of Johnson, H.D. thinks of Azrael, the "Mohammedan angel of Death" (*HD* 21). Azrael, whose eyes may be "amber," directly recalls the amber-eyed Durand, who may be a Moor, and, more obliquely, the Moslem FLN rebels currently fighting in Algeria (*HD* 20, 4).[36] Moreover, it is tempting to attribute H.D.'s sudden anxiety at this point as to whether her spirit-guardians are angels or devils to Pearson's casual description of Johnson as "a handsome devil, rather like a black-coffee Durand."[37] Expressing genuine uncertainty over the beneficence of pre-Christian gods and goddesses—"Astaroth," "Lilith," "Lucifer and Asmodel" (*HD* 17)—she questions the wisdom of her decision to invoke these traditionally demonized figures in previous long poems. She admits, "now I am forced to hold my lines in doubt," and panics over her inability to relocate Asmodel in "Saint's

calendar," "dictionary or reference book" (*HD* 20, 21). As Helios be-
comes Lucifer and Johnson's powers of peace fail to vanquish her despair,
H.D. appears to move into an unstable spiritual world, in which race,
grace, and damnation are divinely correlated. In section 18, she concludes
the sequence with the decision not to "delete" Asmodel from the poem,
asserting

> angels may become devils
> devils may become angels,
> he'd better stay.   (*HD* 21)

The network of associations between Durand substitutes, death, devils,
and the "*feu d'enfer*" also remains in place, however, and will be called
upon again in the poem's last section (*HD* 20).

Journeying to the Interior

> this retreat from the world,
> that yet holds the world, past, present,
> in the mind's closed recess
>
> —H.D., "Grove of Academe"

Where the final version of "Red Rose and a Beggar" stops at section 18,
the first draft goes on for an additional ten sections, three of which ex-
plicitly demonstrate the links between H.D.'s recurring thoughts of death
and the current crises in the Congo and Algeria. For instance, in an orig-
inal section 20, H.D reports of Durand:

> he could brush aside the letter
> and a second that followed after,
> from his Paris desk, loaded with books and paper
> the whole world, and France, in chaos,
> (he has his job there).

And in a section 27 that originally concluded the sequence, she contrasts
her own poetic embracing of passion, mysticism, and myth with Du-
rand's journalistic hardheadedness:

> Bar-Isis, Paris,
> perhaps envied our madness,
> himself, pledged to routine,
> the whole world's disruption
> ~~to be ironed out~~ under supervision,
> with dispatches, reports, ~~ill health.~~[38]

That these lines occur in a whole series of deleted sections underscores the fact that references to contemporary politics are by no means the only material that H.D. chooses to edit from her poem. Such references, however, do constitute the only category of information she systematically excludes from the poem's finished version, and thus it seems fair to ask whether these exclusions were motivated by the nature of the material itself, or simply perpetuated H.D.'s previous modernist practice of mythologizing contemporary history.

Although World War II provides the unmistakable occasion for *Trilogy* and *Helen in Egypt*, both poems do thoroughly absorb the history of the war into various alchemical and ancient mythological systems. In *Vale Ave* (1957), however, H.D. breaks out of this pattern, setting a number of precedents for her subsequent treatment of Durand. In the earlier poem, H.D. meditates on seven meetings she had with Lord Hugh Dowding, Air Chief Marshal during the Battle of Britain, who was removed from his post shortly thereafter and achieved some renown as a Spiritualist. Her poetic accounts of these meetings—in which she sharply juxtaposes mythological identifications ("Circe—/ Gyges") with small, incidental details drawn from their actual encounters ("another cup of tea— a cigarette," a ringing telephone, etc.)—closely anticipate her later accounts of meetings with Durand. But she also squarely places these meetings in the history of her own Spiritualist activities, her Blitz experiences, and Dowding's role in "the great days of the war." In her poem, Dowding is the "Air Marshal" whose "heroic wings held and . . . beat back // the enemy"; through him, "we had survived // the Battle and the threat of the invasion" (pp. 56–59).

In contradicting the precedent laid down by her earlier treatment of Dowding, H.D.'s decision to excise lines openly linking Durand and Johnson to the wars in Algeria and the Congo begins to look less like an attempt to uphold the purity of the mythical method and more like an attempt to suppress a specific content or context. At the same time, however, these acts of editing serve to call the very possibility of undoing the poem's inscription of its historical context into question. For Durand's coverage of "the whole world, and France, in chaos," ostensibly occluded in the poem's final version, continues to govern the logic of the passages that remain. For instance, H.D. begins "Grove of Academe" by retrieving the memory of an averted fall at the award ceremony of the American Academy the previous spring, when St.-John Perse reached out a hand to steady her balance as she slipped on the way back from the podium. In the finished poem, this scene of recovered balance appears to respond directly to the last lines of "Red Rose and a Beggar" where a shaken H.D. vows to "keep my identity / walk unfalteringly toward a Lover" (*HD* 21). But the fantasy also answers to the acute sense of worldwide instability that she articulates in the deleted sections that originally intervened between the two sequences. When H.D. writes to Pearson that she composed "Grove of Academe" as an "*escape* from Part I" meant "to balance intellectually the emotional *Red Rose*," we might assign this further act of balancing, which takes the curious form of an "escape," to the same sense of political instability.[39]

The recent award of the Nobel Prize to St.-John Perse overdetermines the course of H.D.'s "escape" in "Grove of Academe" even further. A *Newsweek* article noting Perse's award reports: "His poetry, the [Swedish] academy said, 'reflects the conditions of our times.'"[40] The praise is likely to strike our own ears as ironic; Perse's poems persistently record fantasies of imperial conquest, drawn in part from memories of his childhood in Guadeloupe and from his years of diplomatic service in Asia.[41] Such fantasies appear painfully at odds with the postwar era of decolonization; as *Newsweek* would report only a week after announcing Perse's award: "In the United Nations these days, nobody—but nobody—loves a 'colonialist.'"[42] Yet it may be just this combination of ascribed historical insight and actual historical disjunction that fuels H.D.'s escape into a world that both is and is not the "world . . . in chaos" that Durand evokes for her.

Significantly, this escape involves both a redefinition of the writer's vocation to include poetry but (it would appear) not journalism, and a "retreat" into the interior reaches of the imagination. H.D. locates the significance of her connection with Perse in the fact "that you write, // even that I have written," and claims that

> my hand worn with endeavour,
> our curious pre-occupation with stylus and pencil,
> was re-born at your touch.   (*HD* 24, 26)

In these lines, she bonds with the poet to the silent exclusion of the journalist. Yet in so doing she also implicitly reasserts the conventional distinction between visionary poetry and journalism that she herself had attempted to break down first in the hybrid genre of *Vale Ave* and the daybook format of *Sagesse* and later in her mythical and alchemical sublimations of Durand's biographical data in "Red Rose and a Beggar."

With the eclipse of the external world whose events occupy the historian and the journalist, H.D. gains access to a more prestigious, internal world in which the artist plays emperor. "If I can do nothing else," she tells Perse,

at least, I can recognize this
unfathomable, dauntless separation,

this retreat from the world,
that yet holds the world, past, present,
in the mind's closed recess.   (*HD* 27)

The terms of this description closely resemble Perse's own description of
his 1930 poem *Anabase* as a "journey to the interior," with, as Peter Baker
notes, its "willed ambiguity between the geographical and spiritual sense
of that phrase." Just as Perse's "Stranger, or Voyager, . . . sets out on a
voyage to the interior presumably involving discovery, conquest, and set-
tlement,"[43] H.D.'s description of poetic creation invokes a poet who not
only gathers the riches of the earth into the private "hold" of the imagi-
nation but also preserves a prewar world of European empire now "past,"
granting it a second "present."[44] And where she earlier desired to "enter
[Durand's] senses," she now takes literal inspiration from the idyllic land-
scapes of Perse's childhood in Guadeloupe:

I breathe the aloes, the acacia
of your senses, tropic red spike,
trumpet flowers, indigo petal-drift

of your remembrance.   (*HD* 30)

Adopting a stance of minuteness, participation, and noncompetition,
she grants Perse exclusive dominion over the stretches of the imagination
in exchange for the right to wander freely in a world unburdened by mod-
ern warfare, civil strife, and anticolonial resistance. "The unfathomable
belongs to you," she writes, "sand, dune, heap and mound, // continent,
empire" (*HD* 40). For herself, it is enough to be

part of your giant-concept
of deserts, the earth entire

with water-fronts, sea-slopes,
storm, wind and thunder-crash.   (*HD* 32)

Although in the very modesty of her stance H.D. may here appear to
borrow her association between the colonial encounter and the making of
art from Perse's superior example, she has her own long and varied history
of aligning the two enterprises. In 1920, she turns to Sappho for inspira-
tion and guidance, describing the Greek poet as "the island of artistic per-
fection, where the lover of ancient beauty (shipwrecked in the modern
world) may yet . . . gain courage for new adventures and dream of yet
unexplored continents and realms of future artistic achievement."[45] Com-
menting on "The Sword Went Out to Sea," she associates the defense of

empire with her efforts to aid the spirit order in saving London from de-
struction during World War II; the novel, she writes, "was aimed at a
Great Secret, the secret that held the Roman empire together, that held the
British empire together."[46] Yet she could also criticize empire for its vio-
lent subjugations. As Susan Friedman has noted, H.D.'s portrayal in her
1927 novel *Palimpsest* of a Roman soldier's attempt finally to "prove Rome
conqueror" by sexually dominating his Greek concubine critiques "the
erotics of empire."[47] In her 1958 poem *Winter Love*, her critique takes on
a more ambiguous form. Helen, a mask for H.D., protests the conven-
tions that confine the Western heroine and female writer to the domestic
obscurity of the "small world of Greece," while permitting the Western
hero and male writer (Ezra Pound) a wide territory of experience and re-
nown. Helen, herself hungry for "escape," asks:

> why should Odysseus leave
>
> unslaked adventure, boundless horizons,
> unconquered citadels for home?   (*HD* 97, 104)

If H.D. here again appears to use exploration and conquest as figures
for achievement and self-realization, elsewhere she makes voyages of dis-
covery and colonial settlement into figures for spiritual quest. In *Trilogy*
she declares,

> *we are voyagers, discoverers*
> *of the not-known,*
>
> *the unrecorded;*
> *we have no map;*
>
> *possibly we will reach haven,*
> *heaven.*   (*T* 59)

And in *Vale Ave*, begun one month after Ghana achieved independence
from Britain, she aligns her long-standing myth of the Isis-search for the
lost companion with the dream of indestructible empire; her late Roman
character Julia, hiding in a tent as her lover fights off "barbaric hosts,"
prays:

> give us a Ship, we'll sail down this wide river,
>
> the sea is not so far, I would forget
> anxiety and ceaseless threat of war,
>
> for we would found a City, greater
> and with more power, even than ancient Rome.[48]

In a discussion of H.D.'s 1951 "Moravian novel" "The Mystery,"
Jane Augustine makes the important point that H.D. traced her belief in

the possibility of a godly and benevolent world order back to the Moravian Church, whose eighteenth-century benefactor, Count Zinzendorf, hoped to form in the New World a global brotherhood, or *Unitas Fratum*, that would cross racial and sectarian lines. As H.D. knew, some of Zinzendorf's contemporaries suspected him of harboring a "secret plan to take over and rule the world." But for believers Zinzendorf held out, in H.D.'s words, "the mysterious plan of a *Jednota*, a unity, a world-unity without war." Moravian colonists in the New World, H.D.'s maternal ancestors among them, turned to Native Americans as allies in their attempts to realize this plan for world peace until wider acts of violence between the two races defeated their joint efforts.[49] It may well be that the fantasy of founding a powerful City on foreign shores, articulated throughout H.D.'s career, originates in the Moravian religious longing for a global brotherhood. Thus, in *Hermetic Definition*, when H.D. celebrates Perse's "*promesse d'îles*" or his "giant-concept / of . . . the earth entire," she may be trying to preserve this spiritual hope for a world peace grounded in nonviolent colonial settlement in the face of the renewed challenges to its viability in Africa; where Perse's own poetry celebrates imperialist acts of exploitation and domination,[50] H.D. explicitly associates the "super-abundance" of his "ποιητής fantasy" with "ecstasy and healing" (*HD* 30, 33).[51]

For the greater part of "Grove of Academe," then, H.D.'s citations of Perse seem to serve two purposes. First, they allow her to escape Durand and the chaotic world evoked in his writing. And they provide an alternative world of ecstasy and healing that may well answer needs emerging from the very period of decolonization that Perse's own evocations of a glorious colonial past are called upon to eclipse. The tropical islands and desert expanses of Perse's world cannot, however, block out the hollow darkness that H.D. continues to associate with Durand's silence and withdrawal. Addressing Perse with the statement "(you are not dead in the darkness)," and later asking of Durand himself "(is he dead in the darkness?)" (*HD* 33, 38), H.D. explicitly doubts the powers of primitivist myth-making and imperialist fantasy alike to exorcize the threat of violence and death that she associates with Durand's trip to Algiers. Near the end of "Grove of Academe," she comes across a passing allusion to Memnon in Perse's poetry that calls this trip to the foreground of her thoughts; the long battle at Troy, in which the Greek hero Achilles killed the Ethiopian warrior-king, mirrors in distorted form the war between French *colons* and Algerian Moslems.

Here, H.D.'s handling of Perse's figure of the Ethiopian king makes clear her increasing distance from Perse's own attitudes toward empire. In *Anabase*, Perse alludes to the myth that Memnon's funeral pillar sings out when struck by the first ray of dawn in a figure equating the sweet sound of his monument with the tinkling of ice in the glasses of conquering pleasure-seekers:

> Tout-puissants dans nos grands gouvernements militaires, avec nos filles parfumées qui se vêtaient d'un souffle, ces tissus,
>   nous établîmes en haut lieu nos pièges au bonheur.
>   Abondance et bien-être, bonheur! Aussi longtemps nos verres où la glace pouvait chanter comme Memnon ...

> Omnipotent in our great military governments, with our scented girls clad in a breath of silk webs,
>   we set in high places our springes for happiness.
>   Plenty and well-being, happiness! For so long the ice sang in our glasses, like Memnon ...[52]

Perse's urbane allusion trivializes Memnon's mythic song in order to suggest the greater power, license, and ease of the military governments that inherit his domains. In contrast, H.D. restores dignity to the figure of Memnon through a fantasy in which she strives for the honor of being the first ray of sun to strike his singing stone (*HD* 42). But in portraying Durand himself as an African warrior—"Bar-Isis, / that Memnon in the desert" (*HD* 39)—she once again slips into representing him as one of the participants in a war that he was in fact on the scene to record. Thus, her use of a mythic hero as a mask for Durand obscures both the content of his account of FLN rebels' efforts to repossess their traditional lands and the very fact that he has written an account at all.

In concealing the nature of his trip to Algiers, H.D.'s mythologized portrait of Durand does not merely distance her poem from the current "chaos" of African decolonization, but actively orders that chaos into an encounter between epic heroes whose pairing upholds the interests of Africa's ancient and contemporary Western colonizers. Furthermore, her very move to restore dignity to the figure of Memnon, far from resisting those interests, again upholds them. H.D. herself understood clearly not only how cultures use myth to justify and glorify their actions, but also how those uses underwrite the very Homeric tradition on which Eliot (following Joyce) based the modernist mythical method. In an arresting speech in "The Sword Went Out to Sea," H.D.'s persona Day-Star, the lover of Pericles, advances the argument that Homer's epics of the Trojan War mask the less honorable history of the Greek sacking of Knossos:

> It was—well, shall we say Achilles who sacked Knossos?
>   Afterwards, they called it Troy, for it reflected little credit on their valiant ancestors that the Greeks had descended from their head-lands, master of a new war-weapon and a new technique, and attacked a defenceless people without warning. . . .

It became legend, it became mythology. A whole hierarchy of heroes was invented, only a shade less heroic than the Greeks, for what credit is it to the warrior caste to have gained a victory over an unarmed, defenceless nation? It was better to forget Crete. It was better to forget Knossos. It might be awkward when our grand-children asked us of our exploits.[53]

When H.D. represents Durand as Memnon, an African warrior "only a shade less heroic" than the immortal Greek who fells him, she mirrors the very strategy she has critiqued in Homer; returning to Homer's war, his heroes, and his example, she substitutes the timeless story of a glorious battle between equals for the less palatable one of African resistance to Western domination and exploitation. Yet for the first time in *Hermetic Definition*—indeed, in her whole poetic career—the conflict between the modernist mythical method and contemporary history, embedded in her use of Bar-Isis, Attis, Azrael, and Memnon as figures for Durand, begins to emerge as an explicit tension or struggle in her writing. Where, in "Red Rose and a Beggar," Ambelain's example allowed H.D. to use even the most resistant biographical material about Durand as support for a series of mythological and mystical identifications, here she exposes the inadequacies of such hermetic definitions. Within the space of four sections, she sharply juxtaposes the mythic aspects she has projected onto Durand with a factual narrative of their actual relationship, in which she spells out her long wait "for another letter," her flight to Perse's poetry when the fantasized love affair between a man "not quite 40" and a woman "over 70" proved unlikely, and her realization in the aftermath of her "*Notre Dame* revelation" that "one can't hurl such findings / in the face of a stranger" (*HD* 39, 41).[54]

The final form of "Grove of Academe" suggests that H.D.'s sense of the emerging contradiction between Durand's actual identity and her mythical personae for him was confined to the context of their personal interactions. The sequence's first draft, however, reveals that H.D.'s concern over the exploding civilian violence in Algeria was also a factor. The back of the page containing the sequence's concluding section bears the following notes (almost certainly inspired by Durand's reports on December 19 and 26 of rioting in Algiers' Casbah):

> casbah—
> Algérie Française
> *colon*
> Algérie Algérienne
> Algérie Musalmane
> F.L.N. rebels—

And in that concluding section itself, H.D. refers to Durand in deleted
lines that appear to follow the intact lines: "I must wait to-day, to-
morrow, or the day after / for the answer":

> the reddest rose unfolds,
> *Seigneur* understand,
> I must stay here,
> where he is,
> somewhere in the desert,
> in Africa anyway,
> ~~& he is now there,~~
> ~~on that continent,~~
> ~~where he is~~
> witness [?] of death's [?] onslaughts.[55]

It is against this background, cut from the poem's final version, that
H.D. stages her abrupt departure from Perse's world, her return "to or-
dinary time-sequence," and her recovery of "the human equation" (*HD*
44, 51).[56]

Yet it is not enough to say that H.D. departs from Perse's world. She
rejects it. Refusing his claim "*Mais Dieu se tait dans le quantième*" in section
17,[57] she defends the terms of worship laid out in *Sagesse*, where she uses
the *calendrier sacré*—or sacred calendar—analyzed in Ambelain's *Kabbale
pratique* to record god's separate manifestations for each day and hour.[58]
With this refusal, she upholds the very possibility of a spiritual life
grounded in the intimate linking of daily events to the ongoing presence
of god. At the same time, H.D.'s defense of god's presence in the days of
the month involves an implicit commitment to her own contemporary
moment, and, with it, to the journalist's appreciation of each day's events
and consequences. She takes her leave of Perse with the assertion:

> I can not step over the horizon;
> I must wait to-day, to-morrow or the day after
> for the answer   (*HD* 44)

In doing so, she relinquishes a poetry committed to prophesying a
wished-for future into being, and accepts instead the lot of living day by
day. With this acceptance, H.D. agrees to wait not only for Durand's an-
swer to her last letter and god's answers to her invocations but also for
time's answers to a temporal world where effects will always wait upon
their causes.

A Season of Long Darkness

it had to go on the full time

　　—H.D., "Star of Day"

A persistent misspelling of Durand's name in her writing about him suggests that H.D.'s very commitment to living in time was tied up in her feelings toward Durand. After May of 1960, she repeatedly refers to the journalist as "Durant," French for "during." This misspelling seems to stem from her ambivalent appreciation of the journalist's own commitment to the dailiness or during-ness of contemporary history, the limited vantage point he could bring to the "supervision" of events, and the humility of his "pledge to routine." Yet if H.D.'s first impulse in *Hermetic Definition* is to offset the chaos of contemporary history with magically omnipotent savior figures drawn from an ancient past, she also recognized that she owed her meeting with Durand to his very focus on "to-day." She writes to Pearson after the poem's completion, "I do think . . . that my E[zra] P[ound memoir] & the later Durant sequence, do keep 'in time' and 'out of time' together. I didn't want to *escape* to-day. To-day gave me the magic & mystery."[59]

As we have seen, the tension between H.D.'s desire to lose herself in Perse's "incomparable challenge // to time—time—time" and her desire to "come back / to ordinary time-sequence" is structured by an underlying struggle between her conflicting desires to deny and to acknowledge Durand's association with the "anguish" of another war. In the poem's last part, "Star of Day," H.D. attempts to effect some reconciliation between these warring terms themselves—to "keep 'in time' and 'out of time' together." In *Trilogy* she achieved this reconciliation by using her "little clock" as a means of ecstatic transport and communion with the Lady (*T* 90). But as its place at her "bed-head" would suggest, her little clock tells a private time, a time fitted to the intimate encounters of the domestic space. In contrast, in "Star of Day," H.D. recasts time as public, world-historical time even as she trades in her figures of lesbian ecstasy for those of maternal possession; the epiphanic encounter now fills time like a fetus stirring to life in the body's own field of dilation and endurance. Not a challenge to time any more, but its changeling, its angel or demon charge, this encounter shares with the violent historical moment that fosters it the indissoluble but unstable bond of mother and child.

H.D. begins the final sequence of her poem by deifying Durand as the Star of Day, whose birth was celebrated each winter solstice at Saïs, the ancient Egyptian burial site of Osiris. At first glance, this identification bears all the signs of a simple return to the very strategies of modernist myth-making she has just rejected at the end of "Grove of Academe"; indeed, H.D.'s allusion to Saïs closely follows the language Ambelain uses to relate the Saïs myth in *Dans l'ombre des cathédrales* (p. 283). H.D.'s choice of this myth, however, also makes direct, albeit muted, reference to the coverage of the riots in Algiers that led to Durand's death. She writes in elegy:

> for you are dead;
>
> they say, Saïs brought forth the Star of Day,
> at midnight when the shadows are most dense,
> the nights longest and most desperate.   (*HD* 45)

In an article appearing in the December 19 issue of *Newsweek* and containing a report from Durand in Algiers, the anonymous lead paragraph runs as follows: "It was a season of raw winds and long darkness. And in the darkest time of the year, from Paris south across the Mediterranean, some felt a strange sense of foreboding, a smell of danger and violence in the air. Almost inevitably, violence exploded in tormented Algeria."[60]

In a letter to Pearson dated December 22, 1960—right at winter solstice—H.D. remarks that Durand "seemed to have had a pretty tough time, (as per *Newsweek*) reporting in Algeria." A week later, in the December 26 issue of *Newsweek*, the lead to Durand's report from the Casbah notes that he was "recovering from the effects of tear-gassing," effects that would shortly bring on his death. H.D. quotes this note in full in her letter of December 28 to Pearson.[61] These documents suggest that H.D. came to associate the myth of the sun's rebirth at winter solstice not just with Durand's death but with the particular circumstances of his death—his unexpectedly fatal assignment in Algiers. Indeed, the florid and apparently unexamined links in *Newsweek* between "the darkest time of the year" and this latest eruption of interracial violence on the "dark continent," when paired with H.D.'s own earlier links between Durand, darkness, and death, compose a dense nexus of racially and politically overdetermined references radiating from her use of the Saïs myth.

In this double allusion to an ancient myth and a contemporary news story, H.D. begins to close the gap that had opened between Durand's actual situation and her mythical deifications of him. Furthermore, with this myth of rebirth she ceases to demand that Durand stand as the primitive bearer of a magical potency great enough to revive an old woman— or a weary West—in their "decline" (*HD* 3, 10). Instead, she takes it upon herself to revive Durand, drawing into her own body Algeria's "season . . . of long darkness," and refiguring it as the womb's life-giving period of gestation. In a tribute not only to the nine months she has carried him in her thoughts but also to her own habitual misspelling of his name, she reviews the course of her acquaintance with Durand as a period not of wasted waiting but of "full time"—a "during" or duration like that of a pregnancy in which hidden life takes root and swells the dying surface of the present moment. "It had to go on the full time," she writes (*HD* 54).

> The experience was unprecedented,
>
> a fire eating me up,
> but a fire to be sustained.   (*HD* 50)

And again: "I have much to sustain me" (*HD* 53). Like *Espérance* at the end of *Winter Love*—the child who slays in drawing life from its mother's milk—Durand's presence in H.D.'s thoughts eats her up, yet in sustaining him she sustains both herself and the epiphanic "fiery moment" whose perfection, she records in *End To Torment*, "can not be sustained—or can it?" (p. 11).

This is not to say, however, that the Saïs myth proves capable of resolving H.D.'s deeply contradictory attitudes toward Durand and decolonization. Reviewing their epiphanic encounter stretched across the fullness of time, she reveals its extended moment to be a space of doubleness, equivocation, and ambivalence. Thus, even as she figures the journalist as her own child, H.D. revives her previous associations between black men, war in Africa, and devils. She rejects the idea that she might have aborted Durand in September, before he resumed coverage of the war, in terms that apply equally to exorcism: "it was too late to cast you out" (*HD* 52).[62] And in the poem's last section, she releases Durand with the ambivalent dismissal:

> Now you are born,
> and it's all over,
> will you leave me alone?
>
> whether you have gone to archangels and lovers
> or to infernal adventures,
> I don't know.   (*HD* 55)

Given the trend in her postwar poetry toward increasingly conservative notions of the child's need for the mother, it is disturbing to discover that this late articulation of the mother's need to be separate from the child coincides with H.D.'s desire to rid herself of the potentially "infernal" messenger of anticolonial resistance. For here it is likely that H.D. alludes to Daphne du Maurier's "hair-raising" book *The Infernal World of Branwell Brontë*, which she was reading with great avidity in early February. She writes to Pearson on February 10, 1961, that this book provided "some resemblance to my own divided personality—or world." H.D.'s obsession with Durand does in fact find a ready correspondence in Branwell's adult obsession with the satanic Alexander Percy of his childhood "infernal world," a fictional British colony in the warring African kingdom of "Angria," whose history he and Charlotte chronicled in elaborate detail. Moreover, Pearson, we recall, had himself described Durand as going through "hell" in "French Algeria" in late December. With the recovery of these intertextual echoes, H.D.'s bid to bring Durand and his fate into the circle of her own body appears to hover between an act of reparation to a victim of colonial violence and a ritual of exorcism that demonizes that same victim.[63]

The final version of *Hermetic Definition* offers a broken and erased account of H.D.'s obsession with Durand, and the ensuing confrontation between his reports on the violence rifling the contemporary period of African decolonization and her own long-standing commitment to modernist myth-making. In neither the lines she keeps, nor in the deleted lines, notes, diary entries and letters from which a more complete picture emerges, is it possible to detect any final resolution to this confrontation. If, in her sudden rejection of Perse's poetic world of "heap and mound, / continent, empire" at the end of "Grove of Academe," we can detect a growing uneasiness with figures of empire or the very project—so dear to high modernism—of a universalizing poetics, H.D. equally refuses to voice any explicit criticism or disavowal of colonialism in this poem. The merging of mythic and contemporary history through the figure of Saïs, while marking a significant reconciliation of a deeply rooted conflict in her poetry, remains considerably more oblique than the final splitting of Durand before angelic and infernal fates, with its unconfronted subtext of racial alienation, exoticism, and demonization.

Throughout this book, I have argued that H.D. attempts in her late poetry to invest the space of epiphany with visionary solutions to contemporary social conflicts, but that these solutions, on inspection, reveal fully historical patterns of political ambivalence and incoherence. In *Hermetic Definition*, H.D. herself appears to stage this very realization as her successive strategies for achieving epiphany repeatedly fail to silence the poem's multiple conflicts. Both her recurring bids for epiphanic resolution and her failure to maintain it can be traced back to two contradictory logics governing H.D.'s use of the inside/outside scheme. According to one logic of this scheme, the violent crossing of a threshold magically transforms a moment of "decline" and death into a moment of sexual fulfillment, healing, and rebirth. This is the logic of ecstasy. In H.D.'s earlier long poems, it governs the transgressive epiphany of a female Christ Child at the conclusion of *Trilogy*, the hallucinatory birth of Horus in *Helen in Egypt*, and the tortuous ecstasy of breast-feeding at the end of *Winter Love*. Here, it governs H.D.'s fantasies of creeping into Durand's cavern and of bearing Durand from her own womb.

According to a second logic of the inside/outside scheme, a reassertion of the barrier between inside and outside secures positive internal values against destructive external forces. This is the logic of the island paradise. In earlier long poems, it governs Kaspar's visionary return to the lost Atlantis near the end of *Trilogy*, and Helen's wish that "the goddess hold me for a while / in this her island, her egg-shell" near the end of "Leuke" in *Helen in Egypt* (*HE* 197). Here, it governs H.D.'s "escape" into "the mind's closed recess" and Perse's "*promesse d'îles*" (*HD* 27, 30). It may also be said to govern H.D.'s revisions of the poem, which, in excluding all explicit references to war in Africa, create a work much closer to her earlier modernist long poems than to the self-reflexive critique of modernism that appears on the pages of the poem's original draft. Although they have worked for H.D. before, both logics fail to bring about resolution or closure in her last poem. This may be because the declared dichotomy between inside and outside, on which these logics each depend, is unable to uphold the additional kinds of difference—between presence and absence, male and female, lover and beloved, parent and child, West and East, contemporary history and ancient myth—with which H.D. would invest it. Thus, as we have seen, much of what H.D. leaves *inside* her final poem can be read as an index of the personal and international conflicts she has ostensibly excluded from it.[64]

The poem's failure to uphold the inside/outside dichotomy itself may also refer to this same array of conflicts. As contemporary events challenged H.D.'s faith in modernist myth-making and a benevolent world order, the similarities between a fantasy of boundary-crossing ecstasy and colonial invasion, on the one hand, and between a fantasy of an island paradise and the buttressing of empire against local and international resistance, on the other, could well have prompted her to doubt the power of these fantasies to heal. Several uncharacteristic stances at the end of "Star of Day" support this supposition. H.D. forgoes the show of messianic promise, creative achievement, and hope that habitually attends the birth scenes in her poetry, and which the myth of Saïs that organizes the sequence gives readers cause to expect. Thus, while she connects her recurring "waves" of depression during the London Blitz to hysterical labor pains and the "birth of a new era," this latest pregnancy, also arising in a period of war, waiting, and despair, carries with it no prophecy or recipe for a better future.[65] She is old, and the age of Aquarius and the House of Friends she has long awaited are not at hand.

In the poem's penultimate lines, H.D. writes:

> I only know,
> this room contains me,
> it is enough for me,
>
> there is always an end.   (*HD* 55)

Once again, this quiet acceptance of her "confinement," as she recovers from the effort of delivering Durand into the next life and prepares for her own death, stands in striking contrast both to her long-standing figures of domestic and maternal entrapment and to the figures of world-annihilating laughter and world-encompassing ecstasy that conclude her two most recent poems, *Sagesse* and *Winter Love*, also written during the postwar wave of decolonization. At a time of bitter territorial struggle in Africa, she finds new adequacy in an enclosed domestic space that does not curtail the woman within so much as illuminate her moderation and wisdom.

Less generously, we might read H.D.'s retreat to her room as one last attempt to escape from a contemporary history whose pain she finds unbearable. But H.D. herself immediately undoes the fantasy of containment and closure that she has just transcribed. The poem ends with an image of the poet that merges the impregnability of the cloister with the grey threshold of dawn:

> now I draw my nun-grey about me
> and know adequately,
>
> *the reddest rose,*
> *the unalterable law* . . .
> Night brings the Day.   (*HD* 55; H.D.'s ellipses)

Whether H.D. hails the mythic rebirth of the Daystar here or "only the days' trial, / reality . . ." is not certain (*HD* 19; H.D.'s ellipses). What is certain, as she marks a dissolving boundary in the turning passage of time, is that the only closure she is now prepared to extend is provisional.

REFERENCE MATTER

Notes

Introduction

1. In this paragraph, I cite works by H.D. in the following order: "The Master," p. 411; *Tribute to Freud*, pp. 36, 37; "The Cinema and the Classics I," p. 33; *The Gift*, p. 17; *T* 25; *End to Torment*, pp. 21, 33; *HERmione*, pp. 223–24; *Nights*, p. 20; Letter to Bryher, April 24 or 25, 1933; *Palimpsest*, p. 220; *Paint It Today*, p. 4; *T* 31. All references in this manuscript to H.D.'s letters, unpublished manuscripts, and personal papers, as well as to the letters of Bryher, Norman Holmes Pearson, and Walter Schmideberg, are to the Yale Collection of American Literature at Beinecke Rare Book and Manuscript Library, Yale University, New Haven, Conn.

2. In this paragraph I cite works by H.D. in the following order: *The Gift*, pp. 77, 91, 106, 57; *Hedylus*, p. 20; *HE* 8; *T* 129, 134, 39, 135; *HE* 15; *Tribute to Freud*, pp. 107, 106; *HERmione*, p. 10; *The Gift*, p. 135; *HD* 3; *Bid Me to Live*, pp. 77, 51; *End to Torment*, p. 6; *Notes on Thought and Vision*, pp. 59, 60, 64.

3. For accounts of H.D.'s early critical reception, see Bryer, "H.D.," pp. 627–31; and Friedman, *Penelope's Web*, pp. 53–55. See also May Sinclair's 1927 review of H.D. in Scott, *Gender of Modernism*, pp. 453–67.

4. Friedman, *Penelope's Web*, pp. 60, 53.

5. Laity, "H.D. and A. C. Swinburne," pp. 221, 223. H.D.'s early (male) psychoanalytic critics unwittingly recast the terms of this opposition in Freudian garb, reading what is "hard, exact, and real" in her writing as a compensation for "penis, mother, father, love—something," or finding in her tropes for "inwardness" "something damp or decaying, cavernous, in a word, insubstantial." See Holland, "H.D. and the 'Blameless Physician,'" p. 476; and Riddel, "H.D. and the Poetics of 'Spiritual Realism,'" p. 449.

6. Here, Susan Stanford Friedman's essay "Who Buried H.D.?" proved groundbreaking.

7. Friedman speaks of H.D.'s "quest for wholeness" and "authentic female voice" in *Psyche Reborn*, pp. 278, x. Ostriker sees Helen in *Helen in Egypt* as "a quintessential woman-as-subject . . . engaged in the recovery of her splintered selves" in "Thieves of Language," pp. 79, 80. DuPlessis conceives of Helen's quest for "inner integration" in dialectical terms, where "conflict and resolution exist in a complex and nuanced balance" in "Romantic Thralldom," pp. 195, 190.

8. Chisholm, "H.D.'s Auto*hetero*graphy," pp. 88, 89; Claire Buck, *H.D. and Freud*, pp. 36, 88.

9. Thus, at the end of "H.D. and A. C. Swinburne," Laity claims that H.D.'s internalizations of modernist views on Swinburne's "depravity" were "momentar[y]" and did not "rule her imagination for long" (p. 235). Similarly, Friedman's acknowledgment of H.D.'s occasional displays of anti-Semitism and racism fades before later claims that H.D. practiced "a modernism of the margins rather than the reactionary center." See DuPlessis and Friedman, "'Woman is Perfect,'" pp. 421–22; and Friedman, "Modernism of the 'Scattered Remnant,'" pp. 102, 116. In the last two chapters of *Penelope's Web*, Friedman sets the dystopic decade of the twenties, when H.D. repeatedly opposed the creative "masculine mind" and the mad, silent, or dying "feminine body" in her writing, against the redemptive decade of the thirties, when she reconceived the grounds of her creative authority in "gynocentric" rather than "patriarchal" terms (pp. 278, 328). And in the last two readings of *H.D. and Freud*, Buck finds *Trilogy* "problematic . . . because the poem identifies the unrepresentable residue [of femininity] as a truth located in individual experience," but celebrates *Helen in Egypt* for "defining the knowledge of woman as something you can know by knowing that you do not know it" (pp. 139, 164). All three critics downplay the possibility of residual negative effects in these positive closing moments.

10. DuPlessis, *H.D.: The Career*, pp. 5, 51.

11. Here and elsewhere, my references to *Hermetic Definition* are to the first, title poem in the volume *Hermetic Definition*, and not to the volume as a whole.

12. Jacobus, "'Tea Daddy,'" pp. 160–61. Jacobus ends her account of Lacan's relationship to Kleinian theory by calling this charge into question, however; citing evidence from one of Klein's early essays, she asserts that "Lacan's unsuspected 'category of the signifier' turns out to have been a guest at [Klein's famous patient] little Dick's tea-party all along" (p. 179).

13. These citations are drawn from Juliet Mitchell's and Jacqueline Rose's respective introductions to *Feminine Sexuality*, pp. 4, 11, 34, 25–26, 18.

14. Rose, *Sexuality*, p. 174. More recently, Rose herself makes note of Lacan's early and unrealized ambition to translate Klein's 1932 *Psychoanalysis of Children*, and remarks, "It seems to me that he was more dependent on her ideas than some of us realised before" ("Hanna Segal Interviewed," p. 208).

15. Jameson, "Imaginary and Symbolic," pp. 355–56. Lacan's debts to and modifications of Kleinian theory are an intermittent focus throughout Part II of this essay.

16. Klein uses the "ph" spelling in "phantasy" to specify unconscious phantasy. I retain her usage when discussing her ideas, but revert to the more common "fan-

tasy" (which carries no distinction between conscious and unconscious unless locally indicated) when referring to the work of Freud, H.D., and others.

17. Doane and Hodges, *From Klein to Kristeva*, p. 26; Jameson, "Imaginary and Symbolic," p. 360; Jacobus, "'Tea Daddy,'" pp. 160–79.

18. Kristeva, *The Kristeva Reader*, p. 95.

19. Kristeva, *Powers of Horror*, pp. 54, 102.

20. Mitchell and Rose, *Feminine Sexuality*, p. 90.

21. Similarly, the Lacanian mirror blanks out the alimentary canal's role in providing the infant with its first terms of judgment; Freud argues that the critical faculty of judgment originates in the infant's impulse to ingest "good" or "useful" items and to "spit out" "bad" or "harmful" ones ("Negation," pp. 236–37). In Kleinian theory, the mutually exclusive categories of good and bad food extend to define the moral options of maternity itself; the mother is good if she feeds, bad if she withholds food (or gives hunger, itself understood as a kind of bad food). One pernicious effect of this Manichean logic is its phobic handling of the fact that the mother eats. In Klein's account, the inevitability of the mother's own hunger ensures her vilification insofar as it marks her unwillingness to hand all the resources available to her over to the infant. The painful simplicity of this scheme is not Klein's own doing; rather, it points to a wider cultural discomfort with the woman who places her own interests above those of others. This discomfort, and the fantasies of maternal nourishment and persecution underwriting it, show up even in feminist criticism; for instance, in her introduction to H.D.'s *Paint It Today*, Cassandra Laity argues that the novel "debates conflicting forms of lesbian love and existence": namely, "an all-consuming mother-love" and "a more nurturing, communal, and less engulfing sister/mother bond" (pp. xxi, xxv–xxvi). Before we pick sides in such a debate, we need to question its organizing assumptions, which exalt the role of nurturing mother (and hence the role of consuming daughter) while condemning the "consuming 'mother'" as "demonic" (p. xxx). As Laity's introduction itself might suggest, the critical conjunction of H.D. and Klein opens up intriguing pathways between H.D.'s work and a growing body of gay, lesbian, and antihomophobic theory that also explores the gendering of the alimentary canal. See, for instance, Moon and Sedgwick, "Divinity," pp. 12–39; Fifer, "Is Flesh Advisable?" pp. 472–83; Stimpson, "The Somagrams of Gertrude Stein," pp. 183–96; Bersani, "Is the Rectum a Grave?" pp. 197–222; Koestenbaum, "The Queen's Throat," pp. 205–34; J. Marcus, "Laughing at Leviticus," pp. 221–50.

22. Thus, Friedman comments that Adrienne Rich "has seen in H.D.'s work a comprehensive critique of the violence at the core of patriarchy," and again that "like Woolf, H.D. connected aggression with patriarchy." See "'I go where I love,'" p. 229, and *Penelope's Web*, p. 340. Friedman discusses H.D.'s matricidal fantasies but again seems to refer these fantasies to conditions peculiar to patriarchy, arguing that "H.D. works through the rage" for her mother "by reflecting on the patriarchal origins of her mother's betrayal" (*Penelope's Web*, p. 343).

23. Rose, *Sexuality*, p. 156.

24. Doane and Hodges argue along similar lines: "Klein hardly ignores the constitutive role of phantasy in the early oedipal stages. But by naturalizing object

choice as a biological constant, Klein is able to align the phantasies of the infant with a grounding 'reality.' In this way, Klein resurrects the positivist view of reality that her own elaborations of the role of phantasy render so problematic" (*From Klein to Kristeva*, p. 15).

25. Butler, *Gender Trouble*, pp. 61–65.

26. The uncritical retention of the nexus of Freudian associations between the feminine (or maternal), the primitive, and the unconscious weakens Dianne Chisholm's otherwise sophisticated and perceptive book, *H.D.'s Freudian Poetics*. Judith Butler has also criticized Lacan for "the pervasive nostalgia for the lost fullness of *jouissance* in his work" (*Gender Trouble*, p. 56). Dominick LaCapra's astute comment that "there is a crucial relation between the conversion of absence into loss and the genesis of the phantasm" suggests a likely source for this "pervasive nostalgia" in psychoanalytic theory ("History and Psychoanalysis," p. 242). For absence to be reconstituted as loss, an idealized (phantasmatic) fullness must be conjured up and set in an idealized past: a simple recipe for nostaglia. If Klein cooks in another kitchen, this may be because her infants experience absence not as loss but as assault.

27. This is not to suggest that Klein desists from all mythologizing in her theories. In bypassing myths of the garden, she squarely embraces myths of the fortunate fall, particularly in her later work. Phyllis Grosskurth follows Dr. Hans Thorner in noting that "her later theories on constitutional envy, the primary importance of the mother, and reparation bear close parallels to the doctrines of original sin, the Immaculate Conception, and Christian atonement" (see Grosskurth, *Melanie Klein*, p. 84). This unacknowledged parallel regains its explicitness in H.D.'s reception of Klein.

28. Rose, *The Haunting*, p. 15.

29. Berque, *Egypt*, pp. 622, 664.

30. In *Hermetic Definition*, H.D. tells Durand: "these lyrics . . . would only embarrass you" (*HD* 16). She writes to Pearson on Sept. 10, 1960, "my poems which I was & am ashamed to show you, deal with Durand." Pearson in turn reassures Frederick Martin at New Directions about the poem, "One can read it certainly, as one can read Yeats, without worrying too much about how literally these things seemed to her" (May 30, 1972). And DuPlessis comments in passing on H.D.'s "irrational, irrepressible desire" for Durand "which she herself calls excessive" (*H.D.: The Career*, p. 125).

31. The Swedish Academy awarded St.-John Perse the 1960 Nobel Prize in Literature because, it said, "his poetry . . . reflects the conditions of our time" ("The Nobel Prizes," p. 60).

32. Rose, *Sexuality*, p. 149.

33. Letter, Pearson to James Laughlin, June 12, 1972. See also Pearson to Peter Glassgold, June 12, 1972.

34. Rose, *Sexuality*, pp. 1–23.

35. Several people provided crucial help in the writing of this introduction. A second look at Harriet Chessman's book on Gertrude Stein and conversations with her on violence and audience got me started. Bruce Hainley's many ideas on anger, grief, gay culture, and remembering the dead grew up next to, and into, my own

thoughts on these subjects. Siobhan Somerville's work on the racialized and gendered body in late nineteenth- and early twentieth-century fictions of passing sharpened my critical interest in the historical implications of H.D.'s representations of race and racial transformation. Michelle Bonnice's essay and conversations on moral education revived my sense of moral dilemmas in my own work. Finally, Beth Povinelli's work on the mutually constitutive cultural roles of body and landscape in a Northern Australian Aboriginal community has prompted me to give new weight to, and to pose new questions about, the body's rhetorical positioning in H.D.'s poems.

Chapter 1

1. *The Gift*, pp. 136–37. Susan Friedman reports that H.D. wrote most of *The Gift* in 1941, adding the last chapter (from which I quote) in 1943; see *Penelope's Web*, p. 364. The death-wish articulated in this added chapter should be aligned with the recurring theme of suicide in H.D.'s writing and life. Barbara Guest derives from *Asphodel* the idea that H.D. gave Bryher a hand in raising Perdita in exchange for her promise not to threaten suicide again, and reports two rumors that H.D. and Bryher each attempted suicide during the war years (*H.D.*, pp. 112, 254). H.D. tells Norman Holmes Pearson that her 1946 breakdown was caused by her mistaken thought that Bryher had committed suicide; she adds, "I was always afraid she would make away with herself, during the Blitz" (letter, Sept. 26, 1946). Diana Collecott reads H.D.'s 1919 poem "I Said" against the backdrop of her relationship with Bryher and Bryher's suicidal despair ("What Is Not Said," p. 247). Susan Friedman discusses H.D.'s literary treatments of suicide in *Asphodel, Paint It Today, Kora and Ka,* and *Nights*; see *Penelope's Web*, pp. 177, 207, 267, 270–78. In addition, figures for both Bryher and H.D. (Irene and Hedylus) contemplate suicide in H.D.'s *Hedylus* (pp. 102, 110, 119). The story "She Is Dead" (June 1941), in which H.D. realizes that she has projected out a dead part of herself and is now free to live, brings this theme into the same time period as her composition of "The Walls Do Not Fall."

2. See Friedman, "'I go where I love,'" pp. 231–32; and Schweik, *A Gulf So Deeply Cut*, pp. 259, 289. Rachel Blau DuPlessis's reading of the opening "argument between spiritual and . . . masculinist-nihilist / materialist positions" in *Trilogy* displays a similar set of assumptions. See *H.D.: The Career*, p. 88.

3. Tylee also points to the increased efforts on the part of the British government to control the population's response to the war, noting that "this was the first war in which psychological warfare was used so efficiently" ("'Maleness Run Riot,'" p. 199). Claire A. Culleton argues on similar lines that because "pictorial postcards were more or less 'invented' during World War I," the images linking women and war on such cards enjoyed an unprecedented circulation ("Gender-Charged Munitions," p. 112). Jane Marcus makes the interesting argument that "the War Office's propaganda posters (and those of British Rail) of nurses, mothers, and wives sending their men to war were a *response* to the overwhelming powerful public iconography of the women's suffrage movement, a challenge to the figures of Amazon Joan of Arc, the virgin warrior and the professional single

woman drawn as the protector of mothers and children"; see "The Asylums of Antaeus," p. 140.

4. Gubar, " 'This Is My Rifle,' " pp. 227–59.

5. Schweik's own reading positions "The Flowering" on a contradictory middle ground between these two categories. Claiming that the poem's final figure of the myrrh bundle offers "a nonviolent, life-affirming, body-affirming *ethics*" associated with the maternal, she acknowledges that myrrh also carries connotations of female violence. But Schweik places this contradiction at the origin of individual pathology, presenting it as the cause of H.D.'s "moral breakdown" after the war (*A Gulf So Deeply Cut*, pp. 269, 286, 290). In contrast, I follow Klein in pathologizing the wider cultural need to enforce a split between women's capacities for aggression and nurture in the first place, and read H.D.'s poem as an attempt to move beyond the false contradiction that ensues from such a splitting.

6. H.D. uses the term "war phobia" in her therapy with Freud. See her letter to Bryher, Nov. 19 or 18, 1934.

7. Norman Holland also detects but does not name Klein's influence in H.D.'s war writings, asserting that this work provides "a graphic illustration of the theory that artistic creativity stems from the wish to reconstitute what has been lost in aggressive fantasy"; see "H.D. and 'The Blameless Physician,' " p. 497. More recently, Dianne Chisholm has "hint[ed] at a thematic connection between H.D. and Klein"; see *H.D.'s Freudian Poetics*, pp. 222–24, 260n15.

8. While my reading of *Trilogy* in the context of the repetitive action of the Freudian death drive was formulated before the publication of Susan Friedman's *Penelope's Web*, her extensive examination of H.D.'s use of repetition in her prose of the twenties and thirties forms an important backdrop to this argument. Friedman proposes to read H.D.'s autobiographically based prose as a self-conscious (re-)staging of the analytic scene in which the narrator, "I now," engages the protagonist, "I then," in a relationship governed by transference, where the goal of writing is to work through repetition to the recovery of repressed memories (pp. 80–99). Yet she argues that two other Freudian models impinge on this therapeutic use of repetition: the *fort-da* game, with its drive for mastery and control of the mother's movements, and the death drive. If, as Friedman argues, H.D. frequently feels compelled to confirm Freud's sense of the deadliness of repetition in her novels, in *Trilogy* she takes on the task of proving him wrong. Again in contrast to my argument, Dianne Chisholm associates "the figure of repetition" in H.D.'s writing not with female aggression but with the *jouissance* of "a primary, feminine masochism"; see *H.D.'s Freudian Poetics*, pp. 157–59.

9. See H.D.'s letters to Bryher, Oct. 5, 1936, and July 27, 1937. After May of 1937, H.D. sought Schmideberg's help only as the need arose; see her letter to Bryher, May 30, 1937. Here and throughout this book, I present nearly exact transcriptions of H.D.'s personal writings, retaining spelling and punctuation anomalies unless such anomalies clearly appear to be typographical errors. I have not, however, reproduced spacing irregularities between words.

10. Friedman, *Penelope's Web*, p. 292.

11. In a letter to H.D. dated June 25, 1958, Bryher gives retrospective notice of Klein's unorthodox focus on aggression. She writes, "One review of modern English books had an interesting comment that Melanie Klein had done most of her

work—a deviation from Freud—on aggression. She had greatly influenced English thought and all the work of 'the angry young men' was concerned not with sex but with aggression. It is interesting."

12. P. King and Steiner, *Freud-Klein Controversies*, p. 34.

13. Ibid., p. 21.

14. In contrast, Juliet Mitchell proposes that Klein's concept of the depressive position, first articulated in a paper delivered in 1934 and published in 1935, "marked the beginning of disagreement among British analysts" (*SMK* 116). As we will see shortly, there is some evidence that suggests Walter Schmideberg made use of this concept in H.D.'s analysis.

15. See H.D.'s letters to Bryher: Oct. 20, 1935; Oct. 26, 1935; Nov. 7, 1935.

16. See H.D.'s letter to Bryher, Oct. 22, 1936.

17. See H.D.'s letter to Bryher, Nov. 10, 1935.

18. See H.D.'s letter to Bryher, Mar. 1, 1936.

19. See H.D.'s letters to Bryher: Mar. 10, 1936; Mar. 12, 1936. In a 1929 essay, Klein argues that "the little girl has a sadistic desire . . . to rob the mother's body of its contents, namely, the father's penis, faeces, children, and to destroy the mother herself. This desire gives rise to anxiety lest the mother should in her turn rob the little girl herself of the contents of her body (especially of children) and lest her body should be destroyed or mutilated. In my view, this anxiety, which I have found in the analyses of girls and women to be the deepest anxiety of all, represents the little girl's earliest danger situation" (*SMK* 92). During March 1936, the same month in which Walter interpreted H.D.'s anger at Bryher's mother, Joan Riviere and Klein gave public lectures on material later used in *Love, Hate and Reparation* (p. vii). There, Klein reiterates her thoughts on infantile phantasies of robbing the mother, and links the infant's closely related "phantasies of exploring the mother's body" to "man's interest in exploring new countries" (*LHR* 103–4). For more material on H.D.'s stealing fantasies, see H.D.'s letters to Bryher, Feb. 16, 1936, Apr. 17, 1936. Bryher's childhood nickname was Dolly; see Guest, *H.D.*, p. 112.

20. See H.D.'s letter to Bryher, Oct. 23, 1936. The "hidden phallus," a term popularized by Klein, refers to infantile phantasies of cannibalistic intercourse, in which the mother eats the father's penis and stores it in her belly (*DPA* 165). The essays in *Developments in Psycho-Analysis*, to which I refer here, are "based primarily on four papers" written by Klein and three of her followers (Joan Riviere, Susan Isaacs, and Paula Heimann); these papers "were originally read in a series of Discussions arranged in 1943 in the British Psycho-Analytic Society with the object of enabling members to clarify their views in regard to [Klein's] work" (*DPA* 4). While these essays refined Klein's theories in the direction of greater subtlety and clarity, for the most part they did not offer significant advances over ideas already in circulation during H.D.'s analysis with Walter Schmideberg. Thus, in providing an account of Kleinian theory, I restrict myself to essays written before or during the period of these discussions in order to provide a sense of the shape Kleinian theory was taking at the time H.D. was directly exposed to it, and to avoid incorporating later theoretical developments into my overview.

21. Friedman reviews H.D.'s records of her discussions with Freud on her unconscious associations between the "primal scene" and "being 'killed' by a man,

the father"; see H.D.'s letter to Bryher, Nov. 18 or 19, 1934, cited in *Penelope's Web*, p. 339.

22. See Bryher's letter to H.D., Sept. 11, 1937, and H.D.'s letters to Bryher: Sept. 28, 1936; Mar. 18, 1936; Apr. 13, 1937. The topic of lesbian overtones in H.D.'s relationship with Perdita was a long-standing one; see H.D.'s letter to Bryher of her dream—discussed with Freud—of kissing the breast of Perdita, posed as Venus on a shell: Oct. 29, 1934. Also see her letter to Bryher of June 8, 1935, in which she notes that Perdita "has evidently fall[en] in love with me, in good Maïdchen in Uniform manner."

23. See Bryher's letter to Walter Schmideberg, Nov. 28, 1936. Edward Glover notes that Kleinian psychoanalysis was sometimes referred to as "the English School" (P. King and Steiner, p. 145).

24. See Grosskurth, *Melanie Klein*, p. 293, for an excerpt from the speech Walter addressed to the Society on March 11, 1942. This speech can be found in full in P. King and Steiner, *Freud-Klein Controversies*, pp. 84–87. Bryher and H.D. may well have read it; in a letter to Bryher dated Apr. 10, 1942, Walter encloses "a speech I made some weeks ago *against* nearly the whole of the British Psychoanalytic society." In this speech, Walter accuses Klein of stealing not only the concepts of "introjection and projection mechanisms, . . . sadism and pre-genital phantasies" from "Freud, Ferenczi [and] Abraham," but also the concept of "Boehm's hidden penis." (As we recall, he used this latter concept in his analysis with H.D.) Melitta later seconded these charges of her mother's plagiarism; see P. King and Steiner, pp. 115–16, 150–51. Whatever truth lay in such charges (which seem a bit over-determined given Klein's wider emphasis on stealing phantasies in the mother-child dyad), the Schmidebergs were alone in making them.

25. See H.D.'s letter to Bryher, Nov. 28, 1936.

26. See Bryher's letters to Walter Schmideberg: Oct. 14, 1936; Sept. 19, 1937; Mar. 3, 1940; Mar. 13, 1940.

27. See Bryher's letters to H.D.: Apr. 15, 1937; Sept. 16, 1937. Unconscious phantasy played a more central and a much earlier role in childhood development for Klein than for Freud. For an overview of their differences, see Segal, *Melanie Klein*, pp. 60–61. In opposition to Freud, Kleinians claimed that our earliest phantasies are nonverbal (*DPA*, pp. 49–50).

28. See Bryher's letter to H.D., July 30, 1936. In her quick reply, dated July 31, 1936, H.D. notes that she is "somewhat sad that he [Walter] is an ice-berg," and continues: "I shall long for all details of him there and at the ps-a [psychoanalytic] hot-bed."

29. See Bryher's letter to H.D., Mar. 18, 1936.

30. See Bryher's letter to H.D., Aug. 3, 1938. In this letter, Bryher also mentions that she "was spoken too, most affably by Queen Victoria Melanie." On Mar. 26, 1940, Bryher again informs H.D. that she has been discussing "the ever prevalent analytical gossip" with Melitta.

31. Friedman, *Psyche Reborn*, p. 134.

32. H.D. discusses her own "carnival aggression" in a letter to Bryher dated Oct. 23, 1936.

33. See H.D.'s letters to Bryher: Nov. 9, 1936; Apr. 17, 1936. See also her letter to Bryher, July 5, 1936.

34. See H.D.'s letters to Bryher: Feb. 4, 1936; Feb. 26, 1936.

35. See H.D.'s letters to Bryher: April 17, 1936; Feb. 11, 1936.

36. See H.D.'s letter to Bryher, Sept. 26, 1936. H.D. would probably have been very vulnerable to charges of bad mothering. Her father died on March 2, 1919, a month before Perdita's birth on March 31; in June and July of 1919, H.D. and Bryher traveled to the Scilly Islands, leaving Perdita in the Norland Nurseries in South Kensington where she would board, with her mother returning to live nearby, in 1919 and 1920 (Guest, *H.D.*, p. 118). Guest notes that H.D. learned of her first pregnancy on the day in August of 1914 that Britain declared war, and argues that this child was not, in fact, "wanted" (pp. 72–73). H.D.'s remark that Walter explains "everything in terms . . . of the Unk [unconscious] and the lost parent," as well as her references to Perdita's intense possessiveness around her, can be aligned with Klein's focus on the child's sense of loss and abandonment during weaning; see H.D.'s letters to Bryher: Jan. 27, 1936; Oct. 23, 1936. H.D. also discussed her own feelings of parental abandonment with Freud. See H.D.'s letter to Bryher, Nov. 27, 1934, where she writes, "So it is perfectly clear I did LOOSE both parents at the age of 3 or 4 and built up my whole love-life on that love and terror mixed, and violence as of war etc."

37. Klein advances her notion of the depressive position in her 1935 essay "A Contribution to the Psychogenesis of Manic Depressive States" (first delivered as a talk in 1934). In the same essay, she carefully spells out the distinction between eating difficulties associated with the paranoid position and those associated with the depressive position (*SMK* 118–19, 121, 127). For an analyst versed in Kleinian theory, H.D.'s symptom of finding her "food hard to chew" would also recall Klein's famous patient Dick, a four-year-old whose anxiety over the destructive power of his own aggression was so great that "he refused to bite [solid food] up and absolutely rejected everything that was not of the consistency of pap; even this he had almost to be forced to take" (*SMK* 100). A Kleinian would probably associate "cleaning the house" with the child's act of reparation to the damaged mother and with its attempt to secure "good internal objects" of a loving, generous mother within itself.

38. H.D. probably had access to both sets of letters; in a letter to Bryher dated May 29, 1940, she reports that she has just dined with the Schmidebergs "and they will come here next week, we meet about once a week, it is a great help and we exchange news and letters." At first glance, Bryher's hilarious tales of a heroine whom she memorably describes as "forty pounds of wriggling Boxer" seem an unlikely spot on which to ground serious discussion of H.D.'s war experiences (Bryher to H.D., Feb. 25, 1940.) But H.D. was already familiar with the impulse to project urgent human fantasies and anxieties onto the antics of dogs. See Susan Friedman's discussion of the time when Freud proposed to give H.D. one of his chow's puppies during her analysis with him and "the drama of the pups enacted procreative fantasies for both of them" (*Penelope's Web*, p. 309).

39. See Bryher's letter to Walter Schmideberg, Apr. 28, 1940, and her letters to H.D.: Apr. 28, 1940; May 14, 1940.

40. See H.D.'s letter to Bryher, May 16, 1940, and Bryher's to H.D., May 30, 1940.

41. See Bryher's letters to H.D., July 29, 1940, and Aug. 3, 1940.

42. See Bryher's letter to Walter Schmideberg, Aug. 10, 1940, and to H.D., Sept. 2, 1940.

43. See Friedman, *Penelope's Web*, p. 340. For letters to Bryher in which H.D. asks after Claudi (whom she repeatedly calls "poor Claudie"), see Feb. 10, 1940; Mar. 5, 1940; May 9, 1940; May 16, 1940; May 31, 1940; June 18, 1940; July 19, 1940; Aug. 16, 1940; Aug. 17, 1940.

44. J. Sandler gave the Controversial Discussions their name, which is now normative, in 1967. Before, they were called the Scientific Meetings and Discussions. Pearl King notes that Melitta "was one of the four Members who signed the proposal calling for [the] Extraordinary Business Meetings. She attended most of these meetings, only missing the one when Glover's letter of resignation was read. However, she came to only one of the Special Scientific Discussions, though she made two written contributions. Following the resignation of Glover, she went to America." Walter "came to all the Business Meetings held in 1942, but did not come to any of the Special Scientific Discussions, or take much part in the Society after Glover had resigned"; see P. King and Steiner, *Freud-Klein Controversies*, pp. 233, xix–xx.

45. Grosskurth, *Melanie Klein*, pp. 297–98. This analogy was all the more starkly enforced by the fact that the meetings of the Society were held in London during the Blitz years because the "continental analysts, . . . as aliens from an enemy country, were not allowed to travel out of the London area" (p. 245).

46. Grosskurth writes, "The Discussions were dominated by women—and what women they were!" Anna Freud, Dorothy Burlingham, Kate Friedlander, Barbara Lantos, Hedwig Hoffer, Barbara Low, Ella Sharpe, and Melitta Schmideberg (though no friend of Anna Freud's) lined against Klein, and Paula Heimann, Joan Riviere, Susan Isaacs, and Sylvia Payne stood with her. Grosskurth further reports that "the continental males . . . were not very effective" and that "the male members of the Klein group were often absent because of wartime duties" (*Melanie Klein*, p. 316).

47. H.D. records a dream in the Hirslanden Journal that suggests that the relationship between Klein and her daughter formed a lasting analogue to H.D.'s own experiences of aggression in the mother-daughter dyad: "Melitta Schmideberg sent me a fascinating book 'The Cat, In the Mysteries of Magic and Religion,' which I have been reading. Last night, there is a small dream-cat and a kitten. The miserable kitten is being cuffed and mauled by its mother. Alas—am I the kitten or am I the cat?" The entry goes on to recall Freud's own comments on the aggression and rivalry displayed by his female dogs (Notebook 2, p. 1: entry for Jan. 26, 1957).

48. Claire Culleton's discussion of women munitions workers during World War I suggests how war propaganda intensified this difficulty by arguing that women could fulfill themselves as mothers precisely by *producing* weapons of destruction; thus, she examines a series of images that suggest that "shell-making is as maternal an act as egg-laying or giving birth" ("Gender-Charged Munitions," p. 111). Culleton's larger survey of munitions imagery offers startling testimony to the cultural accuracy of Klein's accounts of phantasies of maternal aggression; see, for instance, the image of woman-as-cannon exuberantly giving anal or vaginal birth to a stream of explosives (p. 112).

49. Eliot, *Selected Poems*, p. 70.

50. Friedman, *Penelope's Web*, p. 39.

51. Grosskurth, *Melanie Klein*, pp. 115–16. Klein changed her views on the dating of Oedipal conflict in 1945, shortly after H.D. completed *Trilogy*. At this time, she redefined the Oedipus complex "as part and parcel of the depressive position," characterized by a decrease in sadism and the fear of losing the loved object; see Segal, *Melanie Klein*, p. 84. Earlier, she had argued that "the Oedipus conflict begins at a period when sadism predominates" and the infant is still in its paranoid position (*SMK* 96).

52. Segal, *Introduction*, pp. 25–26.

53. For H.D.'s half-humorous record of her own hunger during the war years, see her letter to Bryher, dated Aug. 17, 1942. In her World War II novel "The Sword Went Out to Sea," H.D.'s persona, Delia, reports that "in my delirium . . . I watched in my imagination, migrations of hordes of starving people, driven like cattle in search of pasture. It was only food that mattered." See Book 1, Part 1, sect. 2: 97. On a related note, Jane Marcus argues that it was widespread hunger and not adult heterosexual desire that caused "the breasts of the phallic mother . . . [to] become such important propagandistic signifiers in the literature of war"; see "Corpus/Corps/Corpse," pp. 157–58. For Klein's account of the infant's equation of its "faecal mass with weapons and missiles" and its urine with agents of fire and flood, see *SMK*, p. 96.

54. Donna Krolik Hollenberg has noted on similar lines that H.D. uses the stories of the mollusk and worm "to incorporate hitherto unacceptable feelings of aggression into the female sphere" (*H.D.*, p. 128).

55. Grosskurth cites Klein's 1941 letter to Ernest Jones, in which she names Freud's *Beyond the Pleasure Principle* and *The Ego and the Id* as her greatest inspirations, particularly in the formulation of her theory of reparation. Grosskurth also notes that where "rigid Freudians were most comfortable with Freud's early work, Kleinians were more amenable to his later work, even accepting the death instinct, which most Freudians passed over in embarrassed silence" (*Melanie Klein*, pp. 284, 317).

56. Matt. 13: 46.

57. See H.D.'s letter to Bryher, May 21, 1939. H.D. here refers to James Strachey's article, "Preliminary Notes Upon the Problem of Akhenaten," which relates Akhenaten's cross-dressing to his repressed homosexuality and paranoia. I will return to H.D.'s reception of this article shortly.

58. In my attention to figures of passing in H.D.'s writing, I am indebted to Siobhan Somerville's fine work on images of African-American and gay and lesbian passing in late nineteenth- and early twentieth-century literature. Discussions with her on passing have also stimulated my thinking about the bisexual body.

59. Friedman, "'I go where I love,'" p. 238. Another troubling aspect of H.D.'s ironic connection between gun cartridges and hieroglyphic cartouches is the fact that both are vehicles of breaking and entering. For just as a gun cartridge houses the bullet that punctures the body, cartouches originally provided archeologists with the means to crack the code of the ancient Egyptian hieroglyphic script. As such, the cartouche enabled a repetition in the landscape of language of the violent desecration of the pharaohs' tombs (by ancient grave-robbers and mod-

ern excavators alike) which H.D. evokes in the apocalyptic first section of *Trilogy*, where "ruin opens / the tomb" and "the shrine lies open to the sky" (*T* 3). In *Easy Lessons in Egyptian Hieroglyphics*, a book H.D. owned, E. A. Wallis Budge reviews this history and provides an illustrated demonstration of Champollion's method of decipherment. He notes in passing that "the cartouches . . . are so called because they resemble cartridges" (p. 16).

60. H.D. notes that Amen means "the hidden-one" in Egyptian in "Majic Ring," p. 57.

61. Rev. 1: 14.

62. Shorter, *Egyptian Gods*, pp. 7–8. H.D. owned a copy of this book.

63. Budge, *The Gods of the Egyptians*, vol. 1: 369.

64. After reading this essay, H.D. writes Bryher on May 21, 1939: "Had a wonderful double read in Psycho journal,—did you see the article that followed the Freud? Statue of Akhneton found to be a-sexual, a woman; certain authorities said he WAS a woman; as Queen Hatshepshut, he pretended to be a man. Anyhow, its most interesting, but I expect you have seen all this. I found the Journal full of interesting and suggestive paragraphs. Let me see any others before you have bound." In a discussion that resonates suggestively with this letter, Dianne Chisholm cites the recent argument of Estelle Roith, who claims that Freud avoided citing an early study on Akhenaten (or Ahemhotep) by Karl Abraham in his Moses essays in part out of a need to repress the influential studies on the mother's centrality in childhood development advanced by Abraham's student Melanie Klein. Abraham's own study argued that Ahemhotep's mother, Queen Tiy, initiated Egypt's campaign of monotheistic reform. See Chisholm, *H.D.'s Freudian Poetics*, pp. 222–24; and Roith, *Riddle of Freud*, pp. 170–74.

65. Here, I recall H.D.'s letter to Bryher of Nov. 24, 1934, cited in Friedman and DuPlessis's joint essay, " 'I had two loves separate,' " p. 24. She writes in reference to her therapy with Freud and her writer's block: "I have gone terribly deep with papa. He says, 'you had two things to hide, one that you were a girl, the other that you were a boy.' It appears I am that all-but extinct phenomina, the perfect bi-. Well, this is terribly exciting, but for the moment, PLEASE do not speak of my own MSS., for it seems the conflict consists partly that what I write commits me—to one sex, or the other, I no longer HIDE."

66. Mark 4: 14, 15.

67. For instance, in his discussion of obsessional neuroses, Freud asserts that the "two opposites" love and hate are often found to "have been split apart and one of them, usually the hatred, [has] been repressed." He then cites the case of a man who wanted to pray, " '*May God protect her*,' but a hostile '*not*' suddenly darted out of his unconscious and inserted itself into the sentence; and he understood that this was an attempt at a curse" ("Notes upon a Case," pp. 238–42, 191–93).

68. When Isis's father, Rā, refused to disclose his secret name, which would enable her to become his equal, Isis formed his spittle into a poisonous snake that bit him, and then demanded his name in exchange for his life (Budge, *The Gods of the Egyptians*, vol. 1: 360–63). The myths of Isis's relations with children would also be suggestive to anyone familiar with Kleinian theories of infantile phantasy. On Isis's journey to recover Osiris's limbs, five children die: one by the poisonous sting

of a scorpion when she's refused entrance to a house, one (her own son Horus) by another scorpion when she leaves him unattended, one by fire when its mother interrupts and defeats Isis's attempts to burn away its mortality, one from fear of her loud lamentations, and one from the fright of her angry gaze. She only brings the first two back to life (Frazer, *Adonis Attis Osiris*, vol. 2: 8–10).

69. H.D., *Tribute to Freud*, p. 172.

70. DuPlessis, *Writing Beyond the Ending*, p. 116.

71. Klein makes this major argument in "The Importance of Symbol-Formation," *SMK*, pp. 95–111.

72. Segal, *Introduction*, p. 68.

73. Ibid., p. 76.

74. Ibid.

75. Denise Riley cites an editorial in the *British Medical Journal* for January 1944, which suggests the extent to which both the assumptions and the terms of Klein's account had entered the mainstream of the British medical community by the war years. Entitled "War in the Nursery," the editorial proposes that "destructive impulses let loose in the war may serve to fan the flame of aggression natural to the nursery age . . . the Age of Resistance may thus be prolonged to adult life in the form of bitterness, irresponsibility, or delinquency" (Riley, *War in the Nursery*, p. 1).

76. P. King and Steiner, *Freud-Klein Controversies*, p. 238.

77. Ibid., p. 454.

78. Matt. 5: 38. Joan Riviere and Paula Heimann make this parallel between the Kleinian infant and Mosaic law explicit when they refer to operation of "the talion principle" in the infant's paranoid phantasies (*DPA* 50–51, 159).

79. Gubar, "The Echoing Spell," pp. 207–8; Friedman, *Psyche Reborn*, pp. 220–21.

80. The alchemical "planets" of Mercury, the moon, the sun, and Jupiter (associated with Michael, Gabriel, Raphael, and Zadkiel respectively) are all named directly (*T* 67, 92, 99, 108). "Azrael, // the last and greatest, Death" corresponds to the second alchemical stage of decay and dissolution, ruled by the planet Saturn (*T* 67). "Uriel," of "the red-death" and of "War" (*T* 67, 70), corresponds to the stage ruled by Mars, while "the Venus name," "*Annael, /* peace of God," corresponds to the stage ruled by Venus (*T* ix, 79).

81. Burckhardt, *Alchemy*, pp. 115, 118, 123, 185–191.

82. Friedman, *Psyche Reborn*, p. 252.

83. There is a legitimate distinction to be made between Kloepfer's emphasis on "*language*" and the Kleinian child's preverbal use of symbolic *objects* in its reparation phantasies. Klein, however, directly connects the child's symbol-making activities with his first efforts to "enlarge his vocabulary" (*SMK* 105). H.D.'s alchemical fantasy, in which words take on their own materiality, forms a bridge between Kloepfer's account and Klein's.

84. H.D., *Notes on Thought and Vision*, pp. 67, 65, 60.

85. H.D., *Ion: A Play After Euripides*, p. 58.

86. See H.D.'s letter to Bryher, Mar. 28, 1936.

87. See also Segal, *Melanie Klein*, p. 50.

88. Burckhardt, *Alchemy*, p. 188. This passage orginally appeared in a book entitled *La Parole delaissée* in Bernardus Trevisanus's *Le Voile d'Isis* (Paris: vol. for 1931), p. 461. Burckhardt also includes an excerpt from Nicholas Flamel's fourteenth-century alchemical account, first published in *Bibliothèque des philosophes chimiques* (Paris: G. Salmon, 1741), in which he reports obtaining *materia prima* after years of failure: "Finally I found what I had longed for, and I recognized it at once by its strong smell; and when I had it, I accomplished the work" (p. 180).

89. Taylor, *St. Thérèse*, pp. 149, 179, 190, 193, 194, 312, 350. The book includes the Saint's autobiography, biography, and letters. In "Mythology, Psychoanalysis, and the Occult in the Late Poetry of H.D.," Susan Friedman discusses the importance of the St. Thérèse cult for H.D. (pp. 262, 339–44). In *End to Torment*, H.D. identifies the Saint as one of her female "lost companion[s]" and reports that she used to tell a rosary in conjunction with prayers to the Saint during World War II (pp. 59–60).

90. Taylor, *St. Thérèse*, p. 169.

91. For H.D.'s interpretation of Sappho's phrase, see her poem "Fragment Forty," in *Collected Poems*, p. 173.

92. Miriam Fuchs reads a passage in which H.D. defines her writing as "burning" in a similar way: "H.D. yields to the ongoing, external attacks that could burn her to death, but she also shapes her fear into psychic images of her own creative forces and stamina" (p. 90). H.D.'s association of fire with the force of anger and creativity may be compared to Dianne Chisholm's discussion of H.D.'s association of burning with "a primary, feminine masochism" in *The Gift*; see *H.D.'s Freudian Poetics*, pp. 154–59.

93. For a more extended account of this dream of the Lady, see H.D., "Majic Ring," pp. 98–100.

94. De Rougemont, *Passion and Society*, pp. 85, 56. See also the revised and currently more accessible version, *Love in the Western World*, pp. 71, 46. De Rougemont's *Passion and Society* was a crucial book for H.D. in the early years of World War II. In a letter to Bryher dated May 31, 1941, H.D. thanks her again for the book as she reads it in English translation, and comments that "it is sheer DOPE to me, one of the turning points of my life is the reading of that vol." Friedman reports that H.D. first read the book in its original French in 1939 (*Psyche Reborn*, p. 170).

95. De Rougemont, *Love in the Western World*, p. 90. This passage does not appear in *Passion and Society*, but its gist appears at scattered points throughout the book; see, for example, pp. 117–19.

96. In 1914, Freud defines the compulsion to repeat as the return of repressed libidinal wishes in a register of uncomprehending physical action and symptom-formation rather than conscious verbalization ("Remembering, Repeating," p. 150; "Repression," pp. 154–55). In seeking "to restore an earlier state of things" (*Beyond the Pleasure Principle*, p. 36), the death drive redefines the capacity of the unconscious to conserve its contents as an individual organism's repeating attempts to resist further change by clinging indefinitely to the modifications already imposed on it. By not perishing, early stages of the unconscious insure only that

the individual will not lose his or her own way back to death (pp. 38–39). H.D. alludes to this formulation directly in "The Sword Went Out to Sea," where she speaks of her "stubborn will to keep alive until I could die in my own way" (Book II, sect. 1: p. 28).

97. The jewel carries this same psychoanalytic significance. Freud reports from a conversation with Dora: "Perhaps you do not know that 'jewel-case' ['Schmuck-kästchen'] is a favourite expression for the same thing that you alluded to not long ago by means of the reticule you were wearing—for the female genitals, I mean." To which she is said to have replied, "I knew you would say that" ("Fragment," p. 69).

98. Burckhardt, *Alchemy*, p. 187.

99. See Adalaide Morris's important essay "The Concept of Projection," esp. pp. 424–35, for H.D.'s complex literary use of the several meanings of "projection," including the two I emphasize here.

100. According to secret spiritual meanings encoded in the alchemical work, the alchemist unites his or her own body and soul with god (or the universal spirit) and so confers on them an immortal and "luminous essence" (Hutin, *History of Alchemy*, pp. 109, 114).

101. Burckhardt, *Alchemy*, p. 99.

102. In H.D.'s Artemis dream, the goddess—rainbow-robed and pregnant—appears to another "band of sisters": H.D., Bryher, and Joan Cole. Friedman relates this dream to H.D.'s coded discussion of her conversations with Freud on masturbation; see H.D.'s letter to Bryher, May 26, 1933, and *Penelope's Web*, pp. 321–26. H.D. describes her erotic dream of Perdita in a letter to Bryher dated Oct. 29, 1934; the dream was memorable enough for her to record it again many years later in Notebook 3 of her Hirslanden Journal, entry for Feb. 9, 1957, p. 16. In her autobiography, St. Thérèse also records a highly homoerotic dream which H.D. may have had in mind here. The Saint dreams of "Our Venerable Mother," who "caressed me most tenderly" and "kissed me so lovingly that no words can convey the sweetness of her embrace" (Taylor, *St. Thérèse*, p. 200).

103. As noted earlier, H.D.'s mother's name was Helen.

104. Friedman notes that H.D. associates her father's and grandfather's clocks "with time, which inevitably brings death" in *The Gift*, that Freud interpreted her habit of checking her watch during their sessions as a death wish, and that Julia broods over her husband's war-issue wristwatch in *Bid Me To Live*. *Penelope's Web*, pp. 336, 295, 137. In *Palimpsest*, Raymonde listens to the sound of soldiers' marching feet "keeping pace, keeping time to the terrible rhythm" of "death and birth" (p. 140). Yet two stories written in 1941 link clocks with new life and with lesbian eroticism. In "Warehouse" (Jan. 1941), Bryher fishes through a pile of old family paintings and hands a broken clock to H.D., in whom "the clock released . . . some spring of consciousness"; in need of repair, the clock represents old and new time. In "Pattern," H.D. dreams that she leaves her "little travelling clock" in a bungalow where she has been asleep to visit a house where her mother shows her a piece of H.D.'s own tapestry work. She interprets its unbroken wave and lily design to mean that her life's pattern will not be broken, and concludes, in terms

that anticipate her portrait of the Lady in "Tribute": "My mother is satisfied, pleased with my work and now I find by some miracle, the little clock has come back, it is there, ticking away."

105. H.D., *Nights*, p. 51. In keeping with the lesbian content of the dream of the Lady in "Tribute to the Angels," Dianne Chisholm notes H.D.'s ascription of "large breasts" to this "high-powered deity" in *Nights*, and comments that "the god of her dreams is (also?) a goddess" (*H.D.'s Freudian Poetics*, p. 86).

106. H.D., *Nights*, p. 19.

107. Friedman, *Penelope's Web*, pp. 275–78.

108. Deborah Kloepfer notes similarly that Freud refuses to allow "*adult* relation with the mother, because, in strict Freudian terms, for a woman to become 'adult' means, by definition, to give up the mother" (*Unspeakable Mother*, p. 120). It should be noted that Klein abides by Freud's account in the early parts of her career; see, for instance *SMK*, p. 77. On the other hand, Freud was less condemnatory of homosexuality than Klein, who, as Noreen O'Connor notes, "provides clear statements regarding the necessary pathology of homosexuality" ("Is Melanie Klein the One?" p. 182). But, as Doane and Hodges point out, Klein's "insist[ence] on the innately heterosexual destiny of each sex" is undercut by the fact that most of her work focuses on the period before stable, presumably heterosexual object choices are made, and gives full play to the homosexual trends of infantile phantasy (*From Klein to Kristeva*, pp. 12–13). When Jacqueline Rose asks Klein's disciple Hanna Segal to respond to the "worry that Kleinianism is moralistic and homophobic," Segal makes her own homophobia abundantly clear; see Rose, "Hanna Segal Interviewed," pp. 210–13.

109. Taylor, *St. Thérèse*, p. 200.

110. H.D.'s verbal evocations of portraits of the Virgin call to mind the work of Ruth Kjär, whose own portraits of women Klein analyzed as reparative attempts "to restore her mother and make her new" through art (*SMK* 93).

111. Hutin, *History of Alchemy*, pp. 47, 55.

112. S.v. *Webster's Third New International Dictionary* (1981).

113. Chisholm, *H.D.'s Freudian Poetics*, pp. 122, 128.

114. Ibid., pp. 147–54.

115. Chisholm's analysis of *The Gift*, while it does not argue for Klein's influence, occasionally makes evident Kleinian assumptions in that memoir as well; see in particular *H.D.'s Freudian Poetics*, pp. 135–47. In drawing back from Chisholm's pairing of maternal mourning with a masochistic *jouissance* in H.D.'s war writings, I do not mean to deny the prevalence of masochistic positions of desire in H.D.'s writing more generally. In fact, both masochistic and sadistic fantasies constitute two of the most important, and largely overlooked, aspects of H.D.'s literary imagination. Here again, though, Chisholm would disagree; she associates "egoistic aggression" and "sadistic mastery" exclusively with a heterosexual masculinity that she claims H.D. opposes (pp. 148–49, 155).

116. Schweik's own section on "The Traffic in Myrrh" and her return to Adalaide Morris's article on H.D. and the gift economy helped me to reshape the terms of my argument here; see Schweik, pp. 269–83. My argument also owes a general

debt to Bruce Hainley's moving work on Paul Lynde, the gay closet, guest stars, and remembering the dead.

117. Lewis Carroll, *Alice's Adventures*, pp. 14–23.

118. *Paradise Lost*, Book XI, ll. 833–34, in Milton, p. 452.

119. Gregory, "Rose Cut in Rock," pp. 538, 536.

120. H.D. alludes here and elsewhere in "The Flowering" to Luke 7: 37–50.

121. Taylor, *St. Thérèse*, pp. 350, 194.

122. Reading from Kristevan rather than Freudian premises, Kloepfer offers a similar reading of this line as an indication of the semiotic's simultaneous release from and containment within the bounds of the symbolic or thetic (*Unspeakable Mother*, p. 135).

123. Freud defines the contents of the unconscious as "timeless" and imperishable in *Beyond the Pleasure Principle* and *Civilization and Its Discontents* respectively; see p. 28 of the former, p. 71 of the latter.

124. Friedman credits Adrienne Rich with identifying Kaspar as a persona for Freud (*Penelope's Web*, p. 303, 402n21).

125. For current feminist analyses of ancient Greek links between the permeable female body, the demonic or taboo, and the sacred, see Padel, "Women," pp. 3–19; H. King, "Bound to Bleed," pp. 109–27; and Zeitlin, "Power of Aphrodite," pp. 52–111.

126. Freud's definition of the fetish and his links between it and castration anxiety exclude the possibility of fetishizing the vagina or any other part of the female anatomy. I derive my sense that H.D. is deliberately fetishizing doors in this story not from orthodox Freudian theory, then, but from the supposition that she is here making an unorthodox application of his phallocentric account.

127. Dianne Chisholm also argues that H.D. attempts to revise Freud's account of the *fort-da* game in *The Gift*, and follows Derrida in placing his grandson's game in the larger context of his own mourning for the death of Sophie, daughter to Freud and mother to the little boy; see *H.D.'s Freudian Poetics*, pp. 147–54.

128. Morris, "A Relay of Power," pp. 500, 503, 501.

129. Ibid., pp. 500, 503–4.

130. Taylor, *St. Thérèse*, pp. 241, 251.

131. Ovid, *Metamorphoses*, Book X, pp. 243–51. See also Schweik, *A Gulf So Deeply Cut*, pp. 285–86.

132. Matt. 26:75.

133. Matt. 26:72.

134. In "call[ing] someone quietly to eject her" from his house (*T* 143), Simon enacts Freud's own analogy between a householder's impulse to "order an undesirable guest out of my drawing-room (or out of my front hall)" and the ego's impulse to repress and/or project outwards its own undesirable thoughts ("Repression," p. 153).

135. Matt. 26:11–12. Susan Schweik makes a similar point about Mary's role here—a kind of embalming "in advance"—but reads this moment as one of self-critical meditation "on women's substantial role in encouraging and sustaining war as sacrificial practice" (*A Gulf So Deeply Cut*, p. 286).

136. *Paradise Lost*, Book IV: ll. 305–6, in Milton, p. 285.

137. Milton, p. 49.

138. I thank Roz Carroll for pointing out to me Freud's connections between demonic possession and hysteria. Dianne Chisholm also discusses H.D.'s ongoing use of the figure of the hysteric, and links hysteria with witchcraft and mystical ecstasy; see *H.D.'s Freudian Poetics*, esp. pp. 76–87, 200–13.

139. H.D.'s short story "Before the Battle" (1940) repeats the terms of these letters to Bryher, describing "a sort of rhythm of terror, like rhythm of birth pangs, actually we are in the travail, actually and literally in the sense of the Book of Revelations, we ourselves are begetting this new age" (p. 1). As Friedman notes, H.D.'s earlier novels treat her first pregnancy in similar terms. *Asphodel* links the beat of the fetus's pulse with the "beat of guns" (p. 182), and *Palimpsest* merges the soldiers' marching feet, the joined pulse of mother and child, and the metrical feet of Raymonde's verse in one large "rhythm of pain" (pp. 145–56); cited in *Penelope's Web*, pp. 185, 248.

140. Gen. 3:16. Deborah Kloepfer also reads Kaspar as a kind of surrogate woman, arguing that H.D. uses him as a male intermediary whose presence allows the daughter to explore her own "forbidden access" to incestuous contact with the mother (*Unspeakable Mother*, p. 134). Kloepfer's discussion of the "lesbian sexuality" evoked by the "prenatal harmony, timelessness, and aqueous sensuality" of Kaspar's vision helps to suggest that the vision carries over the theme of an eroticized reunion between mother and daughter established in "Tribute to the Angels" (p. 137).

141. Song of Sol. 1:13. Schweik also notes this reference (*A Gulf So Deeply Cut*, p. 269).

142. H.D.'s childhood religion offered her an important precedent in this multiplication of Christ's sexual identity. As Janice Robinson notes, "according to . . . Moravian theology, Jesus is symbolically both mother and husband. . . . Christ is one body, male and female" (pp. 82, 83). In the Zinzendorf Notebooks, H.D. records Rimius's remark that "they make his Name of the feminine Gender, calling him their Mother, their *Mamma Jesua*," as well as their "Husband with the steaming little Corps!" (pp. 8, 32).

143. Susan Schweik finds a similar complexity in the myrrh figure when she reads it as an "emblem of . . . 'all-at-onceness' " and "a figure of the proverbial 'bundle of contradiction' " (*A Gulf So Deeply Cut*, pp. 284, 289).

144. H.D., "The Sword Went Out to Sea," Book 2, sect. 9:178.

145. Alchemical associations provide further links between Mary Magdalene, myrrh and the desert snowfall here. As noted earlier, purified quicksilver is said to exude a heavenly fragrance and to take on "a fine crystalline lustre" and the whiteness of "snow on top of a very high mountain." In addition, quicksilver is considered "the 'womb' of all metals" and is "also known as 'maternal blood' (*menstruum*), for, when it does not flow 'outwards' and perish, it nourishes the germ in the alchemical womb or 'athanor' " (Burckhardt, *Alchemy*, pp. 188, 81, 140). Donna Hollenberg further notes Barbara Walker's assertion that "in the lore of magic, myrrh was credited with the power to cause menstruation" (*H.D.*, p. 138).

146. Kloepfer, *Unspeakable Mother*, p. 136.

147. See H.D.'s letters to Bryher: Apr. 20, 1936; Nov. 24, 1934.

148. Susan Friedman notes that "in many of H.D.'s texts, heat is associated with heterosexual passion, while cool is connected to its opposite, a lesbian intensity" (*Penelope's Web*, p. 200).

149. Claire Buck takes a similar stance in her reading of this letter itself. She argues that the phrase " 'what I write commits me,' [is] followed by a pause, then 'to one sex, or the other,' the two positions permanently oscillating, not fusing, and thereby undoing any attempt to come out in the open, to 'no longer HIDE.' " Buck's quotation of Marius's response to his female lover Hipparchia in *Palimpsest* (p. 30) is also relevant here: "was she patently beneath his eyes to become sister to herself and brother and changing and interchanging brother, sister, ringing the changes, the interrelations of fourteen distinct and separated entities?" (*H.D. and Freud*, pp. 87, 47). By "The Flowering," H.D. learns to achieve this effect with one word.

150. I owe this line of thought to Bruce Hainley, whose work on gay men's subversive appropriations of the language of flowers has inspired this chapter's conclusion.

151. For instance, Juliet Mitchell rested her early claims to reappropriate Freudian psychoanalytic theory for feminist ends on her ability to demonstrate the unconscious's historical, and therefore reformable, nature. As several of her own readers have argued, the incomplete success of this demonstration jeopardizes her entire project; see her *Psychoanalysis and Feminism*, pp. 361–416; McDonough and Harrison, pp. 14–25; and Kuhn, "Structures of Patriarchy," pp. 51–52.

152. Morris, "Signaling," p. 130.

153. Adalaide Morris makes a similar point when she argues that "although in isolation this practice [of divination and prophecy] may seem apolitical or even anti-political, when used to readjust or confirm social relations, mysticism overlaps with politics." She continues: "Like *The Odyssey, The Aeneid, The Divine Comedy*, and *Paradise Lost, Trilogy* emerges from the midst of cultural crisis, brings myth to bear on history"; see "Signaling," pp. 128, 129.

154. Segal, *Melanie Klein*, p. 153; Riley, *War in the Nursery*, p. 78. Grosskurth notes that Melitta Schmideberg was among the first to make this charge, and cites excerpts from her "scathingly brilliant" presentation to the British Society on Feb. 17, 1937: "Analysis is regarded as an atonement, as a cleansing process, as a religious exercise; getting on in the analysis means doing one's duty, obeying one's parents, learning one's prayers, defecating" (*Melanie Klein*, p. 229).

155. Thus, Doane and Hodges point out that the exclusive focus of Klein and object-relations theorists "on infantile experience precludes attention to other cultural arenas: economic, social, linguistic" (*From Klein to Kristeva*, p. 80). H.D. may have been familiar with this line of critique. Grosskurth cites Melitta Schmideberg's 1971 account that her differences with Kleinians in the 1930's stemmed in part from the fact that she refused to grant unconscious phantasies sole power in determining the infant's development, and instead "paid more attention to the patient's actual environment and reality situation" (p. 213). Klein links the child's phantasies of the gutted maternal body to problems with long division in *Contri-*

butions to Psycho-Analysis, pp. 79–80, and links the same phantasies to colonial conquest (as noted earlier) in *LHR*, pp. 104–5.

156. Doane and Hodges note that the "real" Kleinian mother is "a figure almost empty of agency and subjectivity" (*From Klein to Kristeva*, p. 29). Harriet Chessman makes the same point about the mother's role in Kristeva's theories of the semiotic, where "the mother herself has little access to language of any sort" (*Public Is Invited*, p. 72).

157. Rose, *Sexuality*, p. 16.

Chapter 2

1. Friedman, *Psyche Reborn*, pp. 253–72.

2. Friedman, " 'I go where I love,' " pp. 231–32.

3. Richard W. Hull suggests that World War II directly fueled the drive toward African decolonization: "World War II forced the British and French to reconsider their colonial policies. First, their depleted treasuries could not sustain a strong military presence overseas. Second, both powers, particularly France, owed a great moral debt to African leaders for their wartime military support. Third, the two European wars destroyed the myth of the superior white monolith," increasing anticolonial resistance (*Modern Africa*, p. 117).

4. H.D. links the Quakers' "bare meeting-house" of Amen's dream appearance to "the *House of Friends*" in "Majic Ring," pp. 41–42. H.D. may also have been aware of her indebtedness to ancient Egypt for the art of alchemy, which she takes as her model throughout "Tribute to the Angels"; one conventional etymology for "alchemy" is *al-kimiya*, a derivative of *kême*, meaning "the black land," an ancient Egyptian designation for Egypt (Burckhardt, *Alchemy*, p. 16; Hutin, *History of Alchemy*, p. 12).

5. Berque, *Egypt*, pp. 571, 585–87.

6. For a summary of Egyptian history during this period, see Vatikiotis, *History of Modern Egypt*, pp. 370–93. I follow the schedule of composition for *Helen in Egypt* which H.D. gives in "Thorn Thicket," entry for Aug. 3, 1960, pp. 50–51.

7. Bryher returned to the topic of the Egyptian Revolution in March, reporting to H.D. that "apparently there is a wave of rich Egyptians coming into Switzerland, they escaped from Egypt and had already put their money here," and that "one of them might be interested in Kenwin," Bryher's Bauhaus residence in Switzerland that she was currently trying to sell. See Bryher's letters to H.D.: Feb. 3, 1954; Feb. 26, 1954; Mar. 24, 1954.

8. H.D., "Compassionate Friendship," p. 139. Published in 1955, Newby's *The Picnic at Sakkara* looks back from the recent success of the Egyptian Revolution to its immediate roots in postwar militant Egyptian nationalism. Set in Cairo in the last months of 1946 (p. 205), the novel relates the comic adventures of Mr. Perry, a British English professor who finds himself caught in the middle of the violent student demonstrations staged at the University of Giza during that year. Early in the book, Muawiya Khaslat, one of Perry's students, intervenes on Perry's behalf when a mob of students calling for the evacuation of British troops threatens to kill him (pp. 21–31). Later, however, Khaslat halfheartedly attempts

to assassinate Perry on a picnic to the Tombs of Sakkara at the behest of his comrades in the right-wing terrorist group, the Moslem Brotherhood (pp. 159–61, 210–16). The book ends with Perry's decision to leave Egypt for good and return to England. See Vatikiotis, *History of Modern Egypt*, pp. 358, 360–64, 366–68, 370–71, for an account of the series of student demonstrations—including the 1946 demonstrations at Giza—and the related activities of the Moslem Brotherhood (or Ikhwan) in the years leading up to the Revolution.

9. Friedman, *Psyche Reborn*, pp. 259–60.

10. See DuPlessis, "Romantic Thralldom," pp. 178–203, especially pp. 201–2; and *Writing Beyond the Ending*, pp. 76–83.

11. In placing importance on the detail both in my own argument and in what I assert to be H.D.'s strategy of reading, I owe a general debt to Naomi Schor's *Reading in Detail: Aesthetics and the Feminine*, and a particular debt to her fourth chapter where she argues from Freud that "displacement is then a sort of strategy devised by the unconscious to evade censorship, and the hypersemanticized detail, in turn, becomes a camouflage allowing repressed contents to surface" (p. 71).

12. For a summary of H.D.'s multiple forms of involvement with psychoanalysis from the early twenties onward, see Friedman, *Psyche Reborn*, pp. 17–22, and *Penelope's Web*, pp. 286–93. Sergei Eisenstein ran articles in Bryher's journals, *Close Up* and *Life and Letters Today*, from 1928 to 1946. Although H.D.'s greatest involvement in film spanned the years in which *Close Up* was published, letters to Bryher in 1935 and 1936 bear recurring reports of her enthusiasm for *Life and Letters Today*, and numerous notes on the films she has seen. See in particular H.D.'s letters to Bryher, Dec. 8, 1936 and Dec. 17, 1936. On May 5, 1939, in the month before "Montage in 1938" was launched in serial form, H.D. reports to Bryher: "I love the new L. and L. and am reading it with the last number. I find I always go back and read the old numbers, a great test of the paper's vitality." Because Eisenstein's essays were revised slightly when reissued in Jay Leyda's *Film Form* and *The Film Sense*, I draw on the essays of *Close Up* and *Life and Letters Today* unless otherwise noted; for the reader's convenience, I cite the corresponding passages in Leyda's collections as well. I also posit that H.D. knew Eisenstein's important essay "The Cinematographic Principle and Japanese Culture," published in *transition* in 1930 during a peak period of the *Close Up* circle's own enthusiasm for his work.

13. Here, I consider hysteria as a model for H.D.'s visionary program of reform, not as a model for wider feminist practice. Because the ideas represented by hysterical symptoms conflict with the hysteric's own conscious standards of conduct, they are by definition cut off from the sphere of voluntary political practice. For two nuanced critiques of recent feminists' celebratory appropriations of hysteria, see Clément, pp. 130–36, and Rose, *Sexuality*, pp. 27–47. H.D.'s own war experiences may inform her portrayal of Helen as a hysteric. See letters from H.D. to Bryher for May 30, 1940; June 2, 1940; June 3, 1940, cited in Chapter 1, in which H.D. links her hysterical symptoms of depression at the threat of air raids to her two wartime pregnancies and the birth pains of a new era. H.D.'s links between war, hysteria, birth pain, and a new era will find direct parallels in Helen's "reading" of the lily.

14. Stephen Heath's passing association of Eisenstein's use of filmic "literalisms" with hysteric symptom-formation in a larger discussion on Eisenstein's interest in "inner speech" gave me the idea of reading Freud and Eisenstein as linked influences on *Helen in Egypt* (*Questions of Cinema*, pp. 204–17, 220n54).

15. Friedman, *Psyche Reborn*, pp. 65, 61.

16. See Macpherson, "As Is," *Close Up* 7, 5 (Nov. 1930): 294. This similarity may not be coincidental. Anne Friedberg notes that "early clinical descriptions of 'borderline' patients described many of the qualities which Freud saw in his hysterical patients." See "Writing About Cinema," pp. 146–47.

17. Conversation with Thomas Whitaker, May 9, 1991.

18. Friedman, *Penelope's Web*, p. 358.

19. DuPlessis, "Romantic Thralldom," p. 198. Cited in Kloepfer, *Unspeakable Mother*, p. 138.

20. In contrast to previous chronologies of the poem's opening events, I place the events on the desolate beach before the poem's meditative action begins, and Helen's initial naming of Thetis before rather than after Achilles' attempt to strangle her. After using the present tense in her opening speeches in the temple, Helen adopts the past tense to recount the entire sequence of events that took place during "that first night / on the desolate beach" (*HE* 38), and then returns to the present tense at the beginning of "Pallinode," Book 3, to narrate her subsequent interactions with Achilles (*HE* 1, 6–25, 35 ff). Two headnotes indicate that Helen is alone in the temple when she reviews the beach encounter with Achilles, and that he rejoins her in the temple only after she has finished her account (*HE* 11, 35). In sections 7 and 8 in Book 1 of "Pallinode," Achilles' attack on Helen immediately follows her initial invocations of Thetis (*HE* 13–17). For opposing chronologies, see Friedman, *Psyche Reborn*, p. 60, and DuPlessis, "Romantic Thralldom," p. 193. Jeanne Larsen precedes me in identifying Helen's naming of Thetis as the cause of Achilles' attack ("Myth and Glyph," p. 93).

21. For two opposing positions on the significance of Freud's retraction of the seduction theory for feminists, see Masson, *The Assault on Truth*, and Rose, *Sexuality*, pp. 1–23.

22. Jeanne Larsen also notes the connection between Helen's wounded feet and the "limping Oedipus," but understands this to signify, for Theseus, Helen's female lack of "something unwounded men possess," a notion H.D. herself is said to reject ("Myth and Glyph," p. 94).

23. This ambiguity as to "who it was that dreamed it all"—father or daughter— puts to the reader of *Helen in Egypt* much the same question Alice puts to her cat at the end of Lewis Carroll's *Through the Looking-Glass*: "You see, Kitty, it *must* have been either me or the Red King. He was part of my dream, of course—but then I was part of his dream, too! *Was* it the Red King, Kitty?" (p. 244). Composed in the late 1860's, Carroll's imbricated dream of king and girl precedes by a good 25 years Freud's seduction theory, but by the 1950's H.D. could well have been aware of how Dodgson used his stories of Alice as a masked form of erotic dalliance with Alice Liddell. Carroll's complex use of unconscious reasoning and his heroine's adventures in a puzzling underworld further help to establish the *Alice in Wonderland* tales as precedents for *Helen in Egypt*. In this regard, H.D.'s choice

of the phrase "phantasmagoria of Troy" is interesting. The term for a precinematic form of visual entertainment using a magic lantern and a screen and frequently conjuring up ghostly scenes in exotic Egyptian and Arabian locales, "phantasmagoria" also supplied the title of Carroll's *Phantasmagoria, and Other Poems*, published in 1869. For a fascinating account of eighteenth- through twentieth-century literary appropriations of phantasmagoria shows, which may well provide a distant precedent for the montage structure of *Helen in Egypt* as well as for its thematic concerns, see Castle, pp. 26–61.

24. While critics have not made much of Helen's childhood history of barely averted rape, Rachel DuPlessis suggests that the scene in H.D.'s *The Gift*, in which the young Hilda abruptly escapes from the milk cart of a male stranger, might encode a moment of attempted sexual assault; see *H.D.: The Career*, pp. 78–79. Dianne Chisholm expands on this suggestion in *H.D.'s Freudian Poetics*, pp. 127–28.

25. In *Le Tarot*, a book H.D. owned, Jean Chaboseau identifies the *femme noire* as the black priestess seated at the threshold of the Sanctuary on one of the Tarot cards. The sacred ankh around her neck and the Book of Thoth in her lap link her to Isis, while her darkness is said to represent the obscurity undergone by the hermetic tradition in recent times (pp. 46–47).

26. Budge, *The Egyptian Heaven*, pp. 92, 106. H.D. owned a copy of this book.

27. In a book H.D. owned, Budge recounts Horus's ceremonial assumption of Isis's role in reuniting and reviving the body of Osiris; see *Osiris and the Egyptian Resurrection*, vol. 1: 70–86. Budge also discusses the ancient Egyptians' practice of endowing signs with the spirits and powers of their referents in *The Gods of the Egyptians*, vol. 1: 10.

28. H.D. performed highly complex fusions of the Isis myth with her own life history. As a result, this vision and the terms through which it organizes the rest of the poem draw on many important events in her life. In her unpublished novel "Magic Mirror," she equates "the 1000 (and more)" pilots lost in the Battle of Britain during World War II with the "one still-born child" she lost shortly after hearing of the "*Totenschiff* of the *Lusitania* going down" during World War I (Part 3, sect. 8: 7). During seance sessions with Arthur Bhaduri, H.D. and Bryher used a William Morris table, whose surface was inscribed with a multipetaled flower, to contact several of these dead pilots. H.D. records receiving the message "ne-nu-far" and "water-lis" from a Native American spirit-guide on this same table. See "The Sword Went Out to Sea," Book 1, Part 1, sect. 3: 138; Book 1, Part 2, sect. 5: 247–48. Furthermore, in "Nefert" (Apr. 1941), H.D. associates the Horus lily with "the lotus-years after the last war, those 'lost' years as many of the last war generation, have come to call them."

29. In H.D.'s copy of his bilingual edition of Euripides' *Helen*, Arthur Way translates these lines as follows: "Wherefore delay, O flower of Hellas-land, / To smite, to slay the aliens, and to hurl / Into the sea?" (pp. 600–601).

30. Liddell and Scott, *Greek-English Lexicon*, p. 1070.

31. H.D. was fascinated by the course of the lily symbol through history. In "The Sword Went Out to Sea," she traces the lily through European Renaissance and medieval religious art to ancient Cretan, Aztec, and Egyptian art. She also

attaches significance to the fact that the water lily is native to North America. See Book 1, Part 2, sect. 5: 238–41, 247–48.

32. Perhaps H.D. is also recalling this figure in *Narthex*, where she describes a moment of rebirth in which Raymonde's "mind a lily, rising out of hysteria, saw things clearly" (p. 279). Cited in Friedman, *Penelope's Web*, p. 263.

33. Homans, *Bearing the Word*, pp. 29–32.

34. Thus, in literalizing the figure "to get off on the wrong footing," the hysteric who stumbles signifies an inauspicious beginning, not faulty locomotion. For a similar example, see Freud and Breuer, *Studies on Hysteria*, p. 179.

35. Eisenstein had first introduced his concept of "intellectual cinema" to English readers five years earlier, heralding it as the projected sequel to his current practice of "over-tone montage" in "The Fourth Dimension in the Kino: II." There, he contends that, whereas overtonal montage grows out of "the conflict between the tonal principle of the piece (dominant) and the over-tone," "the intellectual kino will be the kino which resolves the conflict-conjunctions of the physiological and intellectual over-tones" (*Close Up* 6, 4 [Apr. 1930]: 263, 268; *Film Form*, pp. 79, 83). H.D. was probably familiar with the concept of intellectual cinema in its earliest stages, not only because it was being discussed in *Close Up*, but also because Kenneth Macpherson would align his own film *Borderline* (which H.D. acted in, helped to edit, and promoted in writing) with overtonal montage shortly after it was completed. See Friedberg, "Approaching *Borderline*," p. 378. Bryher also discusses Eisenstein's intellectual cinema in her 1929 book, *Film Problems of Soviet Russia*, p. 38. For contrasting views on whether Eisenstein's essays after 1935 broke with his earlier work, see Bordwell, "Eisenstein's Epistemological Shift," pp. 29–46; and Aumont, *Montage Eisenstein*, pp. 151–56.

36. *Life and Letters Today* 13 (Sept. 1935): 187; 13 (Dec. 1935): 174. See also Eisenstein, *Film Form*, pp. 125, 147.

37. *Life and Letters Today* 13 (Sept. 1935): 187; *Film Form*, p. 125.

38. Eisenstein associates the following forms of syncretic thinking with inner speech: the equivalence of a whole and its part, of an object and its image, and of two associated objects.

39. *Life and Letters Today* 13 (Sept. 1935): 190, 191, 193; 13 (Dec. 1935): 172. See also *Film Form*, pp. 130, 131, 134, 142, 143.

40. *Life and Letters Today* 13 (Dec. 1935): 170; *Film Form*, p. 142.

41. "The Cinematographic Principle," p. 98; *Film Form*, p. 37. For a statement of the "significance that the analogy with ideograms had" for Eisenstein's formulation of intellectual cinema, see Ivanov, p. 222.

42. H.D., *Notes on Thought and Vision*, pp. 20, 21.

43. Eisenstein, "Montage in 1938," *Life and Letters Today* 22, 24 (Aug. 1939): 282, 281; see also *The Film Sense*, pp. 31–32.

44. *Life and Letters Today* 21, 22 (June 1939): 101. See also Eisenstein, *The Film Sense*, p. 11. Jacques Aumont offers "global image" as a translation of the Russian term *obraz* used by Eisenstein (p. 176–80); I make use of Aumont's term throughout my discussion in an attempt to prevent the reader from confusing the mental *obraz* with a visual image.

45. *Life and Letters Today* 21, 22 (June 1939): 101; *The Film Sense*, p. 11.

46. *Life and Letters Today* 22, 24 (Aug. 1939): 282, 283; *The Film Sense*, pp. 33, 34.

47. Eisenstein's theory of the global image found a contemporary counterpart in the work of the Russian Formalist critic Boris Eikhenbaum, who, like Eisenstein, turned to Lev Vygotsky's concept of "inner speech" to theorize the viewer's reception of the "film metaphor," which he defined as "a kind of visual realisation of a verbal metaphor"; see Eikhenbaum, "Problems of Film Stylistics," p. 30. Reviewing Eikhenbaum's argument, Paul Willemen suggests his film metaphors might more aptly be called "literalisms" or "verbo-visual puns"; see Willemen, "Reflections on Eikhenbaum's Concept," p. 63. Eisenstein's own interest in such visual literalizations can be traced to his early theater work where he followed other directors in employing circus "eccentrisms" in his productions to intensify the audience's interpretative and emotional response. As Daniel Gerould explains: "The eccentricism of the acting consisted of generalised metaphorical expression of emotions through physical action, combining techniques from *commedia dell'arte* and ancient farce. Portraying astonishment, the actor did not simply give a start—he did a double somersault. All metaphor became literal and physical"; see Gerould, "Eisenstein's 'The Wise Man,'" pp. 90, 96.

48. Friedberg, "Approaching *Borderline*," p. 379.

49. H.D., *The Borderline Pamphlet*, pp. 42–43.

50. Herring spells out that "'images' here . . . mean, not the French meaning, but the screen equivalent of epithet, metaphor and simile" ("Film Imagery," p. 21).

51. The late English publication date of this essay (1949) makes it unlikely that H.D. would have read it. When H.D. joined Bryher and Kenneth Macpherson in Berlin in 1928, however, Eisenstein, Pudovkin, and Pabst were also in the city, and Macpherson was singling out *Potemkin*, currently "going the rounds in its uncut version," for his highest praise; he notes in passing that "the toppling of the upright pram down the steps" was a moment of "sheerest personal terror" ("As Is," *Close Up* 3, 2 [Aug. 1928]: 5, 8, 6). Macpherson also selected a still of "the abandoned pram" as the frontispiece for Bryher's *Film Problems of Soviet Russia*; he titles the still "the most famous scene in the most famous film ever made." It is likely that H.D. talked with Eisenstein directly when the *Close Up* staff met with the "great minds" of German and Russian film in late summer of 1928 (as mentioned in her own *Close Up* article of this period), and it is possible that she heard his ideas on this much-admired scene then. See H.D., "Russian Films," p. 22.

52. Eisenstein, *Film Form*, p. 171.

53. Ibid., pp. 172–73.

54. Aumont provides another example of Eisenstein's attempts to create a global image of revolution in *Montage Eisenstein*, p. 177.

55. More generally, H.D.'s essay "Russian Films" reverberates uncannily with her own concerns in *Helen in Egypt*. She compares Russian films to the Old Testament, which she says "consists of mainly" "tales of murder and rape," just as she will later conflate the Greek drama with "a legend of murder and lust" (*HE* 88). Asserting that "the Russian film at the moment deals with hunger, with starvation, with murder, with oppression, with adultery, with incest, with infanti-

cide, with childbirth, with the very throes of childbirth itself," she places sur-
prising emphasis on Russian Socialist films' treatment of women's experience.
With the exception of hunger and starvation, all the themes listed here will become
central preoccupations in *Helen in Egypt*; see "Russian Films," pp. 18, 19. Also of
note in this context is Bryher's remark in *Film Problems of Soviet Russia* that "*Po-
temkin* and *Ten Days* . . . recall by their austerity and power of compression the
Homeric phrases and the siege of Troy" (p. 30).

56. H.D. may follow Budge in portraying Isis as a black woman. He reports
that "tradition regarded Isis as an African woman, and preferably a woman from
the Sudan" because her retreat to the swamps to bear Horus resembles Sudanese
birthing practices; see *Osiris and the Egyptian Resurrection*, vol. 1: 301–4.

57. Both Bryher and H.D. expressed particular interest in Freud's Moses papers
when they appeared in 1937 and 1939, in German and English respectively. See
Bryher's letter to H.D., July 7, 1937, and H.D.'s to Bryher: May 21, 1939; May
26, 1939. Dianne Chisholm argues similarly that Helen "is, at bottom, Egyptian";
see *H.D.'s Freudian Poetics*, p. 168.

58. Where the myth that Stesichorus and Euripides pass down to H.D. assigns
Helen's false image to the trickery of Greek gods at Troy, while granting her real
body and wifely piety safe harbor in Egypt, H.D. seems to draw out the parallels
between Helen's possible acts of divine impersonation and ancient Egypt's own
status as a land of false images and false gods, jointly condemned under the Mosaic
injunction against image-making recounted by Freud in *Moses and Monotheism*. For
like "the hieroglyphic picture-writing" of Egypt banned under this same injunc-
tion (*Moses and Monotheism*, p. 43), the woman who incites Achilles' rage by mark-
ing her white body with a blackened stick "herself is the writing" (*HE* 22): not
Isis, the mother-goddess herself, but her forbidden substitute, simulacrum, or
sign.

59. *Life and Letters Today* 13 (Dec. 1935): 167; *Film Form*, pp. 135–36.

60. Ibid.

61. *Life and Letters Today* 13 (Dec. 1935): 170; *Film Form*, p. 141.

62. While he never explicitly identifies Egypt's propensity for image-making
with the unconscious, Freud does place pictorial thinking itself "nearer to uncon-
scious processes than . . . thinking in words" (*The Ego and the Id*, p. 21).

63. Freud himself argues just the opposite, asserting that "the pre-eminence
given to intellectual labours" in Jewish life "has helped to check the brutality and
the tendency to violence which are apt to appear where the development of mus-
cular strength is the popular ideal" (*Moses and Monotheism*, p. 115).

64. Dianne Chisholm also discusses Helen's "racial and biological prehistory"
in the context of Freud's *Moses and Monotheism*, whose "mythic historiography"
she contrasts to that of H.D.'s poem. Chisholm argues that "*Helen in Egypt* finds
the sources of Western civilization's progressive discontent in progressive mas-
culinization of mankind and, more specifically, in patriarchal imperialism begin-
ning with the domination and suppression of the Egyptians by the Greeks"; see
"H.D.'s Auto*heter*ography," pp. 101–2. I would challenge this portrayal of H.D.'s
unambivalent anti-imperialism. There is also a problem in saying that "patriarchal
imperialism" began with Greek domination of Egypt. Memphis fell to foreign

Asiatic invaders, the Hyksos, in 1674 B.C., and the Hyksos ruled Egypt for more than a century. During the reign of Thutmose III (1504–1450 B.C.), Egypt itself became an imperial power. See "Egypt, History of," *Encyclopedia Britannica*, 15th ed. (1974), vol. 6: pp. 470–73. In *Moses and Monotheism*, Freud himself notes that "as a result of the military exploits of the great conqueror, Tuthmosis III, Egypt had become a world power. . . . This imperialism was reflected in religion as universalism and monotheism" (p. 21). H.D. refers to "the Princesses of the Hyksos Kings" in *Trilogy*, p. 132.

65. Two patterns emerge in current evaluations of H.D.'s shifting symbolic use of ancient geography. One pattern traces H.D.'s links between Greece, the mother, and pre-oedipal union, while the other traces H.D.'s opposition of Greece and Egypt, in which Greece stands as a violent patriarchal culture, and Egypt as "a symbol of the mother and therefore of fusion, incest, desire and death" (DuPlessis, *H.D.: The Career*, pp. 113–14; and see pp. 18–30, 52–55). See also Friedman, *Psyche Reborn*, pp. 131–32, and *Penelope's Web*, p. 249; and Eileen Gregory, "Scarlet Experience," pp. 86–87. The latter pattern conforms to H.D.'s habitual orientalist conflation of "the West" with virility and strength and "the East" with effeminacy and erotic abandon. In "People of Sparta" (1920), for instance, H.D. imagines a decadent feminizing of the West as Xerxes prepares to invade Greece: "Shall this our earth be a creature of sensuous, high strung, feminine, changeable, fluid character, given first to the lure of the senses, . . . or shall the West prevail?"; see "Notes on Euripides," Part 2, p. 76. For an overview of this pattern of conflation in orientalist discourse, see Said, pp. 180–90, 206. Of course, Freud's analogies evince a similar orientalism. I am proposing, then, not that H.D. here adopts Freud's analogies as an alien symbolic system, but that she absorbs them into an existing version of her symbolic geography.

66. Dianne Chisholm also associates H.D.'s Egypt with the unconscious and the pre-oedipal; see *H.D.'s Freudian Poetics*, pp. 170, 199. H.D.'s gendering of the opposition between Greek intellect and Egyptian dream finds a precedent in "The Sword Went Out to Sea," where she posits that "the mother represents the emotional, creative or dream-self, while the father represents the intellectual, critical or constructive self," and goes on to raise the possibility of thinking "of the buried cities of Crete and Egypt, in terms of the submerged, unconscious mind" (Book I, Part I, sect. 3: 144–45). In *Bid Me to Live*, H.D. again merges the unconscious with "the East" and with a blackened self: H.D.'s persona, Julia, identifies "the gap in consciousness" with the "black-hole-of-Calcutta" and speaks of "her black-Calcutta self" (p. 13).

67. In *Osiris and the Egyptian Resurrection*, Budge reports that "the text of the Metternich Stele suggests that Set had tried to seize his brother's widow for himself, and it states quite clearly that she escaped from the place wherein he had managed to confine her for a time." Thus, he was "defeated in the gratification of his passion for the loving wife of Osiris" (vol. 1: 96).

68. It is interesting to note, however, that it is Horus who suffers Oedipus's self-inflicted punishment of blindness. Horus loses his eye in his fight with Typhon, and in some versions of the myth feeds it to his father to revive him. See Budge, *Osiris and the Egyptian Resurrection*, vol. 1: 82–89. Furthermore, even in the Egyp-

tian myth, the distinction between Typhon and Horus is fragile, as if to acknowledge the fragility of Horus's filial innocence, which the rest of the myth is eager, even designed, to affirm. In the aftermath of their reconciliation, both brother and son guard over Osiris's nightly journey through the land of the dead to protect him from further harm, and in one of their manifestations Typhon and Horus share a common identity. See Budge, *The Gods of the Egyptians*, vol. 1: 467; vol. 2: 241–43.

69. H.D.'s habitual derivation of Trojan culture from Crete and Egypt underwrites her identification of the Trojan Paris with the Egyptian Horus. See "The Sword Went Out to Sea": Book 1, Part 2, sect. 5: 255, and Book 2, sect. 4: 74; and "Compassionate Friendship," entry for Mar. 4, 1955: p. 31. This line of descent will have bearing on her possible use of Paris as a scapegoat for modern Egyptian insurrection, as discussed in the final section of this chapter.

70. Charlotte Mandel precedes me in further relating these lines to "the editing process of a filmmaker"; see "The Redirected Image," p. 43. Pearson also notes that H.D.'s long poems "are almost like verbal renditions of an Eisenstein film track;" see L. S. Dembo, "Pearson on H.D.," p. 439.

71. In "Majic Ring," H.D.'s persona, Delia Alton, discusses how she purposely rearranged her memories in her autobiographical fiction: in this case, how she "worked" "the psychic experience that Gareth [Bryher] and I had had" "into a sequence of reconstructed memories that I made my grandmother tell me, as if in reverie or half-dream or even trance" in *The Gift* (Part 2, sect. 1: 118–19). In a letter to Bryher recounting an important dream analyzed with Freud, H.D. reports on similar lines: "This dream, Freud said, represents the whole of my life in a sequence of detached yet continuous incidents. In that sense it is 'historical,' though the content of the dream is in the main phantasy." See H.D.'s letter to Bryher, April 25 or 24, 1933.

72. Steven Marcus offers an illuminating account of Freud's association of sound narrative practices with mental health ("Freud and Dora," pp. 56–91, especially p. 71).

73. When she presents the myths of ancient Greece as the unreliable memories of the very mythic figures who occupy them, H.D. not only confers on the legends of Troy the same suspect status that Freud would attribute to hysterical memory; she also aggressively contests the status of history or truth that Heinrich Schliemann's archeological discoveries at Troy in the 1870's had conferred on Homer's use of the Trojan myth cycle. Schliemann's discoveries underwrite James Joyce's and Ezra Pound's own claims for historical authority in their respective tributes to Homer, *Ulysses* and *The Cantos*. In contrast, H.D.'s Helen, uncertain that she has even been to Troy, radically undermines male modernists' faith in the accuracy and innocence of archeology as a mode, and metaphor, of historical reconstruction. For an account of Homeric scholarship and tributes in the decades following Schliemann's discoveries, see Kenner, pp. 41–50. H.D. visited Schliemann's excavation site with Perdita in 1932. See H.D.'s letter to Bryher, Apr. 18, 1932.

74. Eisenstein, "The Cinematographic Principle," p. 95; *Film Form*, p. 34.

75. H.D., *HERmione*, p. 71. The narrator anticipates Her's remark in the com-

ment: "Precinematographic conscience didn't help Her. Later conscience would have. She would later have seen form superimposed on thought and thought making its spirals in a manner not wholly related to matter but pertaining to it and the peony petals magnified out of proportion and the people in the room shrunk to tiny insects while the teacups again would have magnified into hemispheres" (p. 60).

76. Here, I concur with Rachel DuPlessis's assertion that "H.D. seems to want the traditional and the transformed stories [of Helen of Troy] to exist simultaneously," but depart from her attribution of this equivocation to H.D.'s "difficulty" as a woman writer in "establishing an authority sufficient to remake a culturally sanctioned story," for reasons stated in the main text; see "Romantic Thralldom," pp. 192–93.

77. H.D.'s oblique allusions to lesbianism through Clytaemnestra produce a particularly rich, if condensed, context for Thetis's speech to Helen. Thetis's comment—"Be still, O sister, O shadow; / your sister, your shadow was near" (*HE* 103)—blurs the opening line of Swinburne's "Itylus": "Swallow, my sister, O sister swallow." In the last lines of Swinburne's poem, Philomela mourns for her sister's son, murdered by his mother in a revenge on his father:

> The voice of the child's blood crying yet
> *Who hath remembered me? who hath forgotten?*
> Thou hast forgotten, O summer swallow,
> But the world shall end when I forget   (p. 49).

Paris's report of "Clytaemnestra's / last words to Orestes, // *remember Iphigenia*" (*HE* 219) echoes and distorts Philomela's lines in interesting ways. Indeed, "Itylus" as a whole, with its themes of memory and forgetting, infanticide, violent resistance to the father's authority, and sororial loyalty and betrayal, stands as an important antecedent to *Helen in Egypt*. For a discussion of H.D.'s renewed interest in Swinburne before beginning *Helen in Egypt*, as well as her use of the "Itylus" poem as a motif in Her's lesbian relationship with Fayne in *HERmione*, see Laity, "H.D. and A. C. Swinburne," pp. 217–40. More recently, Laity herself notes allusions to "Itylus" in *Helen in Egypt*; see her introduction to *Paint It Today*, pp. xxviii, xxxix n. 15.

78. In work published concurrently with an earlier version of this chapter, Donna Hollenberg also notes that "Helen construes an Oedipal relation between Paris and Achilles" and that Paris resists "the old Oedipal story of the son's abandonment by his mother" (*H.D.*, pp. 194, 198).

79. Harriet Chessman discusses a similar preoccupation with mothers who "suppress their daughters' stories through domination and alliance with fathers" in Stein's early fiction (*Public Is Invited*, pp. 75, 35–41).

80. Given H.D.'s use of Lord Hugh Dowding as a model for Achilles, it is noteworthy that she casts Dowding as Oedipus in *Vale Ave* (p. 50), and again associates him with "the Oedipus riddle" in "Compassionate Friendship," entry for Apr. 12, 1955, p. 81.

81. This treatment of Achilles' wound recalls the Moravian hymns that trope Christ's wounds or "side-holes" as vaginas. Janice Robinson notes that the "sym-

bolic overtones" in these hymns "were morbid, not to mention explicitly sexual, in a hysterical kind of way" (*H.D.*, p. 88).

82. Kloepfer makes different use of the same allusion to Freud (p. 166). Claire Buck also argues that "Helen's relationship to her daughter, Hermione, represents a narrative of betrayal, loss and abandonment"; however, she uses Irigaray's account of the construction of femininity to argue that such a relationship distinguishes the daughter's story from the son's, and thus does not note that H.D. associates the same narrative with Achilles and Paris; see " 'O Careless, Unspeakable Mother,' " p. 139.

83. This is H.D.'s own translation. See *Collected Poems*, p. 74.

84. In her emphasis on Achilles' bitterness, H.D. may have been influenced by the ancient Greeks, who made "bitter" anger and grief the paradigmatic feelings of heroes, both male and female. Homer repeatedly ascribes bitterness to Achilles in the *Iliad*. Euripides also makes many of his protagonists bitter, and H.D. further remarks on the "bitterness, . . . that special non-partisanship, non-patriotism that creeps into the dramas of Euripides." See "Notes on Euripides," Part 1, pp. 3–4. In transforming bitterness into love, first in "Tribute to the Angels" and again in *Helen in Egypt*, H.D. may thus be attempting to reform the West's entire heroic tradition and its concomitant glorification of violence and revenge.

85. See, for instance, *HE* 3, 4, 253, 255, 264, 266, 268.

86. This theme of maternal rejection or neglect is extremely widespread in H.D.'s work. Donna Hollenberg has argued that H.D.'s "early fiction depicts the pain of feeling unmothered" (*H.D.*, p. 183). Examples in support of her claim can be found in H.D.'s early story "The Greek Boy," and in her novel *Hedylus*, whose title character complains of his mother's frequent absences and fears she "didn't want me" (p. 21, 111). In *Paint It Today*, Midget speculates that her circle of intimates are "waifs and fugitives" because of the "hatred" their mothers bore them as children (p. 56). In "The Mystery," Saint-Germain retrieves the childhood memory of his mother's abrupt departure; his reverie ends with the question: "Had he ever had a mother?" (chap. 18, p. 132). There is also H.D.'s dream of the abandoned infant Moses, as well as her love of Shakespeare's *The Winter's Tale* and Euripides' *Ion*, with their abandoned children, and of Swinburne's "Itylus," with its murderous mother. H.D. celebrates Freud's statue of Athena as a redeemed version of the abandoning mother: a "Wingless Victory, for Victory could never, would never fly away from Athens" (*Tribute to Freud*, p. 69). The focus on "the lost parent" in her analysis with Schmideberg and the link H.D. made, with Freud, between her bisexuality and the emotional loss of "both parents at the age of 3 or 4" (which resulted in the erection of "my whole love-life on that love and terror mixed, and violence as of war etc.") help to relate this motif back to her own experience. See H.D.'s letters to Bryher: Nov. 27, 1934; Jan. 27, 1936.

87. Haller, "Isis Unveiled," p. 122.

88. Donna Hollenberg also notes that in Helen's encounter with Achilles on the beach, she "is really a grieving mother who is 'stricken, forsaken' " (*H.D.*, p. 186).

89. Homer, *The Iliad*, Book 18, ll. 25–30 (p. 436).

90. Already, such a plot line suggests how conservative the poem's politics are. In its hostile reduction of male homosexual relationships to instances of "forget-

ting women" (*HE* 4), its rejection of the lesbian eroticism associated with Cly-
taemnestra, and its final celebration of the reunited heterosexual couple and the
mother who nurtures her son, *Helen in Egypt* marks its distance from the celebra-
tion of lesbian intimacy and the mother's explicit ties to the daughter in *Trilogy*.

91. In an essay entitled "If Oedipus Was an Egyptian," Estelle Roith pursues
many themes taken up—without knowledge of her essay—in my reading of *Helen
in Egypt*. She derives both Freud's suppression of Jocasta's murderous early rela-
tionship with Oedipus and his antipathy toward the work of Melanie Klein from
his own ambivalent relationship to "his overpowering and seductive mother" and
to Egypt, "the original focus and vehicle of Freud's childhood fantasy life" (*Riddle
of Freud*, p. 164). Dianne Chisholm refers to Roith's argument in *H.D.'s Freudian
Poetics*, pp. 221–23. Roith would no doubt be pleased to learn of H.D.'s own pun-
ning anticipation of her argument. Upon first meeting Freud, H.D. writes that
"this little old mummy of an Oedipus-Rex is right out of my own phantasy
world"; see H.D.'s letter to Bryher, Mar. 5, 1933.

92. Dianne Chisholm argues along similar lines that "the images that have been
rubbed out or written over in the canonical canon are precisely those that surface
hermetically in *Helen in Egypt*, where they haunt the Greek text with their hiero-
glyphic character"; she also argues, however, that such hieroglyphs are "undeci-
pherable" and that Helen "does not perform an actual translation" between Egyp-
tian and Greek characters or texts; see *H.D.'s Freudian Poetics*, pp. 174, 168–69.

93. For a detailed and helpful summary of how H.D. arranged Perdita's up-
bringing, see Friedman, *Penelope's Web*, pp. 224–27.

94. Veith, *Hysteria*, pp. 2–6. H.D. may have discovered this history through
her extensive reading among the British Egyptologists. In fact, as Veith notes, the
oldest extant papyrus, the Kahun Papyrus, explicitly documents various hysterical
symptoms, so that, by the caprice of history, the extant origins of Egyptian writ-
ing and of treatises on hysteria coincide. The Kahun Papyrus is included among
the Petri Papyri, *Hieratic Papyri from Kahun and Gurob (Principally of the Middle
Kingdom)*, ed. by F. L. I. Griffith, 2 vols. (London: Bernard Quaritch, 1897), vol.
1: *Literary, Medical and Mathematical Papyri from Kahun*, pp. 5–11.

95. Donna Hollenberg makes a similar point, characterizing Thetis as "the
mother who is a product of and fosters the patriarchy" and "the unconscious force
behind Helen's self-sabotage." She argues, however, that by the end of the poem,
Helen is able "to redefine Thetis, to transform her" into "a powerful mother, a
mother whose ability to model autonomy is not debased by the present gender
system" (*H.D.*, pp. 202, 192, 197).

96. Marcus, *Virginia Woolf and the Languages*, p. 83.

97. Thus, there is a direct connection between the "ecstasy of desolation" that
overtakes Achilles—numb with the forgotten memory of his mother—on the
beach outside Troy (*HE* 256), the "desolation, destruction" of battlefield itself
(*HE* 243), and the desolate rule of "a warrior race" in Greece (*HE* 90).

98. Artemis's demand that Iphigenia be slaughtered can be contrasted with Hol-
lenberg's portrayal of Artemis as "an island-mother in whose white sphere [Helen]
feels secure" (p. 197). Once again, rather than choose between the two versions,
we need to focus on how the poem enacts the mother's splitting into loving and

destroying selves. For previous discussions of H.D.'s treatments of ambivalence toward the mother, see Friedman, *Psyche Reborn*, pp. 140–42, and *Penelope's Web*, pp. 121–28, 217, 222–24, 245–52, 342–50; DuPlessis, *H.D.: The Career*, pp. 44–55; Kloepfer, pp. 46–51, 117–40.

99. Deborah Kloepfer (*Unspeakable Mother*, pp. 134–36) and Susan Friedman (*Penelope's Web*, p. 256) have argued that H.D. often uses a male figure to tell the daughter's story. Similarly, Claire Buck argues that "Helen has to use Achilles' story, the man's story of his mother, in order to tell a story of her erotic attachment to the mother"; see " 'O Careless, Unspeakable Mother,' " p. 138.

100. H.D. apparently associated Egypt with Klein's good and bad mother as early as 1936. She and Walter Schmideberg related the death of King George V to the death of King Tut and her memories of her 1923 trip to Egypt with her mother and Bryher. She writes to Bryher on Jan. 21, 1936, asking for a copy of *Palimpsest*, which blends events on that trip with an epiphanic vision of a sacred birth-house in the Valley of the Dead: "will you send me one or more Palimps, as I am working on that scene now with Sch., and find I have no Palimp.. I am really at great peace, at least, its awful, but it just evolved to another Chaddie-bad mother and resolves out the good mother, Bvr. [Beaver—Mrs. Doolittle] there in Egypt was so nice and you were so wonderful to us both." Friedman reports that H.D.'s analysis with Mary Chadwick (Chaddie) "seemed to have intensified" H.D.'s suicidal feelings, and notes allusions in the H.D. circle to "Chadwick's sadism" (*Penelope's Web*, pp. 287, 401n6).

101. *Agamemnon*, in Aeschylus, *Oresteia*, p. 63.

102. H.D. uses the witch figure in *The Gift* in ways that are particularly evocative of her later treatment of Helen; like Helen, Mamalie dares to interpret sacred texts literally, and hence is accused of witchcraft by "the stricter Brethren of the [Moravian] church" (pp. 84, 88). Friedman cites H.D.'s identification of her fictionalized selves with witches in *Asphodel* and *Bid Me to Live*. *Penelope's Web*, pp. 172, 174, 184, 186. In addition, Hermione, involved in a lesbian relationship with Fayne, and Rose Beauvais, accused of an "unwholesome" friendship with Blanchfleur, are both associated with witches in *HERmione* and "The Sword Went Out to Sea" respectively. See *HERmione*, p. 165; and "The Sword," Book 2, sect. 13: 274–77.

103. As noted earlier, H.D. uses this phrase in *Bid Me To Live*, p. 13.

104. DuPlessis makes much the same point in "Romantic Thralldom," pp. 201–2.

105. According to Denise Riley, Bowlby's theories of "maternal deprivation" posited that "mothers ought never to leave their children, on pain of inflicting serious psychic damage if they did" (*War in the Nursery*, pp. 95, 100). Riley argues against the impulse to hold Bowlby solely accountable for the conservative nature of his clinical findings; she claims that "the theories of Kleinian psychoanalysis, couched in terms of the innateness of aggression, were wide open to being 'borne out' by behavioural observations. The course adopted by Bowlby was neither unpredictable nor surprising in its directions" (p. 106). Here, I would align myself with Janice Doane's and Devon Hodges' objection that Riley "does not fully appreciate the extent to which Winnicott" and later British theorists like Bowlby

depart "from Klein's notions of the infant" (*From Klein to Kristeva*, p. 83n9). They argue, I think rightly, that Klein "eschewed" the tradition of "prescriptions for mothers" which Winnicott and others "encouraged" (p. 31). Furthermore, Riley's insistence on the radical distinction between "British Kleinianism" and "Freud's psychoanalysis" sets Klein up as the point where all the trouble starts, and hence lets Freud slip from the hook of Riley's own critique (pp. 79, 107).

106. Friedman briefly discusses H.D.'s finances and Bryher's gifts to her, ranging "from checks to books and clothing, from cruises to major medical bills," in *Penelope's Web*, p. 395n14. Because Bryher adopted Perdita in 1928, when she was nine, it is likely that Bryher's money also played a significant role in Perdita's upbringing. On Jan. 18, 1955, Bryher writes urging H.D. to "safeguard your capital": "I am very sorry to have to ask you to read the enclosed letter from Mr Lancester, but I must, because we are all getting very worried over the situation in South Africa, as they want to break away from England, and if they did, it might freeze or you might lose part of the value of the securities there." In "Compassionate Friendship," H.D. notes while discussing her will: "This money in England or/and Canada and Africa is a direct gift, Bryher's overwhelming generosity" (entry for Feb. 22, 1955, p. 18). At some point during the decade, Bryher's brother, John Ellerman, went to live in South Africa, which may have contributed to her decision to invest in the region; see Bryher's letter to H.D., Apr. 19, 1959.

107. H.D., *Palimpsest*, pp. 6–7, 29.

108. My proposal that H.D. may have shared a literary investment in empire with other (male) modernist epic poets should be contrasted with Susan Friedman's portrayal of H.D.'s "effort to feminize the epic" in *Helen in Egypt*, and her "rejection of male epic models" that foreground "the destructive aspects of the masculine—war, armies, death, and betrayal"; see "Gender and Genre," pp. 206, 222, 214.

109. Hamilton, *Mythology*, p. 30.

Chapter 3

1. For previous readings of the poem, see Quinn, "H.D.'s 'Hermetic Definition,'" pp. 51–61; Friedman, *Psyche Reborn*, pp. 145–51; DuPlessis, *H.D.: The Career*, pp. 124–30; and Hatlen, "Recovering," pp. 141–69. For Durand's interview with H.D., see "Life in a Hothouse," pp. 92–93.

2. Eliot, *Selected Prose*, p. 77.

3. Biographical data on H.D. is drawn from Silverstein, "Herself Delineated," pp. 32–45; on Alexis St.-Léger Léger from Benét, *Reader's Encyclopedia*, p. 622, and Little, *Saint-John Perse*, pp. 1–7; and on Lionel Durand from his obituary in *Newsweek*, "Epitaph: A Reporter," p. 62. In *End to Torment*, H.D. quotes from an entry on Pound that appears in the edition of Benét's *Reader's Encyclopedia* that I cite here (p. 31); Benét's entry on Léger includes the remarks by Eliot that I quote above. H.D. knew little about Durand's life until he died. For a focused account of H.D.'s "creation of some of the literary models from which modernism developed," see Pondrom, "H.D.," pp. 73–97.

4. Friedman, "Modernism of the 'Scattered Remnant,'" pp. 116, 94. In an es-

say of comparable importance employing the same analytical scheme, Jane Marcus studies Djuna Barnes's treatment of "the black, lesbian, transvestite, or Jew[ish]" body in *Nightwood*. Marcus claims that the novel "center[s] the marginal," and that "Djuna Barnes identifies with all outsiders" ("Laughing at Leviticus," pp. 221, 232, 229). Marcus notes that she wrote the essay in 1983–84 (p. 397).

5. DuPlessis, *H.D.: The Career*, p. 124.

6. Aldon Lynn Nielsen precedes me in challenging Friedman's assumption that opposing political perspectives are mutually exclusive for H.D. Where Friedman contends that H.D.'s use of irony in her novel *HERmione* to portray her former patronizing attitudes toward African-Americans precludes a continuation of such patronage in the present, Nielson argues that it is "possible to be ironic" and "patronizing" at the same time (*Reading Race*, p. 87).

7. hooks, *Feminist Theory*, Preface.

8. Ibid. hooks does consider the negative consequences of the double vision of oppressed groups in her brief discussion of "internalized racism" (p. 55).

9. Rose, *The Haunting*, pp. 176, 210.

10. Laplanche and Pontalis, "Fantasy," pp. 14, 17; Rose, *The Haunting*, p. 7.

11. H.D., *Vale Ave*, p. 18.

12. The Algerian War provides a remarkably apt occasion for H.D.'s late questioning of her modernist poetics. Fredric Jameson invokes the "emblematic date of 1884—the year of the Berlin Conference, which parcelled Africa out among the 'advanced' powers"—to link the emergence of imperialism with that of modernism, and further links "the end of modernism . . . with the restructuration of the classical imperialist world system"; see "Modernism and Imperialism," p. 6. In this process of restructuration 1960, the year in which H.D. began her poem, marked a crucial juncture. Dubbed by *Newsweek* "Africa's Year of Freedom," 1960 saw sixteen African colonies and trust territories gain their independence. See "Africa: Hate . . . Hope," p. 38; and Hull, *Modern Africa*, pp. 87–88. It should be noted, however, that Edward Said takes issue with Jameson's alignment, arguing that "imperialism itself was a continuous process for at least a century and a half *before* the scramble for Africa"; see "Yeats and Decolonization," p. 6.

13. Eliot, *Selected Prose*, p. 177.

14. For example, Hazel Carby notes that during the 1920's "British colonizers in Nigeria dismissed all traditional forms of social organization that they found as 'organized anarchy' " ("White Woman Listen!" p. 225).

15. Woolf, *The Waves*, p. 167–68.

16. See Pearson's letter to H.D., July 26, 1960.

17. On Aug. 9, 1960, H.D. notifies Pearson of her new subscription to *Newsweek* "as from Aug. 1." H.D. was at this time already receiving back copies of *Time* and *The Listener* from Bryher. Though correspondence from earlier years does not suggest that she was an avid follower of international news, in this period she writes to Bryher, "I read too much *news*—& see T.V. & rush up to AFN at 9." This claim is substantiated by the increasing frequency with which she notes world events in her correspondence. See H.D.'s letter to Bryher, Sept. 24, 1960.

18. For instance, in a letter to Pearson dated Sept. 21, 1960, H.D. remarks on the T.V. coverage of the anticommunist "mob" protest over Khrushchev's visit to

New York City: "It is like 20 years ago." She may have been reflecting a media evaluation of current events; identifying Cuba, the Congo, West Berlin, and the high seas and airways as trouble sites between the United States and the Soviet Union, *Newsweek* refers to "a whole series of East-West 'incidents,' clashes of a kind that might once have started wars." See "K's Four-Front 'War,' " p. 35. After Durand's death, H.D. explicitly relates the Algerian War to her own traumatic memories of World War II and the Holocaust; see 1961 Diary, entry for June 1.

19. For letters commenting on Perse's award, see Bryher to H.D.: Oct. 27, 1960; Nov. 2, 1960; H.D. to Bryher: Oct. 30, 1960; Nov. 29, 1960.

20. H.D.'s letter to Pearson of Jan. 6, 1961, refers to Durand's report in *Newsweek*, Dec. 26, 1960. See "Algeria: 'You-you-you-you,' " p. 26.

21. Denis de Rougement describes the burning of the Cathars in *Passion and Society*, p. 97. H.D. marked this passage in one of her many rereadings of the book.

22. H.D., "Thorn Thicket," entry for Apr. 9, 1960, p. 43. H.D. reports to Pearson that Durand identified himself as French in a letter dated Mar. 5 (a slip for Apr. 5), 1960. While H.D.'s critics have assumed that Durand was "dark-skinned" (DuPlessis, *H.D.: The Career*, p. 125), published photos make clear that he was not. After meeting Durand a second time, H.D. herself notes twice that "he was *not* as dark as I had visualized." See H.D.'s letter to Pearson, May 15, 1960, and her letter to Bryher, May 16, 1960. Photographs of Durand appear in *Newsweek* articles, "As People Overseas See It," p. 46, and "Epitaph: A Reporter," p. 62. In recording that he had been born a Haitian, however, Durand's obituary appears to have confirmed H.D.'s ongoing sense that "he was not French at all" (Diary, 1961, entry for May 21).

23. Ambelain, *Dans l'ombre*, pp. 72, 73.

24. At the end of "Red Rose and a Beggar," H.D. portrays Durand as "a Lover, / the *hachish supérieur* of dream," a substance she has just connected with "*fleur de chanvre,* / from India" (*HD* 21, 18).

25. Friedman, *Penelope's Web*, pp. 152, 154. To some degree, H.D. associated Durand with Lawrence's dark god because she associated him with Lawrence himself and with *Bid Me to Live*, the book in part about Lawrence whose publication occasioned Durand's first interview with her. In a "Thorn Thicket" entry for Oct. 27, 1960, H.D. writes that "Durant again is the Rafe [Aldington] or Rico [Lawrence] image of *Madrigal* [*Bid Me to Live*]. He took away a photograph of myself of that period and so seemed to superimpose himself on the book" (p. 53).

26. Friedman, *Penelope's Web*, pp. 154, 155, 164.

27. Friedman, "Modernism of the 'Scattered Remnant,' " p. 114.

28. Snead, "European Pedigrees," p. 236. Marianna Torgovnick makes the further point that when Lawrence turns from associating the primitive with femininity in novels like *Women in Love* to associating it with masculinity in *The Plumed Serpent*, the primitive itself takes a turn "from the degenerative to the regenerative" (*Gone Primitive*, p. 163). H.D. seeks a parallel regeneration in her primitivist fantasies of Durand, but in doing so risks the possibility that the primitive will revert to its more negative associations with death.

29. Ambelain, *Dans l'ombre*, pp. 195–96. This line reads in English translation: "Assist, aid, and favor the action of Nature."

30. See Pearson's letter to H.D., Dec. 31, 1960, and H.D.'s to Pearson, Jan. 6, 1961.

31. See Pearson's letter to H.D., Sept. 7, 1960.

32. "Olympic Rivals," p. 81.

33. *Hermetic Definition*, Notebook 1, Part 1, sect. 13. H.D.'s confusing pagination and dating system, her many revised and crossed-out pages, and her use of empty back pages to draft the first sections of "Grove of Academe" in the first notebook of the *Hermetic Definition* manuscript make it very difficult to reconstruct for another reader where the passages I cite can be found. I have decided simply to transcribe whatever pertinent information (section number, page number, and/or date) appears on a given page in the hopes that another reader can use these multiple indexes to find the passages in question.

34. Murray, *Euripides*, p. 113. H.D owned a copy of this book.

35. The python is an established figure of war for H.D. Friedman writes of H.D.'s account of the London Blitz in *The Gift*: "Snakes and [bomber] planes merge in Chapter 4 in the image of 'the vilest Python whom Apollo, the light, slew with his burning arrows'" (*Penelope's Web*, p. 339).

36. H.D.'s association of Azrael with "Judgement" and the "bondage" of desire in section 17 also refers back to her earlier association of Durand with a scene of "Judgement" and imprisonment in section 9. Friedman reads this fantasy of Durand as Judge against H.D.'s diary entry for June 1, 1961, which links judging with masculinity. For her the fantasy represents his "masculine" power to condemn H.D.'s literary achievement, "nearly paralyz[ing] her capacity to write" (*Psyche Reborn*, pp. 148, 313n39). But in the same entry H.D. goes on to link this power to judge with Durand's "astute weighing, essaying of world events. 'Will not the Judge of all the world do right?'" These remarks might suggest that the judgment fantasies involving Durand and Azrael in "Red Rose and a Beggar" encode another allusion to Durand's political coverage of "world events" in Africa, though it is not clear whether H.D. had already come up with this set of associations while writing her poem.

37. Further support for H.D.'s associations between racial difference and the spirit world can be found in a deleted set of lines for a section 20 of "Red Rose":

> God, God, who has sown this wheat?
> just anyone? someone was here before,
>
> someone ploughed furrows,
> no race apart, angels, demons,
> not even daemons, particularly gifted.

Hermetic Definition, Notebook 1, Part 1, sect. 20: dated Sept. 9 and Oct. 25 [1960].

38. *Hermetic Definition*, Notebook 1, Part 1, sects. 20 (p. 23), 27: dated Oct. 18 [1960]. In section 26 of the same sequence, dated Sept. 24, H.D. again makes passing reference to war in Africa when she speaks of

> Isis, the enchantress,
> above the first *Notre Dame* door,
> simplicity and unity,
> even in a world at war,
> knowing that Michael will not fail,
> leading ~~Azrael's death's~~ heaven's cohorts. . . .

39. See H.D.'s letters to Pearson: Mar. 13, 1961; Feb. 17, 1961. In "Grove of Academe," H.D. anticipates this alignment of "emotion" with Durand and "intellect" with Perse when she declares in section 2

> there is nothing visionary
> nor ecstatic here,
> only recognition,

before telling Perse that his

> mind's thought and range
> exceeds mine
> out of all proportion   (*HD* 25).

H.D.'s use of the emotion/intellect dichotomy here harks back to "the Manichean allegory" that Abdul R. JanMohamed follows Frantz Fanon in ascribing to Western imperialist discourse. In this allegory, "Europeans are rational and intelligent, while Orientals are emotional and sensuous" ("Economy of Manichean Allegory," p. 99).

40. "The Nobel Prizes," p. 60.

41. For a reading of Perse's influence on Geoffrey Hill, which characterizes both T. S. Eliot and Perse as poets of "imperial and at times imperious dreams," see Dodsworth, "*Mercian Hymns*," p. 61. For a critical rejection of the notion that *Anabase* celebrates "l'aventure impériale française en Orient," see Antoine, "Saint-John Perse," p. 154. For a detailed account of Perse's poetic references to earlier empires, see Cellier, "Mots et savoirs," pp. 229–47.

42. "The U.N. . . . An 'Empire' of Its Own," p. 50. In some sense, however, such ironies pervaded and defined the conditions of the time. For instance, U.N. Secretary-General Dag Hammarskjöld, a co-translator of Perse's "Chronique" into Swedish, was reported to have used his influence to secure the Nobel Prize for Perse in the same months that he sent U.N. troops into the newly independent Congo to "restore order," at first as neutral observers, and later by force. See "The Nobel Prizes," p. 60.

43. Baker, "Sexuation of Poetic Language," pp. 109–10.

44. Such a reading gains support from the manuscript of the first draft (Notebook 1, Part 2, sect. 4, p. 28, dated Nov. 1) which records:

> this retreat from the world,
>
> that   the world
>   yet holding   ~~the~~   past, present,
> in the closed recess of your mind's secret.

I take the indicated excisions and additions to mean that the second line originally read: "yet holding the past present."

45. H.D., *Notes on Thought and Vision*, p. 67.

46. H.D., "Compassionate Friendship," entry for Feb. 19, 1955, p. 6.

47. Friedman, *Penelope's Web*, pp. 241–43. Elsewhere in the same novel, however, H.D. appears to applaud a notion of empire when it takes the form of cultural domination or hegemony. Thus, the concubine's ostensible victimization in bed with the soldier ironically masks a greater triumph, for, as she says: "The conquered must inevitably conquer. Not Rome, Marius, but finally the whole world. Greek must rule. Not Rome only but the world" (*Palimpsest*, pp. 29, 74–75). In this connection, it is important to note that H.D. regarded Greece's own colonial history with equanimity. In "The People of Sparta," she describes Athens as a "begetter of poets and lover of poets from furthest island and foreign coast, daring colonizer of the Asian sea-board, Athens, a city set forever on a hill"; see "Notes on Euripides," Part 2, p. 76.

48. H.D., *Vale Ave*, pp. 40, 41. On the page opposite an entry for Oct. 2, 1958, in her Hirslanden Journal, Notebook 4, H.D. notes that she wrote the poem between April 5 and May 13, 1957. The British newsweekly *The Listener* (which H.D. draws on for her image of the Scops owl in *Sagesse* in June 1957) ran a five-part series entitled "South of Sahara" from March 21 to April 18, 1957. The series, which was written by William Clark, speaks to the implications of Ghana's independence for British Africa as a whole, under such rubrics as "The Road to Independence," "Black and White—Can Partnership Succeed?" and "The Needs of Nationalism."

49. Augustine, "Modernist Moravianism," pp. 65, 70, 69. For a discussion of H.D.'s portrayal of Moravian history in *The Gift*, see Friedman, *Penelope's Web*, pp. 346–47. Friedman argues that H.D. celebrates the "biracial communities, . . . rituals of peace, and . . . fair treaties" which Moravians and American Indians created together, but also mourns the Moravians' eventual betrayal of "their special 'Gift' of peace to the world."

50. While evidence for this claim abounds, I will cite just two examples from *Anabase*: " ' ... Roses, pourpre délice: la terre vaste à mon désir, et qui en posera les limites ce soir? ... ' "; and: " ... lois données sur d'autres rives, et les alliances par les femmes au sein des peuples dissolus; de grands pays vendus à la criée sous l'inflation solaire, les hauts plateaux pacifiés et les provinces mises à prix dans l'odeur solennelle des roses... " (Perse's ellipses). (In Eliot's translation: " ' . . . Roses, purple delight; the earth stretched forth to my desire—and who shall set bounds thereunto, this evening?' " and: " . . . laws enacted upon other shores, alliances by marriage in the midst of dissolute peoples, great territories auctioned away beneath the inflation of the Sun, the highlands subdued and the provinces priced in the solemn odour of roses. . . ") See Perse, *Collected Poems*, pp. 108–9, 118–21. H.D. selects the phrases *"roses, pourpre délice"* and *"l'odeur solonnelle des roses"* for use in her own poem (*HD* 22, 33).

51. Here, the very move to recast Perse's secular and hedonistic portrayals of empire in spiritual terms is simply the most pronounced indication of H.D.'s wider intent to bring his poetry into line with her own postwar visionary writings.

Thus, H.D.'s modest self-effacement before the achievement of Perse functions as a mask for less humble intentions. The images of roses, goddesses, islands, snow-owls, scented flowers, desert sand, moments of grace and the reviving dead which she draws from Perse's "ποιητής fantasy" are his in word only. Minor, floating details in his work, they are in fact far more recognizable as the long-standing staples of H.D.'s poetry. Detaching Perse's lines and phrases from their original contexts and rearranging them in her own, H.D. remakes the poetic corpus of the latest Nobel Prize recipient in her own image. Burton Hatlen and Gary Burnett also remark on H.D.'s strategy of "tell[ing] her own story . . . through the masks of the poets she reviews"; see Burnett, *H.D.*, p. 22, and Hatlen, "Recovering," p. 156.

52. Translation by T. S. Eliot, from *Anabase*, in Perse, *Collected Poems*, pp. 118–19. Perse's ellipses.

53. "The Sword Went Out to Sea," Book 2, sect. 4:74. Here again, though, we need to distinguish H.D.'s condemnation of military aggression from a blanket condemnation of colonialism. Earlier in the same novel she identifies Troy as a Cretan colony like Mycenae (Book 1, Part 1, sect. 5:255).

54. Vincent Quinn precedes me in noting the tension between H.D.'s contradictory portrayals of Durand. He argues that Durand is "present as both human being and symbol; in the first part his symbolic role predominates, and here [in "Grove of Academe"] his reality is stressed" ("H.D.'s 'Hermetic Definition,'" p. 58).

55. *Hermetic Definition*, Notebook 2, Part 2, section 18, dated Dec. 24 [1960]. Two words in the last line of this deleted passage are illegible; thus, my readings for "witness" and "death's" are tentative. The deleted lines appear alone on the left page (typically left blank) opposite the lines included in the final poem; I am assuming they succeed the last lines of the following page.

56. Here I extend Hatlen's point that "to live in the human equation is to live in time" by arguing that to live in time is to live in contemporary time and in history. Likewise, I follow Hatlen in arguing that Durand "has come to represent" "the human world" by the end of "Grove of Academe," but again define this "human world" as a contemporary and international, rather than an ahistorical and personal, world; see Hatlen, "Recovering," pp. 165, 158.

57. The line is from Perse's then most recent poem, *Chronique*, and reads, in Robert Fitzgerald's translation, "But God does not dwell in the date or day"; see Perse, *Collected Poems*, pp. 580–81.

58. H.D. notes her use of "the *Calendrier Sacré* of Robert Ambelain" in "the Owl Sequence" in the Hirslanden Journal, Notebook 4, entry for Jan. 5, 1958.

59. See H.D.'s letter to Pearson, Apr. 29, 1961.

60. "Into the Eye of the Storm," p. 31.

61. See H.D.'s letters to Pearson: Dec. 22, 1960; Dec. 28, 1960. See also "Algeria: 'You-you-you-you,'" p. 26.

62. DuPlessis (*H.D.: The Career*, p. 129) and Hatlen ("Recovering," p. 165) also associate these lines with the exorcism of "an invading demon."

63. For letters mentioning du Maurier's *The Infernal World*, see H.D. to Pearson: Feb. 10, 1961; H.D. to Bryher: Feb. 1, 1961, and Feb. 8, 1961. H.D.'s other

reading during this period is equally suggestive. In early January she appears to have read and enjoyed Isak Dinesen's memoir, *Shadows on the Grass*, in which fond tributes to former Somali and Kenyan servants (one of whom later participated in the Mau-Mau revolts in Kenya) double as a nostalgic celebration of prewar British colonialism in East Africa. For references to Bryher's gift to H.D. of "the short Blixen" and "the Dinisen Africa book," see H.D.'s letter to Bryher, Jan. 10, 1961, and Bryher's to H.D., Jan. 14, 1961. H.D. mentions another book on Africa that I have been unable to identify; in a letter to Bryher dated Feb. 18, 1961, she writes: "Again, thank you for *Spade* book. I am enchanted, especially now, with all this Africa frenzy."

64. For an important discussion of H.D.'s early poetry that examines her complex use of the motifs of "clairvoyant ecstasy," figured as the pleasures and dangers of the crossed threshold, and the " 'private space' of imagination," figured as "a liminal 'island' set apart from ordinary life," see Gregory, "Rose Cut in Rock," pp. 548, 544, 532. Gregory places these characteristic approaches to the inside/outside scheme in the context of lesbian literary, erotic, and mystical contact and exchange. As such, her argument helps to suggest the concrete ways in which the inside/outside scheme itself takes on "contradictory implications" for H.D. over time, functioning as yet another palimpsest in which the radical and conservative aspects of her visionary poetic project are alike inscribed.

65. See H.D.'s letters to Bryher: May 30, 1940; June 2, 1940; June 3, 1940.

Works Cited

Frequently cited works are listed, with full bibliographic information, in Abbreviations, p. x.

Abel, Elizabeth. *Virginia Woolf and the Fictions of Psychoanalysis*. Chicago: University of Chicago Press, 1989.

Aeschylus. *Oresteia*. Trans. Richmond Lattimore. Chicago: University of Chicago Press, 1953.

"Africa: Hate . . . Hope." *Newsweek*. Aug. 22, 1960: 38–41, 44.

"Algeria: 'You-you-you-you.'" *Newsweek*. Dec. 26, 1960: 31.

Ambelain, Robert. *Dans l'ombre des cathédrales*. Paris: Editions Adyar, 1939.

Antoine, Régis. "Saint-John Perse et l'Asie Orientale." In Antoine Raybaud and Henri Colliot, eds., *Espaces de Saint-John Perse 1–2*, pp. 151–66.

"As People Overseas See It." *Newsweek*. Dec. 12, 1960: 46.

Augustine, Jane. "Modernist Moravianism: H.D.'s Unpublished Novel *The Mystery*." *Sagetrieb* 9, 1–2 (1990): 65–78.

Aumont, Jacques. *Montage Eisenstein*. Trans. Lee Hildreth, Constance Penley, and Andrew Ross. Bloomington: Indiana University Press, 1987.

Baker, Peter. "The Sexuation of Poetic Language in Saint-John Perse's *Anabase*." *French Forum* 12, 1 (Jan. 1987): 109–18.

Benét, William Rose, ed. *The Reader's Encyclopedia: An Encyclopedia of World Literature and the Arts*. New York: Thomas Y. Crowell, 1948.

Berque, Jacques. *Egypt: Imperialism and Revolution*. Trans. Jean Stewart. London: Faber and Faber, 1972; New York: Praeger, 1972.

Bersani, Leo. "Is the Rectum a Grave?" In Douglas Crimp, ed., *AIDS: Cultural Analysis / Cultural Activism*, pp. 197–222. Cambridge, Mass.: MIT Press, 1988.

Bordwell, David. "Eisenstein's Epistemological Shift." *Screen* 15, 4 (Winter 1974/75): 29–46.

Bryer, Jackson R. "H.D.: A Note on Her Critical Reputation." *Contemporary Literature* 10, 4 (Autumn 1969): 627–31.

Bryher. *Film Problems of Soviet Russia*. Territet, Switzerland: Pool, 1929.

———. Letters to H.D. and Walter Schmideberg. Beinecke Library, Yale University, New Haven, Conn.

Buck, Claire. *H.D. and Freud: Bisexuality and a Feminine Discourse*. New York: Harvester Wheatsheaf, 1991.

———. " 'O Careless, Unspeakable Mother': Irigaray, H.D. and Maternal Origin." In Susan Sellers, ed., *Feminist Criticism: Theory and Practice*, pp. 129–42. Toronto: University of Toronto Press, 1991.

Budge, E. A. Wallis. *Easy Lessons in Egyptian Hieroglyphics*. Vol. 3 of *Books on Egypt and Chaldea*. 23 vols. London: Kegan Paul, Trench, Trübner, 1902.

———. *The Egyptian Heaven and Hell*. Vol. 22 of *Books on Egypt and Chaldea*. 23 vols. Chicago: Open Court; London: Kegan Paul, Trench, Trübner, 1905.

———. *The Gods of the Egyptians: Or Studies in Egyptian Mythology*. 2 vols. Chicago: Open Court; London: Methuen, 1904.

———. *Osiris and the Egyptian Resurrection*. Vol. 1. 2 vols. London: Philip Lee Warner; New York: G. P. Putnam, 1911.

Burckhardt, Titus. *Alchemy: Science of the Cosmos, Science of the Soul*. Trans. William Stoddart. Baltimore: Penguin, 1971.

Burnett, Gary. *H.D. Between Image and Epic: The Mysteries of Her Poetics*. Ann Arbor, Mich.: U.M.I. Research Press, 1990.

Butler, Judith. *Gender Trouble: Feminism and the Subversion of Identity*. New York: Routledge, 1990.

Cameron, Averil, and Amélie Kuhrt, eds. *Images of Women in Antiquity*. London: Croom Helm, 1983.

Carby, Hazel V. "White Woman Listen! Black Feminism and the Boundaries of Sisterhood." In *The Empire Strikes Back: Race and Racism in 70s Britain*, comp. Center for Contemporary Cultural Studies, pp. 212–35. London: Hutchinson, 1984.

Carroll, Lewis. *Alice's Adventures in Wonderland and Through the Looking-Glass*. Ed. with intro. by Roger Lancelyn Green. Oxford: Oxford University Press, 1982.

Castle, Terry. "Phantasmagoria: Spectral Technology and the Metaphorics of Modern Reverie." *Critical Inquiry* 15 (Autumn 1988): 26–61.

Cellier, Pierre. "Mots et savoirs: présence des grandes civilisations dans l'oeuvre poétique de Saint-John Perse." In Antoine Raybaud and Henri Colliot, eds., *Espaces de Saint-John Perse 1–2*, pp. 229–47.

Chaboseau, Jean. *Le Tarot: essai d'interprétation selon les principes de l'hermétisme*. Paris: Editions Niclaus, 1946.

Chessman, Harriet Scott. *The Public Is Invited to Dance: Representation, the Body, and Dialogue in Gertrude Stein*. Stanford, Calif.: Stanford University Press, 1989.

Chisholm, Dianne. "H.D.'s Auto*heterography*." *Tulsa Studies in Women's Literature* 9, 1 (Spring 1990): 79–106.

———. *H.D.'s Freudian Poetics: Psychoanalysis in Translation*. Ithaca: Cornell University Press, 1992.

Clark, William. "South of Sahara" (five-part series). *The Listener.* "A New Leader in Africa," Mar. 21, 1957: 461–62; "The Road to Independence," Mar. 28, 1957: 501–2; "Black and White—Can Partnership Succeed?" Apr. 4, 1957: 542–44; "Town, Mine, and Village," Apr. 11, 1957: 589, 604; "The Needs of Nationalism," Apr. 18, 1957: 623, 643.

Clément, Catherine. "Enclave Esclave." In Elaine Marks and Isabelle de Courtivron, eds., *New French Feminisms: An Anthology,* pp. 130–36. Amherst: University of Massachusetts Press, 1980.

Collecott, Diana. "What Is Not Said: A Study in Textual Inversion." *Textual Practice* 4, 2 (Summer 1990): 236–58.

Culleton, Claire A. "Gender-Charged Munitions: The Language of World War I Munitions Reports." *Women's Studies International Forum* 11, 2 (1988): 109–16.

Dembo, L. S. "Norman Holmes Pearson on H.D.: An Interview." *Contemporary Literature* 10, 4 (Autumn 1969): 435–46.

De Rougemont, Denis. *Love in the Western World.* Trans. Montgomery Belgion. Rev. ed. Princeton: Princeton University Press, 1983.

———. *Passion and Society.* Trans. Montgomery Belgion. London: Faber and Faber, 1940.

Dinesen, Isak. *Shadows on the Grass.* New York: Random House, 1961.

Doane, Janice, and Devon Hodges. *From Klein to Kristeva: Psychoanalytic Feminism and the Search for the "Good Enough" Mother.* Ann Arbor: University of Michigan Press, 1992.

Dodsworth, Martin. "*Mercian Hymns,* Offa, Charlemagne and Geoffrey Hill." In Peter Robinson, ed., *Geoffrey Hill: Essays on His Work,* pp. 49–61. Milton Keynes, Eng.: Open University Press, 1985.

Du Maurier, Daphne. *The Infernal World of Branwell Brontë.* Garden City, N.Y.: Doubleday, 1961.

DuPlessis, Rachel Blau. *H.D.: The Career of That Struggle.* Bloomington: Indiana University Press, 1986.

———. "Romantic Thralldom in H.D." *Contemporary Literature* 20, 2 (Spring 1979): 178–203.

———. *Writing Beyond the Ending: Narrative Strategies of Twentieth-Century Women Writers.* Bloomington: Indiana University Press, 1985.

DuPlessis, Rachel Blau, and Susan Stanford Friedman. "'Woman is Perfect': H.D.'s Debate with Freud." *Feminist Studies* 7, 3 (Fall 1981): 417–30.

Eikhenbaum, Boris. "Problems of Film Stylistics" (1927). Trans. Thomas Aman. *Screen* 15, 3 (Autumn 1974): 7–32.

Eisenstein, Sergei M. "The Cinematographic Principle and Japanese Culture (With a Digression on Montage and the Shot)." *transition* 19–20 (Spring–Summer 1930): 90–103.

———. *Film Form: Essays in Film Theory.* Trans. and ed. Jay Leyda. San Diego: Harcourt Brace Jovanovich, 1949.

———. "Film Form, 1935—New Problems." *Life and Letters Today* 13 (Sept. 1935): 185–93; 13 (Dec. 1935): 167–75.

———. *The Film Sense.* Trans. and ed. Jay Leyda. San Diego: Harcourt Brace Jovanovich, 1947.

————. "The Fourth Dimension in the Kino." *Close Up* 6, 3 (Mar. 1930): 184–94; 6, 4 (Apr. 1930): 253–68.

————. "Montage in 1938." *Life and Letters Today* 21, 22 (June 1939): 93–101; 22, 24 (Aug. 1939): 272–84.

Eliot, T. S. *Selected Poems*. New York: Harcourt Brace Jovanovich, 1934.

————. *Selected Prose of T. S. Eliot*. Ed. with intro. by Frank Kermode. New York: Harcourt Brace Jovanovich, 1975.

"Epitaph—A Reporter." *Newsweek*. Jan. 23, 1961: 62.

Fifer, Elizabeth. "Is Flesh Advisable? The Interior Theatre of Gertrude Stein." *Signs* 4, 3 (Spring 1979): 472–83.

Frazer, Sir James George. *Adonis Attis Osiris*. Vol. 2, Part 4 of *The Golden Bough: A Study in Magic and Religion*. 12 vols. 3rd ed. London: Macmillan; New York: St. Martin's Press, 1966.

Freud, Sigmund. *Beyond the Pleasure Principle* (1920). Vol. 18 of *The Standard Edition*, pp. 3–64.

————. "A Case of Paranoia Running Counter to the Psycho-Analytic Theory of the Disease" (1915). Vol. 14 of *The Standard Edition*, pp. 263–72.

————. *Civilization and Its Discontents* (1930). Vol. 21 of *The Standard Edition*, pp. 59–145.

————. *The Ego and the Id* (1923). Vol. 19 of *The Standard Edition*, pp. 3–66.

————. "Female Sexuality" (1931). Vol. 21 of *The Standard Edition*, pp. 223–43.

————. "Femininity." *New Introductory Lectures on Psycho-Analysis* (1933 [1932]). Vol. 22 of *The Standard Edition*, pp. 112–35.

————. "Fetishism" (1927). Vol. 21 of *The Standard Edition*, pp. 149–57.

————. "Formulations on the Two Principles of Mental Functioning" (1911). Vol. 12 of *The Standard Edition*, pp. 213–26.

————. "Fragment of an Analysis of a Case of Hysteria" (1905 [1901]). Vol. 7 of *The Standard Edition*, pp. 3–122.

————. "From the History of an Infantile Neurosis" (1918 [1914]). Vol. 17 of *The Standard Edition*, pp. 3–123.

————. "Hysterical Phantasies and Their Relation to Bisexuality" (1908). Vol. 9 of *The Standard Edition*, pp. 157–66.

————. *The Interpretation of Dreams* (1900). Vols. 4–5 of *The Standard Edition*.

————. *Jokes and Their Relation to the Unconscious* (1905). Vol. 8 of *The Standard Edition*.

————. *Leonardo da Vinci and a Memory of His Childhood* (1910). Vol. 11 of *The Standard Edition*, pp. 59–137.

————. *Moses and Monotheism: Three Essays* (1939 [1934–38]). Vol. 23 of *The Standard Edition*, pp. 3–137.

————. "Negation" (1925). Vol. 19 of *The Standard Edition*, pp. 235–40.

————. "A Note upon the 'Mystic Writing-Pad'" (1925 [1924]). Vol. 19 of *The Standard Edition*, pp. 227–32.

————. "Notes upon a Case of Obsessional Neurosis" (1909). Vol. 10 of *The Standard Edition*, pp. 153–320.

————. *The Question of Lay Analysis: Conversations with an Impartial Person* (1926). Vol. 20 of *The Standard Edition*, pp. 183–258.

————. "Remembering, Repeating and Working Through (Further Recommendations on the Technique of Psycho-Analysis II)" (1914). Vol. 12 of *The Standard Edition*, pp. 147–56.

————. "Repression." *Papers on Metapsychology* (1915). Vol. 14 of *The Standard Edition*, pp. 143–58.

————. "A Seventeenth-Century Demonological Neurosis" (1923 [1922]). Vol. 19 of *The Standard Edition*, pp. 69–105.

————. *The Standard Edition of the Complete Psychological Works*. Trans. under the general editorship of James Strachey. 24 vols. London: Hogarth Press, 1955–64.

————. *Three Essays on the Theory of Sexuality* (1905). Vol. 7 of *The Standard Edition*, pp. 125–245.

————. "The Unconscious," in *Papers on Metapsychology* (1915). Vol. 14 of *The Standard Edition*, pp. 159–216.

Freud, Sigmund, and Joseph Breuer. *Studies on Hysteria* (1893–95). Vol. 2 of *The Standard Edition*.

Friedberg, Anne. "Approaching *Borderline*." In Michael King, ed., *H.D.: Woman and Poet*, pp. 369–90.

————. "Writing About Cinema: *Close Up* 1927–1933." Ph.D. diss., New York University, 1983.

Friedman, Susan Stanford. "Gender and Genre Anxiety: Elizabeth Barrett Browning and H.D. as Epic Poets." *Tulsa Studies in Women's Literature* 5, 2 (Fall 1986): 203–28.

————. " 'I go where I love': An Intertextual Study of H.D. and Adrienne Rich." *Signs* 9, 2 (1983): 228–45.

————. "Modernism of the 'Scattered Remnant': Race and Politics in the Development of H.D.'s Modernist Vision." In Michael King, ed., *H.D.: Woman and Poet*, pp. 91–116.

————. "Mythology, Psychoanalysis, and the Occult in the Late Poetry of H.D." Ph.D. diss., University of Wisconsin, 1973.

————. *Penelope's Web: Gender, Modernity, H.D.'s Fiction*. Cambridge, Eng.: Cambridge University Press, 1990.

————. *Psyche Reborn: The Emergence of H.D.* Bloomington: Indiana University Press, 1981.

————. "Who Buried H.D.?: A Poet, Her Critics, and Her Place in 'The Literary Tradition.' " *College English* 36, 7 (Mar. 1975): 801–14.

Friedman, Susan Stanford, and Rachel Blau DuPlessis. " 'I had two loves separate': The Sexualities of H.D.'s *Her*." *Montemora* 8 (1981): 7–30.

Fuchs, Miriam. "H.D.'s *The Gift*: 'Hide-and-Seek' with the 'Skeleton-Hand of Death.' " In Janice Morgan and Colette T. Hall, eds., *Redefining Autobiography in Twentieth-Century Women's Fiction: An Essay Collection*, pp. 85–102. New York: Garland, 1991.

Gerould, Daniel. "Eisenstein's 'The Wise Man.' " In Ian Christie and David Elliott, eds., *Eisenstein at Ninety*, pp. 89–100. Oxford: Museum of Modern Art, 1988.

Gilbert, Sandra M. "Soldier's Heart: Literary Men, Literary Women, and the Great War." In Margaret Higonnet et al., eds., *Behind the Lines: Gender and the Two World Wars*, pp. 197–226.

Gregory, Eileen. "Rose Cut in Rock: Sappho and H.D.'s *Sea Garden*." *Contemporary Literature* 27, 4 (1986): 525–52.

———. "Scarlet Experience: H.D.'s *Hymen*." *Sagetrieb* 6, 2 (Fall 1987): 77–100.

Grosskurth, Phyllis. *Melanie Klein: Her World and Her Work*. New York: Alfred A. Knopf, 1986.

Gubar, Susan. "The Echoing Spell of H.D.'s *Trilogy*." *Contemporary Literature* 19, 2 (Spring 1978): 196–218.

———. " 'This Is My Rifle, This Is My Gun': World War II and the Blitz on Women." In Margaret Higonnet et al., eds., *Behind the Lines: Gender and the Two World Wars*, pp. 227–59.

Guest, Barbara. *Herself Defined: The Poet H.D. and Her World*. Garden City, N.Y.: Doubleday, 1984.

Haller, Evelyn. "Isis Unveiled: Virginia Woolf's Use of Egyptian Myth." In Jane Marcus, ed., *Virginia Woolf: A Feminist Slant*, pp. 109–31. Lincoln: University of Nebraska Press, 1983.

Hamilton, Edith. *Mythology* (1940). New York: New American Library, 1969.

Hatlen, Burton. "Recovering the Human Equation: H.D.'s 'Hermetic Definition.' " *Sagetrieb* 6, 2 (Fall 1987): 141–69.

H.D. *Asphodel*. Ed. Robert Spoo. Durham, N.C.: Duke University Press, 1992.

———. *Bid Me to Live (A Madrigal)*. New York: Dial Press, 1960.

———. *The Borderline Pamphlet*. *Sagetrieb* 6, 2 (Fall 1987): 29–49.

———. "The Cinema and the Classics I." *Close Up* 1, 1 (July 1927): 22–33.

———. *Collected Poems 1912–1944*. Ed. Louis L. Martz. New York: New Directions, 1983.

———. "Compassionate Friendship." Typescript. H.D. Papers. Beinecke Library, Yale University, New Haven, Conn.

———. Diary, 1961. Ms. H.D. Papers. Beinecke Library, Yale University, New Haven, Conn.

———. *End to Torment: A Memoir of Ezra Pound*; with *Hilda's Book* by Ezra Pound. Ed. Norman Holmes Pearson and Michael King. New York: New Directions, 1979.

———. *The Gift*. New York: New Directions, 1982.

———. "The Gift." Typescript. H.D. Papers. Beinecke Library, Yale University, New Haven, Conn.

———. "The Greek Boy." [Early Stories II] Typescript. H.D. Papers. Beinecke Library, Yale University, New Haven, Conn.

———. *Hedylus*. Stratford-upon-Avon: Shakespeare Head Press, 1928.

———. *Hermetic Definition* Notebooks. Ms. H.D. Papers. Beinecke Library, Yale University, New Haven, Conn.

———. *HERmione*. New York: New Directions, 1981.

———. "Hirslanden Journal." Ms. H.D. Papers. Beinecke Library, Yale University, New Haven, Conn.

———. *Ion: A Play After Euripides* (1937). Redding Ridge, Conn: Black Swan Books, 1986.

———. Letters to Winifred Bryher and Norman Holmes Pearson. Beinecke Library, Yale University, New Haven, Conn.

———. "Magic Mirror." Typescript. H.D. Papers. Beinecke Library, Yale University, New Haven, Conn.

———. "Majic Ring." Typescript. H.D. Papers. Beinecke Library, Yale University, New Haven, Conn.

———. "The Master." *Feminist Studies* 7, 3 (Fall 1981): 407–16.

———. "The Mystery." Typescript. H.D. Papers. Beinecke Library, Yale University, New Haven, Conn.

———. *Narthex*. In Alfred Kreymborg, Lewis Mumford, and Paul Rosenfeld, eds., *The Second American Caravan*, pp. 225–84. New York: Macaulay, 1928.

———. *Nights*. New York: New Directions, 1986.

———. "Notes on Euripides, Pausanius, and Greek Lyric Poets." Typescript. H.D. Papers. Beinecke Library, Yale University, New Haven, Conn.

———. *Notes on Thought and Vision & The Wise Sappho*. San Francisco: City Lights Books, 1982.

———. *Paint It Today*. Ed. with intro. by Cassandra Laity. New York: New York University Press, 1992.

———. *Palimpsest*, Rev. ed. (1926). Carbondale: Southern Illinois University Press, 1968.

———. "Russian Films." *Close Up* 3, 3 (Sept. 1928): 18–29.

———. "The Sword Went Out to Sea." Typescript. H.D. Papers. Beinecke Library, Yale University, New Haven, Conn.

———. "Thorn Thicket." Typescript. H.D. Papers. Beinecke Library, Yale University, New Haven, Conn.

———. *Tribute to Freud* (1974). New York: New Directions, 1984.

———. *Vale Ave*. In James Laughlin with Peter Glassgold and Frederick R. Martin, eds., *New Directions in Prose and Poetry No. 44*. New York: New Directions, 1982.

———. "Within the Walls." [Short Story Collection] Typescript. H.D. Papers. Beinecke Library, Yale University, New Haven, Conn.

———. Zinzendorf Notebooks. Ms. H.D. Papers. Beinecke Library, Yale University, New Haven, Conn.

Heath, Stephen. *Questions of Cinema*. Bloomington: Indiana University Press, 1981.

Herring, Robert. "Film Imagery: Eisenstein." *Close Up* 3, 6 (Dec. 1928): 20–30.

Higonnet, Margaret, Jane Jenson, Sonya Michel, and Margaret Collins Weitz, eds., *Behind the Lines: Gender and the Two World Wars*. New Haven, Conn.: Yale University Press, 1987.

Hirsh, Elizabeth A. " 'New Eyes': H.D., Modernism, and the Psychoanalysis of Seeing." *Literature and Psychology* 32, 3 (1986): 1–10.

Holland, Norman N. "H.D. and 'The Blameless Physician.' " *Contemporary Literature* 10, 4 (Autumn 1969): 474–506.

Hollenberg, Donna Krolik. *H.D.: The Poetics of Childbirth and Creativity*. Boston: Northeastern University Press, 1991.

Homans, Margaret. *Bearing the Word: Language and Female Experience in Nineteenth Century Women's Writing*. Chicago: University of Chicago Press, 1986.

Homer. *The Iliad*. Trans. Robert Fitzgerald. New York: Anchor Books, 1975.

hooks, bell. *Feminist Theory from Margin to Center*. Boston: South End Press, 1984.

Hull, Richard W. *Modern Africa: Change and Continuity*. Englewood Cliffs, N.J.: Prentice-Hall, 1980.

Hutin, Serge. *A History of Alchemy*. Trans. Tamara Alferoff. New York: Walker, 1962.

"Into the Eye of the Storm." *Newsweek*. Dec. 19, 1960: 31–32.

Ivanov, Vjačeslav Vsevolodovič. "Eisenstein's Montage of Hieroglyphic Signs." In Marshall Blonsky, ed., *On Signs*, pp. 221–35. Baltimore: Johns Hopkins University Press, 1985.

Jacobus, Mary. " 'Tea Daddy': Poor Mrs. Klein and the Pencil Shavings." *Women: A Cultural Review* 1, 2 (Summer 1990): 160–79.

Jameson, Fredric. "Imaginary and Symbolic in Lacan: Marxism, Psychoanalytic Criticism, and the Problem of the Subject." In Shoshana Felman, ed., *Literature and Psychoanalysis: The Question of Reading: Otherwise*, pp. 338–95. Baltimore: Johns Hopkins University Press, 1982.

———. "Modernism and Imperialism." *Field Day Pamphlet No. 14*. Lawrence Hill, Derry: Field Day Theatre, 1988.

JanMohamed, Abdul R. "The Economy of Manichean Allegory: The Function of Racial Difference in Colonialist Literature." In Henry Louis Gates, Jr., ed., *"Race," Writing, and Difference*, pp. 78–106. Chicago: University of Chicago Press, 1986.

Kenner, Hugh. *The Pound Era*. Berkeley: University of California Press, 1971.

King, Helen. "Bound to Bleed: Artemis and Greek Women." In Averil Cameron and Amélie Kuhrt, eds., *Images of Women*, pp. 109–27.

King, Michael, ed. *H.D.: Woman and Poet*. Orono, Me.: National Poetry Foundation, 1986.

King, Pearl, and Riccardo Steiner, eds. *The Freud-Klein Controversies 1941–45*. London: Tavistock/Routledge, 1991.

Klein, Melanie. *Contributions to Psycho-Analysis 1921–45*. London: Hogarth Press, 1948.

Kloepfer, Deborah Kelly. *The Unspeakable Mother: Forbidden Discourse in Jean Rhys and H.D.* Ithaca: Cornell University Press, 1989.

Koestenbaum, Wayne. "The Queen's Throat: (Homo)sexuality and the Art of Singing." In Diana Fuss, ed., *Inside/Out: Lesbian Theories, Gay Theories*, pp. 205–34. New York: Routledge, 1991.

Kristeva, Julia. *The Kristeva Reader*. Ed. Toril Moi. New York: Columbia University Press, 1986.

———. *Powers of Horror: An Essay on Abjection*. Trans. Leon S. Roudiez. New York: Columbia University Press, 1982.

"K's Four-Front 'War.' " *Newsweek*. Aug. 1, 1960: 35–36.

Kuhn, Annette. "Structures of Patriarchy and Capital in the Family." In Annette Kuhn and AnnMarie Wolpe, eds., *Feminism and Materialism*, pp. 42–67.

Kuhn, Annette, and AnnMarie Wolpe, eds. *Feminism and Materialism: Women and Modes of Production*. London: Routledge and Kegan Paul, 1978.

LaCapra, Dominick. "History and Psychoanalysis." *Critical Inquiry* (Winter 1987): 222–51.

Laity, Cassandra. "H.D. and A. C. Swinburne: Decadence and Sapphic Modernism." In Karla Jay and Joanne Glasgow, eds., *Lesbian Texts and Contexts: Radical Revisions*, pp. 217–40. New York: New York University Press, 1990.

Laplanche, Jean, and J.-B. Pontalis. "Fantasy and the Origins of Sexuality." *The International Journal of Psycho-analysis* 49, 1 (1968): 1–18.

Larsen, Jeanne. "Myth and Glyph in *Helen in Egypt*." *San Jose Studies* 13, 3 (Fall 1987): 88–101.

Liddell, Henry George, and Robert Scott. *A Greek-English Lexicon*. Revised and augmented by Sir Henry Stuart Jones with the assistance of Roderick McKenzie. Oxford: Clarendon Press, 1940. 9th ed., 1978.

"Life in a Hothouse." *Newsweek*. May 2, 1960: 92–93.

Little, Roger. *Saint-John Perse*. London: Athlone Press, 1973.

McDonough, Roisin, and Rachel Harrison. "Patriarchy and Relations of Production." In Annette Kuhn and AnnMarie Wolpe, eds., *Feminism and Materialism*, pp. 11–41.

Macpherson, Kenneth. "As Is." *Close Up* 3, 2 (Aug. 1928): 5–11.

———. "As Is." *Close Up* 7, 5 (Nov. 1930): 293–98.

Mandel, Charlotte. "The Redirected Image: Cinematic Dynamics in the Style of H.D. (Hilda Doolittle)." *Literature/Film Quarterly* 11, 1 (1983): 36–45.

Marcus, Jane. "The Asylums of Antaeus: Women, War, and Madness—Is There a Feminist Fetishism?" In H. Aram Veeser, ed., *The New Historicism*, pp. 132–51. New York: Routledge, 1989.

———. "Corpus/Corps/Corpse: Writing the Body in/at War." In Helen M. Cooper, Adrienne Auslander Munich, and Susan Merrill Squier, eds., *Arms and the Woman: War, Gender, and Literary Representation*, pp. 124–67. Chapel Hill: University of North Carolina Press, 1989.

———. "Laughing at Leviticus: *Nightwood* as Woman's Circus Epic." In Mary Lynn Broe, ed., *Silence and Power: A Reevaluation of Djuna Barnes*, pp. 221–50. Carbondale: Southern Illinois University Press, 1991.

———. *Virginia Woolf and the Languages of Patriarchy*. Bloomington: Indiana University Press, 1987.

Marcus, Steven. "Freud and Dora: Story, History, Case History." In Charles Bernheimer and Claire Kahane, eds., *In Dora's Case: Freud—Hysteria—Feminism*, pp. 56–91. New York: Columbia University Press, 1985.

Martin, Biddy, and Chandra Talpade Mohanty. "Feminist Politics: What's Home Got to Do with It?" In Teresa de Lauretis, ed., *Feminist Studies/Critical Studies*, pp. 191–212. Bloomington: Indiana University Press, 1986.

Masson, Jeffrey Moussaieff. *The Assault on Truth: Freud's Suppression of the Seduction Theory*. New York: Penguin, 1985.

Milton, John. *Complete Poems and Major Prose*. Ed. Merritt Y. Hughes. Indianapolis, Ind.: Odyssey Press, 1957.

Mitchell, Juliet. *Psychoanalysis and Feminism*. New York: Vintage Books, 1975.

Mitchell, Juliet, and Jacqueline Rose, eds. *Feminine Sexuality: Jacques Lacan and the école freudienne*. Trans. Jacqueline Rose. New York: W. W. Norton, 1985.

Moon, Michael, and Eve Kosofsky Sedgwick. "Divinity: A Dossier, A Performance Piece, A Little-Understood Emotion." *Discourse* 13, 1 (Fall–Winter 1990–91): 12–39.

Morris, Adalaide. "The Concept of Projection: H.D.'s Visionary Powers." *Contemporary Literature* 25, 4 (Winter 1984): 411–36.

———. "A Relay of Power and of Peace: H.D. and the Spirit of the Gift." *Contemporary Literature* 27, 4 (1986): 493–524.

———. "Signaling: Feminism, Politics, and Mysticism in H.D.'s War Trilogy." *Sagetrieb* 9, 3 (Winter 1990): 121–34.

Murray, Gilbert. *Euripides and His Age*. London: Butterworth, 1931.

Newby, Percy Howard. *The Picnic at Sakkara*. New York: Knopf, 1955.

Nielsen, Aldon Lynn. *Reading Race: White American Poets and the Racial Discourse in the Twentieth Century*. Athens, Georgia: University of Georgia Press, 1988.

"The Nobel Prizes: . . . But None for Peace." *Newsweek*. Nov. 7, 1960: 60.

O'Connor, Noreen. "Is Melanie Klein the One Who Knows Who You Really Are?" *Women: A Cultural Review* 1, 2 (Summer 1990): 180–88.

"Olympic Rivals—'Everyone is Equal.'" *Newsweek*. Aug. 29, 1960: 81.

Ostriker, Alicia. "The Thieves of Language: Women Poets and Revisionist Mythmaking." *Signs* 8, 1 (Autumn 1982): 68–90.

Ovid. *Metamorphoses*. Trans. Rolfe Humphries. Bloomington: Indiana University Press, 1955.

Padel, Ruth. "Women: Model for Possession by Greek Daemons." In Averil Cameron and Amélie Kuhrt, eds., *Images of Women*, pp. 3–19.

Pearson, Norman Holmes. Letters to H.D. and New Directions. Beinecke Library, Yale University, New Haven, Conn.

Perse, St.-John. *Collected Poems*. Bollingen Series 87. Princeton: Princeton University Press, 1971.

Pondrom, Cyrena N. "H.D. and the Origins of Imagism." *Sagetrieb* 4, 1 (Spring 1985): 73–97.

Quinn, Vincent. "H.D.'s 'Hermetic Definition': The Poet as Archetypal Mother." *Contemporary Literature* 18, 1 (Winter 1977): 51–61.

Raybaud, Antoine, and Henri Colliot, eds. *Espaces de Saint-John Perse 1–2*. Aix-en-Provence: Université de Provence, 1979.

Riddel, Joseph N. "H.D. and the Poetics of 'Spiritual Realism.'" *Contemporary Literature* 10, 4 (Autumn 1969): 447–73.

Riley, Denise. *War in the Nursery: Theories of the Child and Mother*. London: Virago Press, 1983.

Robinson, Janice S. *H.D.: The Life and Work of an American Poet*. Boston: Houghton Mifflin, 1982.

Roith, Estelle. *The Riddle of Freud: Jewish Influences on His Theory of Female Sexuality*. London: Tavistock, 1987.

Rose, Jacqueline. "Hanna Segal Interviewed by Jacqueline Rose." *Women: A Cultural Review* 1, 2 (Summer 1990): 198–214.

———. *The Haunting of Sylvia Plath*. Cambridge, Mass.: Harvard University Press, 1992.

———. *Sexuality in the Field of Vision*. London: Verso, 1986.

Said, Edward W. *Orientalism*. New York: Pantheon, 1978.

———. "Yeats and Decolonization." *Field Day Pamphlet No. 15*. Lawrence Hill, Derry: Field Day Theatre, 1988.

Schmideberg, Walter. Letter to Winifred Bryher. Beinecke Library, Yale University, New Haven, Conn.

Schor, Naomi. *Reading in Detail: Aesthetics and the Feminine*. New York: Methuen, 1987.

Schuyler, Sarah. "Double-Dealing Fictions." *Genders* 3 (Fall 1990): 75–92.

Schweik, Susan. *A Gulf So Deeply Cut: American Women Poets and the Second World War*. Madison: University of Wisconsin Press, 1991.

Scott, Bonnie Kime, ed. *The Gender of Modernism: A Critical Anthology*. Bloomington: Indiana University Press, 1990.

Segal, Hanna. *Introduction to the Work of Melanie Klein*. London: Hogarth Press, 1973.

———. *Melanie Klein*. Ed. Frank Kermode. New York: Penguin, 1981.

Shorter, Alan W. *Egyptian Gods: A Handbook*. London: Kegan Paul, Trench, Trübner, 1937.

Silverstein, Louis H. "Herself Delineated: Chronological Highlights of H.D." In Susan Stanford Friedman and Rachel Blau DuPlessis, eds., *Signets: Reading H.D.*, pp. 32–45. Madison: University of Wisconsin Press, 1990.

Smith, Paul. "H.D.'s Flaws." *Iowa Review* 16, 3 (Fall 1986): 77–86.

Snead, James. "European Pedigrees / African Contagions: Nationality, Narrative, and Communality in Tutuola, Achebe, and Reed." In Homi K. Bhabha, ed., *Nation and Narration*, pp. 231–49. London: Routledge, 1990.

Spivak, Gayatri Chakravorty. *In Other Worlds: Essays in Cultural Politics*. New York: Methuen, 1987.

Stimpson, Catharine R. "The Somagrams of Gertrude Stein." In Michael J. Hoffman, ed., *Critical Essays on Gertrude Stein*, pp. 183–96. Boston: G. K. Hall, 1986.

Strachey, James. "Preliminary Notes Upon the Problem of Akhenaten." *The International Journal of Psycho-Analysis* 20, 1 (1939): 33–42.

Swinburne, Algernon Charles. *The Best of Swinburne*. Ed. Clyde Kenneth Hyder and Lewis Chase. New York: Ronald Press, 1937.

Taylor, Rev. Thomas N., ed. and trans. *St. Thérèse of Lisieux, the Little Flower of Jesus*. London: Burns, Oates and Washbourne, 1927.

Torgovnick, Marianna. *Gone Primitive: Savage Intellects, Modern Lives*. Chicago: University of Chicago Press, 1990.

Tylee, Claire M. "'Maleness Run Riot'—The Great War and Women's Resistance to Militarism." *Women's Studies International Forum* 11, 3 (1988): 199–210.

"The U.N. . . . An 'Empire' of Its Own—The Trusteeships." *Newsweek*. Nov. 14, 1960: 50–51.

Vatikiotis, P. J. *The History of Modern Egypt: From Muhammad Ali to Mubarak*. 4th ed. London: Weidenfeld and Nicolson, 1991.

Veith, Ilza. *Hysteria: The History of a Disease*. Chicago: University of Chicago Press, 1965.

Way, Arthur S., trans. and ed. *Euripides*, vol 1. 4 vols. London: William Heinemann; New York: G. P. Putnam, 1912.

Willemen, Paul. "Reflections on Eikhenbaum's Concept of Internal Speech in the Cinema." *Screen* 15, 4 (Winter 1974/75): 59–70.

Woolf, Virginia. *The Waves.* San Diego: Harcourt Brace Jovanovich, 1931.

Zeitlin, Froma I. "The Power of Aphrodite: Eros and the Boundaries of the Self in the *Hippolytus.*" In Peter Burian, ed., *Directions in Euripidean Criticism: A Collection of Essays*, pp. 52–111. Durham, N.C.: Duke University Press, 1985.

Index

In this index "f" after a number indicates a separate reference on the next page, and "ff" indicates separate references on the next two pages. A continuous discussion over two or more pages is indicated by a span of numbers. *Passim* is used for a cluster of references in close but not consecutive sequence.

180n7, 200nn20,22, 207nn76–78,
208nn82,88, 209nn92,95,98,
210nn99,102
Helios, 161–62. *See also* Apollo
Hermes Trismegistus, 55
Hermione, 102, 105, 131, 133–34, 136,
140, 208n82, 210n102
Herring, Robert, 118, 203n50
Heydt, Erich, 95, 97
Hidden phallus, 28, 185n20, 186n24
Hieroglyph, 1, 12–13, 41–42, 98, 101,
110–23 *passim*, 129, 135, 189n59,
204n58, 209nn92,94; lotus, 105, 109–
15, 119, 122, 131–39 *passim*, 159,
199n13, 201nn28,31
Hirsh, Elizabeth A., 3, 101
History, 1–7 *passim*, 14–15, 33, 69, 89,
122, 129, 138; and epiphany, 5, 16,
89–90, 152, 171, 173–74; and psycho-
analysis, 9–11, 122; and the uncon-
scious, 15, 86, 89, 197nn151,155; and
myth, 96–97, 148, 152–53, 159–75
passim, 201n28, 204n64; and fantasy,
99, 106, 108–09, 126–28, 140, 151–52,
157–59, 164–65, 175, 206n71; and
journalism, 152, 162, 167, 170–71. *See
also* Body: historical; Motherhood:
and history
Hodges, Devon, 8, 91
Hoffer, Hedwig, 188n46
Holland, Norman N., 179n5, 184n7
Hollenberg, Donna Krolik, 189n54,
196n145, 207n78, 208nn86,88,
209nn95,98
Homans, Margaret, 114
Homer, 134, 141, 168–69, 206n73; *The
Iliad*, 98, 138, 208n89
hooks, bell, 151, 212n8
Horus, 102, 110–11, 113–14, 120–21,
124–25, 130, 132, 137–39, 143, 154–
60 *passim*, 168f, 175, 191n68,
201nn27–28, 204n56, 205nn67–68,
206n69
Hull, Richard W., 198n3, 212n12
Hunger, 2, 29–39 *passim*, 46–54 *passim*,
71, 181n21, 189n53, 203n55
Hutin, Serge, 193n100, 194n111, 198n4
Hyde, Lewis, 77
Hyksos, 74, 205n64
Hysteria, 6, 11–12, 18, 81–83, 93, 95,

111, 114, 123–24, 133, 140, 145–47,
175, 196n138, 200n16; and memory,
17–18, 82, 105, 109, 115, 126–27. *See
also* Body: hysterical; Identification,
hysterical; Literalization: and hysteria;
Reordering; Seduction theory; Symp-
tom: hysterical

Identification, hysterical, 98, 107–8,
121, 133
Imperialism, 13, 121, 160, 166, 204n64;
and Britain, 6, 142, 146–48, 153, 166,
212n14, 218n63; and psychoanalysis,
11, 13. *See also* African decoloniza-
tion; Bryher: views on empire; H.D.:
views on empire; Modernism: and
imperialism; Motherhood: and impe-
rialism; Perse, St.-John: and empire
Incest, 124, 203n55, 205n65; father-
daughter, 15, 106, 108–9, 145–46; les-
bian, 27, 62–64, 66, 84–85, 89, 91,
131, 181n21, 186n22, 193n102,
196n140
Infantile phantasy, 8, 26–37 *passim*, 44,
54–55, 90–91, 140, 180n16, 181n24,
186n27, 190n68. *See also* Stealing
phantasies
Inner speech, 115–17, 124, 200n14,
203n47
Intellectual cinema, 98, 115–21 *passim*,
202n35
International Congresses (1936, 1938),
29
Introjection, 37–38, 186n24
Iphigenia, 102, 104, 131, 141, 144,
209n98; *Iphigenia at Aulis*, 134
Irigaray, Luce, 208n82
Irony, 34, 38, 41–42, 49, 53
Isaacs, Susan, 28, 185n20, 188n46
Isis, 50–51, 80, 105, 107, 110, 114,
119–21, 123–24, 129–31, 137–39,
143–44, 146, 156, 160, 166, 190n68,
201nn25,27, 204n56, 205n67, 215n38;
family of, 6, 97–98, 107, 125, 130,
142; and grief, 6, 12, 137; myth of, 98,
124f, 130, 201n28
Ivanov, Vjačeslav Vsevolodovič, 202n41

Jacobus, Mary, 180n12, 181n17
Jameson, Fredric, 8, 12, 181n17, 212n12

Library of Congress Cataloging-in-Publication Data

Edmunds, Susan.
Out of line : history, psychoanalysis, and montage
in H.D.'s long poems / Susan Edmunds.
    p.   cm.
Includes bibliographical references and index.
ISBN 0-8047-2370-2 (cloth : acid-free paper) :
    1. H.D. (Hilda Doolittle), 1886–1961—Criticism
and interpretation.   2. Literature and history—
United States—History—20th century.   3. Women
and literature—United States—History—20th
century.   4. Femininity (Psychology) in literature.
5. Psychoanalysis and literature.   6. Body,
Human, in literature.   I. Title.
PS3507.0726Z63   1994
811'.52—dc20
94-13823   CIP

  ∞ This book is printed on acid-free paper.
It was typeset in 10/12 Bembo by Wilsted & Taylor.